Sex Business TOKYO

By
ALTA EVA BOURNE

© 2021 Alta Eva Bourne & Night Star.
All rights reserved.

No part of this publication may be reproduced, stored in a retrieval system, or transmitted, in any form or in any means – by electronic, mechanical, photocopying, recording or otherwise – without prior written permission.

ISBN: 978-0-9943358-0-7 (Paperback)
ISBN: 978-0-9943358-1-4 (E-book)

Dedication

This book is dedicated to the Voice within Angela,
and indeed the voice
within us all, if we would only bother to listen.

CHAPTER ONE
'Letting Go.'

~~

It was a hot February morning, in 1985, as the 747 Jumbo taxied to its take-off position. The plane nestled readily on the tarmac of Sydney's Kingsford Smith Airport. A man and a woman stood atop the platform of the observation deck.

Almost at once, the plane lurched forward. It began its hurried pace down the runway; through the side window images of the terminal flickered by. Angela Krukowski looked out and saw the last visual pictures of her boyfriend Theo, and sister Lynn. It was an emotional moment for Angela, for they were the two closest people in her life.

Then with a bump, the plane lifted off the ground, and the airport building disappeared. Slowly a tear rolled down Angela's cheek as she cramped her neck to catch a final glimpse of her family and home. Before she knew it, the plane had ascended high into the sky, and thick clouds blanketed the airport's distant image below.

Angela began to cry as she whispered to herself, "This trip will be different, this time, I'll be gone for a long time."

The people sitting nearby were a little embarrassed, for they were almost all Japanese and weren't traditionally given to public displays of emotion. The plane levelled off, and the passengers relaxed and unfastened their seat belts. In a short time, Angela became a little more at ease.

It wasn't her first flight, for Angela had flown alone many times, in fact too many times. The flight attendants served afternoon coffee and cake. It settled her nerves, allowing her to rest. She had exhausted herself in preparation for this significant trip.

Minutes turned into hours, and the flight became just another monotonous voyage into the darkness. The film onboard began over the airy hum of the plane as Angela drifted into a deep sleep. She dreamt about her dance tours, how she had travelled throughout South East Asia and Australia, dancing in cabaret shows. Angela was a professional dancer and an excellent one at that. Yet, there wasn't a great deal of work for a dancer. Angela had spent a total of three years travelling and working, only to return home with very little to show for it. She always gave every performance her complete dedication. Unfortunately, dancing wasn't quite as profitable as most people were led to believe. Still, it was her dream, the dream of stardom.

Angela always dreamt in vivid colours, and the vision she had on board this flight was no exception. It was a collage that included the cabaret-style feathers, the veils, the audience, and the lights. It gave her a sense of peace. As the plane bumped its way through the turbulent night sky, images of Theo emerged. Theo was obviously Greek, small-framed, oddly handsome, and emotionally volatile. Angela had been in love with him for several years, but more recently, things were different. Yet, she only remembered the good times they'd shared.

The sleepy sojourn also revealed times with Barb, her best friend. They had like sisters ever since high school. They shared every experience together and believed in each other's aspirations as much as their own. Barb had always considered Angela to be very talented and knew she'd be famous one day. A few years ago, after a holiday in Japan, Barb married a Japanese Buddhist monk and lived in Japan's small country area. Barb had always loved the idea of Japan, and she so wanted to have children.

Then there was Lyn, Angela's sister. She was more than a sister, for she was a best friend too. Lyn had been very emotional about Angela's leaving. Still, she was happy also, for the realization of Angela's plans were at hand. As Angela slept, a smile spread across her face as the beauty of the dream unfolded. Then after the vision had passed, other images formed. These were sad impressions and scattered memories of the times of no work and very little money when there was only hope to live on.

Suddenly the plane hit a large air pocket, and with an enormous jolt, Angela woke, shook her head and looked around. Angela sighed while thinking about what may be ahead, for the uncertainty was daunting. However, the excitement and possibilities were far more tantalizing. There was no itinerary, just five hundred dollars and a plan to succeed where many before her had failed. Angela couldn't speak Japanese and had never been to Tokyo before, but alas these were minor considerations. Most importantly, Angela believed in herself and her vision.

Most of the other passengers rested as Angela began to write. At first, writing a letter to her family explaining why she had left without a dance contract. The real reason wasn't so much stardom as the chance of a good life. Australia offered very little for Angela, perhaps a position in an unemployment line, the odd show for a birthday party, and her family's consoling company. However loving her family was, Angela had decided to sacrifice that security to achieve something she longed to possess, financial and career security. There was another reason, but it was one she couldn't articulate in those personal letters – the recent violence she'd experienced at the hands of Theo.

Most people on board slept through the flight. However, Angela read a Tokyo travel book, marking the places of entertainment in the city and the metropolitan area carefully. The plan was to visit the recreation centres and seek work as a dancer. In fact, Angela had performed several dance episodes on television, and people considered her very exciting. The Japanese loved cabaret and blonde women; Angela believed she had the perfect combination of both. She was tall, blonde, pale-skinned, blue-eyed and beautiful and possessed intelligence to match, albeit with some naivety thrown in.

Angela looked around and saw that she was the only blonde headed person on board the flight. This inconsistency would be something Angela would have to get used to if she lived in Tokyo. In any case, she loved the attention, liked to be different, and loved to be noticed in a crowd.

The sun began to rise, and the beautiful red clouds could be seen as they scattered fresh sunlight against the ocean. It was a majestic sight.

The captain announced, "We will be arriving at Tokyo Narita Airport in approximately thirty minutes. I do hope your flight has been enjoyable and that you will fly with us again."

Angela could feel the butterflies swarming her stomach. The tears of Australia and her friends had dried some hours ago, and now it was time to be excited, for the Japanese experience was about to begin.

The plane touched down softly as if landing on water. It was a combination of snow and rain, wintertime in Japan, wet and freezing. Most of the people on board had been Japanese tourists visiting Australia for a summer holiday. They were adequately prepared with wet weather gear and fur coats. However, Angela was wearing a mini skirt and a very light cotton top. In the overhead locker, she had a warm jacket, but it wouldn't be enough to withstand the blizzard outside.

As the passengers disembarked, Angela had the sense that a very unusual journey had begun. Her feeling of excitement was overpowering, but at the same time, there was an element of emotional insecurity. It was clear that Angela's plan wasn't going to be an easy one, but like all good ideas, it was going to work, one way or another. She'd make sure of that.

It seemed to take hours to get through customs at Narita Airport. When the customs officials saw the Australian passport, she was pushed straight through. No checking was necessary. This was the first indication that Australians were generally deemed as trustworthy. The passengers then boarded a limousine bus to Tokyo as the city was about an hour's drive from the airport.

Afterwards, Angela arrived at a ryokan, a small Japanese inn, with a prearranged one-week booking. It was in Shinjuku, a rather large sub-city of Tokyo. It was great to get inside out of the snow, wind, and rain. She was freezing, and her clothes were wet. Angela spent the first twenty-four hours in bed cuddled up with a warm electric blanket and wrapped in a thick eiderdown quilt. After the hibernation period, she emerged out of the room to the surprise of the innkeeper. He'd said that he thought Miss Angela may have been a bear, in broken English because she had slept so long!

That night Angela planned to visit Shinjuku's entertainment area and try every nightclub within sight. That would prove to be a very daunting task. After an early dinner, the necessary things were packed: show photographs, publicity, videotape, and photocopies of her passport. Everything was neatly placed into a little bag. Then Angela rugged herself up and marched down the road with a map of the entertainment centre. It was quite an incredible sight, Tokyo at night with a virtual sea of people and lights. Futuristic and voluminous. Spruikers were standing outside clubs yelling and screaming in a language that seemed incomprehensible. But all Angela could see was the lights and, strangely, it was as if they all spelt out, 'ANGELA.'

Instinctively she knew that this place was her city and somehow, in some way, it would become just that. It was something she knew in her heart but didn't know what form it would manifest.

Angela had an unusual relationship with a voice inside her mind. It was a very personal thing. Some suggested that the *Voice* was a kind of spiritual guide. Although she perceived the Voice as a person, as if in the next room. To Angela, it was as if she could read his or her thoughts and feel what the Voice was feeling. As if someone was very close but remained unseen. That was her explanation of this unusual relationship. To Angela, the Voice was as real as you or me. Barb who first suggested that the Voice may be a long since departed relative who was there to guide Angela in her times of need. Others believed it may be something more sinister.

The Voice softly uttered, "Tokyo will be your home, Angela. Don't worry, you won't be alone, I will always be with you."

Angela always felt apprehensive about telling people that a voice actually spoke to her. She had once told Barb, "You know they lock people away who hear voices inside their head, if I were to tell people what I really heard, they'd think I was crazy." But Barb and Lyn knew very well that Angela was relatively sane; perhaps more so than most.

That night, Angela went from club to club, presenting the dance poster and uttering a few Japanese words to introduce herself that she had learnt especially for the occasion. Most people were amazed to see Angela as she was rather striking and a little larger than life. However, their responses were always negative, for the clubs didn't take foreign shows anymore. Most Tokyo nightclubs only had hostesses these days.

Cabaret shows were a thing of the past. The 'thing' of the moment was 'Karaoke,' a Japanese entertainment where someone from the audience would sing to prepared music with lyrics scrolling on a screen. The modern style, of female entertainment, were the hostesses, who'd sit very charmingly pouring drinks and chatting with the men to entertain them between and after their business negotiations. Sadly, there was very little need for dancers, except at some sleazy establishments, namely the strip-clubs in Kabukichō or Asakusa. Undaunted Angela pushed on to dozens of clubs, one after the other. After a few hours, the clubs all looked the same. They were usually small rooms with hostesses, tables, and very surprised Japanese businessmen, whose eyes nearly popped out of their head when she entered the room.

Many men exclaimed, "Â, bikkurishita!" (What a surprise!).

They gazed at her as if she was from another planet, an Amazonian one. Japanese people had been a very isolated race. They were one of the few modern societies that were slow to internationalize. Most Japanese people couldn't speak English and had very little interaction with foreigners. So, Japan appeared as the last horizon.

By four o'clock in the morning, Angela had been to some thirty or forty clubs. Her feet were aching, and she was famished. Determined to press on nonetheless, visiting a few more places farther outside the central area. It was impossible to go to all the clubs. Tokyo was incomprehensibly vast to a foreign person. Literally thousands upon thousands of nightclubs scattered throughout the city. God only knows how people would find their way around in an emergency, such as an earthquake or fire.

It wasn't until five-thirty that Angela wearily returned to the ryokan and soaked in a bath for two hours while contemplating her next move. Determined, she resolved to repeat the same process every night until there was a success. Some club owners wanted her show, but they weren't allowed to have foreign shows anymore. The Japanese Immigration Department had ruled out permission for many dancing visas, for they considered dancers a low moral standard. Only large clubs that were owned by big hotels could hold such dance visas. These companies had the power to persuade the government to grant their permission requests. The next move was to visit those large clubs, forgetting the little hostess bars, Karaoke bars and nightclubs.

The next evening, Angela repeated the sequence. She aimed only those places that seemingly had the power to obtain work permits. The response was much the same, but they were nonetheless very delighted to meet her. Many of them offered hostess work. After travelling around Asia dancing for several years, it really wasn't a compromise that she was prepared to make. Angela was a dancer who wanted to dance. Later she sat in a little cafe talking to some Japanese men about the Tokyo nightclub system until dawn. Tears formed in her eyes as the sun rose. Her thoughts drifted back home to Australia, with the images of Lyn going about her typical day to day life, without Angela. But in fact, she would be asleep at that time in the morning.

Just then, Angela realized she had drifted away and returned to the conversation only to hear the mutterings of the Japanese men. They spoke in 'Japlish,' almost an English dialect with a thick Japanese accent. Angela understood very little but smiled a lot. The men appreciated the company of a Gaijin (foreign person) and so paid for her noodles. Then, leaving wearily once more, she returned to the 'o-furo' (Japanese style bath) at the ryokan. It had been an unusual experience, meeting so many Japanese men.

"Where are you from? What is your country? What is your name? How old are you?" They all seemed to ask the same questions. It was as if they had all read the same books or had been to the same schools, but they were all pleasant enough. It was surprising that they were friendly and uninhibited towards foreign people, particularly to a beautiful foreign blonde-headed woman.

One man said to Angela, "Oh, so you're looking for a job! Well, you're young, beautiful, and blonde, in Tokyo I don't think you'll have much trouble." Then he smiled, picked up his briefcase and slowly walked away.

Thinking to herself, "But I've been to so many places. They all said *no*, how can it be that the people said yes, yet the clubs say no?"

That night, Angela decided to be a tourist and not try so hard, just relax a little and find out more about Japanese customs by talking with people. That was the best way to learn more about Tokyo.

She caught the subway to Ginza, a fashionable sub-city of Tokyo. It was a little bit like Double Bay in Sydney or Rodeo Drive in Los Angeles, the upper-class area where the people with money frequented. It was impressive and expensive. Angela loved the feeling of Ginza; it seemed to call to her in some way, but there was virtually no cabaret there. There was a sense of familiarity with Tokyo as if she had been there before, perhaps in a dream. That night was spent wandering around, locating the right hotels, and contacting the nightclubs' managers. Each one had its own booking agent and surprisingly enough were usually situated overseas. There was no success at Ginza either. The same problem seemed to come up, time and time again. Angela was only one person, and an entertainment agent would contract group. They were big companies, either located in the United States or Europe, which left Angela's solo dance act pretty well out in the cold.

"Why don't you go to the strip clubs for work?" one club manager suggested.

"No, thanks," Angela replied with dismay.

In fact, more recently, Belly Dance work had been hard to find in Australia. So, Angela had worked as a stripper in Kings Cross for the Greek Mafia. The money was pitiful. One Mafia leader even fell in love with her. When she refused his sexual invitation, he'd violently threatened, "I will give you a *headache*, you'll never forget!" She ran out the door with the homicidal man pursuing close behind, then he'd punched her car as she'd drove away. Needless to say, Angela lived each day in Australia in fear that the threat may one day become a reality. So, she vowed never to work as a stripper or for the organised crime again. It was another reason why she had left.

Tokyo was a large city, indeed. Angela had never been to such a place before. Compared to Sydney, Tokyo was enormous. During the daytime, Angela went to the large department stores. She gazed in all the shops, at the prices, the quality and quantity of goods. From time to time, she'd hear the same Japanese word uttered, "Sugoi!" Angela didn't know what it meant and thought it must be some form of greeting. Practically every second or third Japanese man who looked at her exclaimed, "Sugoi Gaijin!"

Later that afternoon at the ryokan, Angela talked to the bilingual Japanese man who ran the inn. He said, 'Sugoi' was a complimentary word that meant marvellous, extraordinary, and referred to her beauty. 'Gaijin' was simply a foreigner. She began to hear them more frequently. In fact, Sugoi was heard so often, it began to echo in the back of Angela's mind as she lay down to sleep each night.

"Sugoi! Sugoi!" It was as if someone was calling her.

Angela continued going to different nightclubs seeking work. It was always the same story, lots of hostess work. There was also public relations work but was it really public relations work? She never did know and were these really just hostess jobs? Apparently, so it seemed. It was a Japanese custom to have hostesses who were merely that. Yet, in other countries, even in Australia, the word 'hostess' had many connotations, some of them being sexual. However, was Japan so different? Hostesses were like modern 'Geisha'. Geisha traditionally didn't provide any sexual services. Still, they would entertain and be with a man to stimulate his every need, except sexual. As time passed and attitudes changed, Geisha became corrupt, especially with the influence of the 'Yakuza,' or Japanese Mafia. Geisha had been replaced by low-level hostesses, who may or may not provide sexual services dictated by the Yakuza, who ran the establishment.

The Yakuza was very influential in early times and something of a legend in modern Japan. However, many people had told Angela before arriving, the Yakuza were dead. They were a thing of the past. In the back of her mind, Angela still knew from her experiences that there was Mafia wherever night clubs were. But the extent of that organised crime was unknown.

It had been a week now since Angela had arrived in Japan and she had seen most of the nightlife centres. Although, she had only visited very few clubs, for there were literally too many. The club owners Angela did see all seemed to like her, but there was no legitimate employment opportunity. Some places did have dancers but only for big shows. Angela could arrange such a troupe, but that would take time and money. One booking agent even suggested contracting her to put together a cabaret show with a dozen girls for the following year, but that meant an enormous amount of money and time.

Alas, each night, Angela prayed before laying her head down to sleep. Her inner strength was like steel, and nothing could change that. If the Voice convinced Angela of something; then, nothing could change her mind. Angela believed in the words that came to her at night, more than life itself. So much so, she'd cast her lot with every phrase of the Voice many times before. The anonymous Voice had told her that this place would be her home, but it was uncertain for how long. The Voice had also said that she would realise her dream, but to be patient and not give way to doubt. 'D' stood for doubt, and doubt represented the Devil. Doubt is the Devil of the modern world, to Angela at least. Somehow, in some way, she knew things would work out, it was just a matter of believing.

Angela knew the Japanese people wanted to see more of her, from their reaction on the street. This was an opportunity to show the world what she was actually made of.

In the past, Angela's performances were always short, and

the engagements were relatively infrequent. The audiences were small, although the appreciation was high, yet the facilities were usually inadequate. When the Australian television stations did use her dancing, they never paid, it was exploitation labelled as self-promotion.

That's what it takes to get to the top, being used, ripped off and abused. That kind of experience helps someone make it or break it. Angela had broken it and now wanted to make it. Angela was realistic yet not prepared to compromise. The word compromise in the entertainment industry was considered the same as selling out. Angela possessed a real positive attitude towards life, every plan, every direction, and every purpose had to produce a positive result. If it wasn't positive, it wasn't part of the scheme of things.

Night after night, Angela spent in the entertainment areas amidst the lights, clubs, people, and action. There was plenty of excitement in Tokyo's streets, mostly when Angela was around, for it was as if the camera was on her every move. It felt as if everyone were there just to look at her, and all she had to do was stand and smile. Dozens of men would stare at her, ogling and sometimes even giggling like schoolboys. Angela would look around to check that they were, in fact, looking at her.

Usually, it was groups of young men. It was hard to understand their reaction to her. "Is it just because I'm a foreign girl?" she'd say. Angela possessed a captivating beauty, which is not so easily found in many women, combined with intense sexuality and a voluptuous figure. For reasons that seem inexplicable, the Japanese loved Angela's appearance. They loved that real honest beauty mixed with vibrant sexuality.

Many men introduced themselves on the street, "Hello! My name is... I'd like to talk with you, have dinner with you, or do anything with you." Pleading as she passed by. At first, Angela accepted most of the civilized offers from reasonably nice looking and polite men. Dinner and coffee became something of an occupation. The days were filled with virtually full-time dates. It was an excellent way to learn about Japan. Angela would spend time having dinner with a man, going to a movie or for a drive or doing anything they wanted to do. Just as long as there was no touching involved, and they paid for everything. They would give her information on where the best place would be to find work while many promised to talk with a friend in the entertainment business. It was strange how so many had friends in the film and television business.

Japan was a very odd place, in so many ways. One custom that fascinated Angela was that the Japanese never did anything on their own in a company. They made decisions as a group. They've been brought up in groups and lived in groups. When a decision is to be made, virtually the whole group must agree. Otherwise, it's abandoned. Angela began to realize she had to belong to a group to advance her career employment prospects. That meant she would have to know many people, the right people. She wanted to influence people in prominent positions, in such a way to provide a chance for permanent club work and perhaps television. We are not talking about some little club down a back street, but a great nightclub. A place that would put her name up in lights or a television station would put her dancing on the screen and pay the appropriate fee.

Those goals needed leverage, and this could come through an introduction to the right people. Japanese people are reliant on the opening. To know the right people, Angela had to be introduced appropriately, and so began a chain of presentations. Angela met people who seemed, at first, to be directly involved in the entertainment industry. Going out on dates with these men and talking with them about show business, seemed like an excellent place to start. Alas, they were always interested in one thing. They didn't state it openly until the end of the evening. Still, it was always Angela, not her dancing, nor her talent that they wanted.

Many men said, "You're so gorgeous - I must have you." Others offered lusty sums of money and promises of a better life if she agreed to be their mistress.

Angela gave a standard reply, "I'm not like that!"

However, for the Japanese, it was not entirely an insult. Some Japanese women would consider a large quantity of money offered for sexual favours a compliment, even though they'd most likely refuse. Angela had never been a prostitute. The closest she'd ever come was striptease and, as far as she was concerned, her striptease was a strip illusion act, for she would only undress to topless. It was just an act on stage. Angela was an actress and a dancer; any strip act she did was acting and mostly dancing.

The dates multiplied, as did the days. The men became numerous, and a trend began to emerge. They were all handsome, wealthy, and sophisticated. These men had everything, but why did they all want Angela?

"There are so many beautiful women - so many beautiful Japanese women. Why do you want me? Is it just the blonde hair and blue eyes?" she asked many times.

However, she never got an answer. Each night, purely out of loneliness, the dates would last longer. Instead of insisting on being home at twelve, she'd stay and go to a nightclub. And sometimes she would drink a little too much. Angela was trying as hard as she could, but it wasn't working out the way she'd planned. Life was becoming a mixture of confusion and unfamiliar feelings. Sure, the excitement was still there, she felt it burn inside. But something else was there, only she couldn't quite put her finger on it. While dancing at the nightclub one night, Angela felt terrific. The crowd had let her have the dance floor as she forgot herself and danced up a frenzy. Everyone loved it. Angela never usually gave free shows, but after three brandy-and-lemonades, she didn't care if she got paid or not. She just wanted to dance.

The nightclub manager said, "Please come again! You're great?" Then offered her a member's card and added, "You will never pay for anything here."

It was hardly a job, but still, it was at least some kind of recognition. Angela now knew that Japanese people loved her dancing when they were given a chance to see it. The nightlife action in Tokyo was mesmerising. It was much better than anywhere else she'd been, yet the Japanese didn't understand dance. Angela watched them dance, they looked like little robots with no natural rhythm. As a mass of people, they had no talent as dancers. In fact, they couldn't actually dance. While watching television at the ryokan, the dancers had no natural grace, just lousy choreography. They certainly needed Angela.

It was apparent that Angela needed to learn the Japanese language. 'Sugoi' was always heard, but now there were other words like, 'Kirei,' (beautiful) and 'Daisuki,' (big like) and dozens of different phrases all about her. People were talking about her wherever she went. They never seemed to say bad things. One can tell by people's attitudes if someone is nasty, even if it's a pretence. Angela, despite her naivety, was a good judge of character. Often one didn't have to understand the language to understand the meaning. Angela was polite enough to thank people, even if she didn't know what they'd said for she knew they were friendly, just by the look in their eye.

Many people, who could speak English, pleaded, "Please stay in Japan, please don't go back." There was a new trend towards internationalising Japan in the '80s. So many businessmen had taken English lessons, yet the pronunciation needed much improvement.

Angela replied to one person, "Perhaps I could become an English teacher, as some foreigners do for a short time, till I find a dancing job." It seemed like a starting point.

So, the next day was spent arranging interviews through the newspaper, teaching English to businessmen. The reaction was good as Angela was a native English speaker and considered intelligent, apart from the fact she was lovely to look at. This way, she could continue to search for dancing work while making enough money to survive. Alas, there was only one problem, the English schools were usually run by conservative people, and they didn't think she was a suitable teacher.

The Gaijins in Tokyo, what little numbers there were, didn't like Angela's glamorous appearance and overt sexuality. Yet the Japanese adored her. There was a strange anomaly here. It was as like being caught between two worlds, a world of enchantment and a world of disapproval. The world of rejection belonged to the people of her own kind. The world of magic was full of people of an unknown exotic language and unfamiliar customs. Angela's heart cried out for acceptance, so she didn't want to go back to Australia. All that was needed was to find a way to make it happen, in Tokyo.

The Voice said, "Forgive me, Angela, this world is an evil place, and sometimes new dreams are built on broken ones. But remember, I am always with you. Nothing will ever hurt you, just believe in *me*."

The next night, Angela went to Ginza again, an exciting place with beautiful lights, where everyone was superbly dressed. Angela wasn't wearing designer clothes, but it didn't matter, for they never noticed what she was wearing, just her face, for they loved her look.

"Are you a Hollywood movie star?" many excitedly inquired.

They admired her face, lips, and hair. Sometimes, strangers would walk up to Angela in the street, and touch her as if she was a doll or a mannequin. In Western terms, it's vulgar, but the Japanese possessed a strange naiveté. They seemed innocent about many things and often weren't conscious of their actions. They had a genuine curiosity to know if she was real. It was as if she was some type of high-tech Android or something Japanese scientists had developed, or at least that's how it felt to Angela.

One afternoon Angela was walking down a street in Harajuku, a little trendy and fashionable suburb when a television crew came along and spotted her. Quickly setting up the camera, they started filming her as people gathered to watch. She knew one thing, wherever there were cameras, there was an audience; so, she threw off her jacket and started to dance wildly. It was just some current affairs program, but it didn't matter. It became a dance performance and would be sensational on television, even though she never got a chance to see it.

"Another free show," she giggled, "Oh well - I've done so many, what's one more? Perhaps it will lead to something."

It would most certainly lead to something, but it would not be what Angela had in mind. That night she went to Ginza, once more. It was becoming a habit. Ginza was a great place where to look for nightclubs and meet men without the sleaze of Shinjuku, Asakusa, or the other low-class areas. Everything Angela needed appeared to be at Ginza.

All she had to do was catch the subway, it was only about hyaku-ni-ju-en (¥120, A$1.20), very reasonable. However, after midnight, the subway system in Tokyo shuts down. If one were caught somewhere far from home, then it would mean taking a taxi. A taxi ride in Tokyo is a little bit like buying a first-class ticket on an international flight. Angela believed she could never afford to take a cab. Moments before the subway closed each night, she'd leave Ginza just as the real action was beginning.

Angela's money was running low. Although the ryokan booking had been extended and paid for in advance, there was almost nothing leftover. Fortunately, nearly all her food was paid for by the men whom she dated but, as time went on, the money seemed to dwindle away quickly. Something would need to happen soon, or Angela may not have enough to live on, and not even have enough to leave Tokyo.

Late one evening, while purchasing a subway ticket back to Shinjuku, a man walked up and asked, "Ga'day. You're Australian, aren't you?" It was almost as if he was a long-lost friend. He was a Japanese man indeed, but one who spoke perfect Australian style English.

"Yes! I'm from Sydney," Angela replied happily.

"I was in Sydney last month. I'm going back in a couple of weeks, I've been to 'Down-under' many times. I love Australia! I actually feel like I'm at home when I'm in Aussieland!"

It was nice to meet someone who knew all about her homeland and could speak English fluently. He added, "Let's go have a drink and talk. I know an excellent place in Shinjuku."

"Why not," Angela replied.

Together, they went for a drink at a skyline bar. The view of Tokyo from the 23rd story of an elegant hotel was breathtaking. Angela told her story. How she'd come to Japan to find stardom. The man's reaction wasn't verbal for he was too busy admiring her. As if she was a Goya painting or something to devour visually, but not to be touched. The Japanese had an eloquent attitude, she loved it, and it made her feel very safe.

Everyone had said, "Tokyo is the safest city in the world." As far as Angela could tell, it was, and there had no reason to think otherwise.

Angela felt comfortable with this man, and so had another

drink. French liqueur was her favourite drink, even though it was a little stiff. This man was not like the others. And so, she had a little bit more to drink than with other men. Feeling so relaxed, Angela believed she could trust this Australian like Japanese man. However, all the experiences Angela ever had with Australian men were not always safe ones. Perhaps it was merely homesickness. The men back home always tried their luck, attempted to get her into bed. Sex was the only thing they were usually only interested in. The one guy who ever really treated Angela with respect was Theo, in the beginning anyway.

Angela believed that Japanese men weren't like the Australian men and allowed herself to be lulled into a false sense of security while agreeing to another drink, and yet another. It was now time for the bar to close, and Angela was drunk.

"Please, can you take me to my ryokan?" Angela asked with a hiccup.

"Sure, we'll catch a taxi. Don't worry. It's okay."

In the taxi, the man seemed like a close friend.

"I don't want to take you to your ryokan. How about we go to a hotel room and just talk? We won't do anything. I've only just met you!" he whispered softly.

"It's a funny thing that we should go to a hotel and just talk. Most men would want to make love. I don't want to," Angela replied.

Just at that moment, Angela's thoughts turned to Theo. They had been together for a few years now, but the last year or so he'd beaten her numerous times, for insignificant things. In fact, the most recent time, he'd struck her so hard that he cracked several ribs and completely dislocated her shoulder. Yet she took him back, believing he wouldn't do it again. Theo had been clinically diagnosed with Schizophrenia and refused to take medication. Angela still loved him but was afraid of his episodes. She loved him so much she didn't want to see the man she once knew degenerate into a mad man. Tokyo seemed like the right choice for many reasons. However, it was lonely, but she was adamant.

"No! I want to go home!" Angela stated boldly, but the man directed the taxi driver to a 'love hotel', around the corner.

A 'love hotel' is a Japanese hotel that is purely designed for couples to have sex. It's rented by the hour, and each room has videos of sexual exploits of many kinds. A bar, a vibrating bed, spa, or big bath for two people, all types of little sexual curiosities, mirrored ceiling, and some even have nightclub lights. Angela had read about them in the tourist manual but hadn't thought she'd ever see the inside of one.

Before she knew it, Angela was lying on a bed in the hotel room, with her head spinning from too much 'Cointreau'. The man embraced her and started to rip off her clothes. The gentleman seemed to disappear as this other creature emerged.

"Men are men, no matter where they're from," Angela stated aloud. In this case, she was right. She screamed, "No! Don't! Stop it!"

Strangely, the man stopped. He wasn't about to rape her but was trying to force Angela into bed and under the covers. He insisted that they would not do anything she didn't want to. Finally, Angela agreed to lie under the covers with her underwear on, as long as he didn't touch her, and they just talked.

Then, while he was climbing into bed, Angela rushed over and tried to open the door. The doors were all computer locked. Once a girl enters a love hotel room with a man, she can't get out alone. The person who booked the room must call the desk on the phone, and then they would unlock the door remotely. Angela always suffered from claustrophobia and, even though drunk, that feeling of entrapment engulfed her.

"Don't worry, it's all right, we're just going to lie here and talk, we won't do anything. I have a friend who is in the film industry. Perhaps I can get you into movies. Trust me! I love you; I won't hurt you," the man pleaded.

Too much alcohol, loneliness and fear of failure made Angela particularly vulnerable on this occasion.

"All right then. I will lie between the covers, but that's all," Angela retorted.

As time passed, she began to get a bit sleepy and started to doze off while listening to him murmuring about his job, wife, and personal problems. The man didn't care to help anyone into films, in the end, he just wanted to take advantage of a beautiful Australian girl in Tokyo who was alone.

Suddenly, the man exclaimed, "Watch out for the Yakuza! You are young and beautiful, they will try to catch you, be very careful. They are extremely dangerous!"

Automatically, Angela opened her eyes. It was a surprise to hear the word that she had read about so many times. The two terms which were most prevalent in Japanese history books were Geisha and Yakuza. Angela was curious but apprehensive.

The man continued, "Sure, Yakuza isn't as bad as it used to be, they've become more up-market, more high-class and so more powerful. You never know who the Yakuza is until they catch *you*. You must be very careful." He seemed concerned, even after his rather aggressive behaviour before.

Then he slowly tried to remove Angela's bra. It became difficult to stop him, alas with little success. He was strong and had managed to take off all her clothes, except the panties. The panties were very tight, and Angela managed to keep them on. Of course, by now the man had removed his own clothing as well. Then he tried very hard to make love to Angela while attempting to remove the panties simultaneously.

Angela insisted they just cuddle and be friends. It was challenging to get out of this situation. The man was too powerful, and the door was locked. It seemed the love hotels were purely designed for men, in particular, Japanese men. No one could indeed break-in, but Angela was only concerned with getting out!

"It's okay. I promise to get you a job. It's all right, trust me, and we can be lovers. I have a wife sure, but I don't love her. I love you. You're beautiful and everything I've ever wanted. Please believe me!" the man exclaimed dramatically.

Angela's knew that this man wanted sex, and that's all. For one brief moment, there didn't seem to be any way out of this situation. Still intoxicated, she agreed to allow him to only touch her breasts. The man accepted but continued to try everything else.

As the morning drew closer, the man jumped on top of her

and tried penetration. Angela jumped out of bed, quite upset. The alcohol had now worn off. She threatened to pick up something and hit him across the head if he persisted. Reluctantly he accepted. How could he refuse? Angela was tall and quite ominous standing there in a fit of anger. Then he began to get dressed and admitted defeat. She could go now as it was time for him to go home to his wife.

"Are you really going to help me?" Angela asked.

"Sure, I'll help you. Phone me next week - perhaps we can go away for a couple of days. Mount Fuji's beautiful in the wintertime. I'll take you there, and you can meet my film director friend, personally."

"As long as there's no sex, okay?"

"Yes, we're just friends. Although I love you, I must be patient and wait for you to love me," the man added, in a low tone.

Angela sighed, "This is a very unusual situation, but I will accept your invitation."

The night had ended quite abruptly, and the day had begun soberly. Willingly, Angela walked back to her hotel, which was very close by. Strangely, she had never noticed the love hotels before, but walking in the crisp morning air so many were visible with their bright neon lights. It was as if they stood out for the first time. Some were go-sen-en (¥5,000, A$50.00) an hour. There were cheaper ones. However, all night cost ranged between ni-man-en (¥20,000, A$200) to go-man-en (¥50,000, A$500), for a beautiful one. It was now apparent that the love hotels were clustered together in the same area.

The inn where Angela stayed was, of course, a ryokan and not a love hotel. It was refreshing to get back to a regular bed and a standard room with windows. Even though it wasn't glamorous, it was still home for the time being.

That day Angela rang the man who she'd been with the previous night. He remarked, "I've spoken to my friend. I'm sorry, but he can't help you. But I'll keep trying. In the meantime, don't forget our date next week."

It was clear he just wanted to use Angela. All the men she'd dated were all the same in different ways — situations designed to manipulate her into bed in one way or another.

It was now Sunday, the day of rest. Angela decided to put her problems aside and walked into Shinjuku's Kabukichō to see a movie during the daytime. There were so many different Western films playing, in English with Japanese subtitles. Although the ticket price was quite pricey at ni-sen-go-hyaku-en (¥2,500, A$25.00). Angela's budget was stretched yet the desire to see something resembling home was overpowering.

After the movie, Angela sat outside the 'Mister Donut' shop in the centre of Kabukichō and watched the world go by.

Kabukichō is just like Kings Cross. The same type of people, the same sort of attitude, sleazy and low-class. However sophisticated the Japanese were in their dress, those places always had the same style, and it couldn't be covered up with lights and paint. It shone through like a neon sign, 'sleaze area'. Angela thought, "It's daytime. Nothing awful can happen here, and besides, I don't see any Yakuza. There just seems to be a lot of single guys looking for someone to pick up." Many men who walked past, ogled at her and uttered a few words in Japanese. Angela didn't understand what they'd said but understood the intention. Some even confronted her, to no avail.

Sometimes she'd hear the word 'sex,' but just ignored it. She plugged in her Walkman headphones to block out the world, watched the colourful pictures and the people's faces as she listened to Australian rock music. Just then to her left, she noticed a very distinguished-looking man in a suit. He looked Chinese, but it was difficult to tell. The man stood there, staring at her. He wasn't quite like the others as he had more style and didn't seem to be trying to pick up anyone. He merely admired Angela from a distance. Afterwards, Angela decided to go for a stroll. She walked up the street; then, walked past the man who had been admiring her earlier.

"Excuse me," the man uttered.

"You speak English," Angela replied. "Yes, what is it?"

"May I walk with you? I would like to talk to you."

Angela nodded. After all, it was a public street. Casually, they began to chat. The man asked the most likely things, "What is your country, your name?" It was a like 'name, rank and serial number'.

Angela had replied before he spoke. "I'm from Australia, my name is Angela, I am twenty-eight, and I'm here looking for a dancing job. Is there anything else you would like to know?"

"That's strange you should talk like that! I'm just trying to be friendly." He seemed a little embarrassed. His hands fidgeted as he spoke while he looked at the ground. The man wore glasses and was clearly sweating on the palms and temples.

"I didn't mean to be like that, I'm just sick of men asking the same questions and wanting the same thing," Angela told him.

"Do you want me to go away?"

"I really don't have much else to do. Perhaps we can just walk around and talk." The truth was she was lonely.

"What would you like to do?"

"I would like to go shopping and buy some groceries. But I don't know where the supermarkets are, and besides it's Sunday, I don't even know if the supermarket is open?"

The man laughed and replied, "Haha! This is Japan, the supermarkets are always open. In fact, everything is always open, all the time if you know where to go. And in Shinjuku, you can find anything you want, twenty-four hours a day. Let me take you to a place I go to. It's very cheap and has lots of different food." He seemed a practical, a down-to-earth sort of person. He wasn't over flattering or complimentary but secretly admired Angela. Despite his containment, she knew what he was thinking just by the look in his eye. As time passed, Angela insisted on returning to her hotel.

The man accepted that and then presented his card, "My name is Mr Ono. I would like to call you if I have your permission."

"Ono-san, is that how it's said?" Angela replied. "Oh, and I'm Angela."

"Hai (yes). That is correct, Miss Angela."

Angela knew she'd need a friend in Tokyo and so took the card, thanked the man, replied, "I'm staying at this hotel," and presented the telephone number. "Perhaps, you can ring me some time."

Ono-san was quite surprised that she should give her telephone number so quickly. Apparently, it wasn't a Japanese custom, for women should be very cautious. However, in Australia, it was customary that you gave them your telephone number if you liked someone. It didn't mean anything, only that you'd like to see them again. Ono-san wasn't handsome like some of the others, but he wasn't pushy either. More like a puppy dog that would follow you around. The other men held onto tightly as if she was some precious object that may disappear at any instant. Whereas Ono-san was too shy to look at her for too long or stand too close.

Ironically, Ono-san would prove to be one of the causes of Angela's broken dream. This man was unassuming and ineffectual. However, Ono-san, along with many other Japanese men, would change Angela's plans for the future in such a way she never thought possible.

Ono-san uttered, "I will call you," as he gave a deep bow and backed away.

The next couple of days were pretty uneventful for Angela. English teaching interviews in the daytime and haunting the nightclubs of Ginza, Asakusa, Akasaka, Shinjuku, Ueno, Shibuya, Ikebukuro and many other locations in the evening. Angela now knew Tokyo very well, almost like the back of her hand. She'd only been there two weeks but already knew every entertainment area, perhaps even more so than most Japanese.

Strangely enough, Kings Cross in Australia was an unsafe place. People got knifed, robbed, and all sorts of nasty things happened. However, Japan seemed to be a very safe place, especially in Tokyo. It was said to be the safest city in the world, or that's what Angela believed, and that's the way it appeared on the surface.

All the job interviews for teaching proved unfruitful, and all the clubs refused with a sigh. The reply was always the same.

"We cannot obtain a visa for you. Very sorry."

Many places suggested striptease clubs, which meant she would be dancing illegally without a visa and working for the Yakuza. Which would be dangerous.

In this problematic situation, most people would just return to Australia. But Angela wasn't like most people.

Some men had said, "Angela, you're too beautiful to be an exotic dancer, and you must be careful. Tokyo is not as it seems. Nothing in Japan is as it seems."

Tokyo felt very safe. A place where Angela could live without complications. It gave her the freedom to move around, go sightseeing, or meet anybody without any anxiety. While other cities, Angela had visited seem to possess an air of impending danger. Tokyo didn't have that threat. Anyway, she knew that the Voice would never let her get into a dangerous situation. So, she trusted the Voice enough to go into the streets of a foreign country late at night, alone. These were places where some Japanese people would never go. Angela walked past many groups of young men, only to hear their 'wolf whistles' and Japanese mutterings of 'Sugoi' and 'Kirei'. She never feared them, for their response was a positive one. They were always excited to see her. Sure, there was the occasional creep who'd follow her around, but she was tall, and most Japanese men were shorter. So, Angela gave the impression she could take care of herself. However, she never ventured into dark places. If someone were following, Angela would only walk past the nearest police station. That usually did the trick.

Despite the many dinner dates, Angela's funds had dwindled to very little indeed. And that night there was an accidental meeting with yet another man.

"You are beautiful! You are just like my dream. I've just come back from America."

Angela's response was pretty unemotional. There'd been many introductions with Japanese men, and so she waited for the same questions and the same motive. This man didn't care to ask any questions.

The man quickly opened his wallet, "I have a thousand American dollars. Please, come to my hotel room for a couple of hours, and I'll give you this money for sex."

Angela was surprised. The man was so blatant and direct. He didn't waste time with small talk but was straight to the point. Interestingly enough, he wasn't sleazy and was very well dressed.

The man apparently didn't mean to be offensive. As far as he was concerned, it was merely a business negotiation.

"I'm not for sale!" Angela responded, defiantly.

"I don't want to buy you. I just want to pay for your services."

Angela thought for a moment and replied, "That is a strange but honest way to put it." She had always seen prostitution as forfeiting one's soul, and there never seemed anything positive about it.

People always said, "Don't sell your soul Angela, whatever you do!"

Angela's most prized possession was her soul, and she had believed that the girls who stood on the street of Kings Cross had bargained with the Devil. They had needle marks on their arms and did 'around the world' for forty dollars. It wasn't much of a future for those poor girls who started off as potential models to end up as skid row junkies. Evidently, they'd sold their souls. There was no doubt about that, but was it for sex or drugs? In any case, the point was that in Angela's experience prostitution always had a derogatory image, and she'd ever felt that it was morally wrong. God wouldn't love her if she were to do that, or so she believed.

"No, thanks. I need the money, but no thank you," Angela replied, holding onto her purse tightly. Inside there were one hundred Australian dollars, along with the return portion of an air-ticket to Australia. The ticket was dated for one month, and her room rent was now due, but Angela still said, "No."

"But I don't understand why not? Are you married?" the man inquired.

"No, I'm not."

"Then let's go. We won't do anything you don't want to do."

"Definitely not," Angela replied and walked away. As she did, the man quickly ran up and pushed a business card into her hand.

"My name is Sato. This is my telephone number. If you ever change your mind, please call me. I'd be happy to see you next time."

Angela's impulse was to throw that card in the garbage along with all the other cards men had given her for the same purpose. So many men had offered money to Angela for sex, and she had not accepted. This time was no exception, or was it? After all, this was Tokyo and just maybe for once in her life if things got desperate, she would have to do something repulsive. Instinctively she pushed that business card into her purse.

"Just in case, only as a last resort," she thought, "Only in a matter of life or death."

Soon afterwards, Angela forgot about the man and continued on her merry way. It was club after club, and encounter after encounter. So many men with the same intention tried to negotiate sex, only to be courteously refused. Angela quickly walked away from all those invitations and then returned to her cold lonely room at the inn. Looking in the mirror, she noticed her shoes had worn through, and the skirt had started to fray. There were no stockings left, and the cold snow of Tokyo had dampened the imitation fur coat. In reality, the image was that of a poorly dressed person, with a broken dream and no money. Yet underneath it, that movie star face, and voluptuous body still glistened.

Opening her purse, Angela noticed the card with the name 'Sato' and the nearby hotel's telephone number. She quickly scrunched it up, threw it in the garbage, and started to cry. Weeping, "Never in a million years." Then threw herself on the bed as those tears began to stream down like rain.

The Voice knew her heart, "Don't cry, Angela. Everything will be all right, trust *me*."

She lay on the bed for hours thinking about home. Thinking about the good times with her family, the trips away and images of the past. They were things she had almost forgotten — the death of her father some twelve months prior and the death of her grandfather some years before. There was only her mother and sister who remained. She felt responsible for her family. If something happened to her, there'd be no one for them. The family needed Angela, for she was the prodigal daughter and the last of the family line.

Money was her most significant issue. Angela had put herself in serious debt, together with the funeral expenses and now the trip to Japan. The credit cards had been utterly exhausted.

Responsibilities were mounting. It felt as if a concrete slab lay on Angela's head and kept pushing down. Angela couldn't return to Australia, there were too many debts to meet, and without work that meant bankruptcy, and failure. What was she to do? Surely *God* would provide the answer. It must come soon for there was only enough money to last two more days in Tokyo.

Lying in bed later that night Angela dreamt of the death of her father. She recollected that he had said something one Sunday afternoon. He had come over for dinner and passed by one of the street girls in Kings Cross. Angela's father was a loving man; William was his name. He had a genuine heart and had been a dancer as well.

William said caringly, "Those girls standing on the street, it's sad you know, most of them are nice kids who were never given a break." He believed that there was no sin on their part for they were simply victims of a society that had dealt them a wrong hand. William had always been a non-judgmental type of person. Angela remembered everything about him that Sunday as she visualised his beautiful smile. It was as if her father was there, consoling his daughter. He used to always say, "It'll be alright love."

That night during another dream, Angela saw images of her name up in lights. It was also an auditory vision, the words called to her, "Sugoi Gaijin." It was all about her.

"Ring, ring!" The house telephone vibrated as Angela quickly awoke. It was Ono-san. He apologized for the early call and suggested that they meet for lunch that day. He had a job proposition, teaching English. Angela quickly accepted, thanked him for his consideration and agreed to meet at one of the restaurants nearby. The meeting was pretty superficial.

Ono-san stated, "I have a teaching job for Miss Angela. One hour per week!" The job paid ten thousand yen, or ichi-man-en (¥10,000, A$100), for one hour.

This meant Angela would have to travel for three hours there and back by train. It would probably take up the full day, but it was money, and it was a job. Angela politely accepted.

Ono-san insisted they go out to dinner and celebrate that night. So, at eight o'clock, Ono-san took Angela to a nightclub. Afterwards, they went for a late supper, where they drank and listened to music. As they talked, Ono-san confessed that he was in love with Angela and wanted to make love to her. He was no different to all the others except for one small detail, this man had offered this desperate girl work. Angela wanted to say 'no' but didn't want to offend him or risk losing her new teaching position. So, she tried to be friendly and told him that there was a boyfriend whom she was in love with. Ono-san seemed to understand but still attempted to kiss and touch her, nonetheless. Angela politely refused, but he persisted. Eventually, after much struggling, Angela allowed one kiss, purely as a means of keeping him at bay.

Angela sighed. "I'm tired, please take me home." They then left the club. In the taxi, Ono-san wrapped his arms around his prize and forced his hand inside the low-cut blouse to touch her soft white breast. Grabbing hold of one breast firmly, he pulled her tightly in and excitedly exclaimed, "I must have you. You are now mine."

Angela shouted, "Stop! I want to get out" and removed his hand from beneath her clothing as her anger mounted.

Ono-san said, "It's all right. I'll take you home." Pausing briefly, he added, "If you want me to help you, then you must be nice to me." It seems that Ono-san wasn't so shy after all. "Do you understand Miss Angela?"

Angela stated firmly, "No, I don't understand. I don't get you or your kind." She climbed out of the taxi and began wandering down the street that led to the ryokan. Sadly, the realisation started to sink in that there weren't many people who were prepared to help her out of generosity alone.

Many men said, "Be nice to me." 'Being nice,' had enormous overtones of sexual gratitude. "But I am nice to you," Angela often replied, only it wasn't what they meant.

'Being nice' was a polite way of saying, "Let me have sex with you." The time was at hand when this Australian woman's naiveté was about to vanish, forever.

It was very late by the time Angela arrived back at the ryokan. The snow was falling softly, and the side of the inn had water dripping down the wall forming into little stalactites. Angela stood in the cold and gazed at the stars. She loved the stars, for it was like looking into God's eyes. The longer one stood there, the colder it became. She knew that this time was a turning point in her life but wasn't sure what to do.

Whether to return to Australia or try once more to find a life and dance work in Japan. Was it possible to stay here and weather the storm, get what she could and be smart enough and just careful enough not to get into anything that she couldn't get out of?

Angela wondered, "The future is so vast and so unknown, what will happen?" If only she could glimpse into the crystal ball of her own destiny. That night she gazed at the moon, for it seemed to possess a purity of whiteness or was it in Angela? Was it always there, without her realising it? The beauty of the moon is its purity, and the reflection of the sunlight upon it gives it an almost spiritual presence. Yet, if one looked carefully, one could see the markings of its existence, the scars of its age, and the indentations of objects that have impacted against it throughout time. That didn't take away its beauty, it was a stellar aberration and not merely something overhead.

The next few days passed uneventfully. The same thing happened everywhere. Men would introduce themselves, present their cards with telephone numbers and ask if they could call for a dinner date, or 'something'. Angela collected them all. It was a little bit like collecting postage stamps. Looking in her bag the cardholder had expanded to its full size, and now cards were spilling out. There was an enormous quantity, at least ninety cards, all within a brief time in Japan. Most of them were businessmen, wealthy and reasonably sophisticated. It was now time to clean out the bag. Angela took all the cards and put them in a little box, placed them in her travel bag under the bed as mere souvenirs of the trip to Japan. In fact, that's all they'd ever be, reminders of how attractive the Japanese men thought Angela to be.

The evening of the next day was the teaching job. It was quite a long trip by train outside Tokyo to a country town on the borderline near the mountains. It was a gorgeous place. The people were friendly and amazed to see a blonde Gaijin. Everywhere she went, people giggled with excitement and watched her every move.

In the train looking out the window, the reflection of their faces could still be seen, glaring back. They were looking for something in the Gaijin, yet they didn't know what. Angela didn't know either, but whatever it was she had it, and they liked it.

Arriving at the little town, Angela telephoned Ono-san, who promptly came and collected her. They drove to a big building where many students were living. Apparently, it was some type of arrangement for students to have English conversation classes on the weekend. Angela was to be their new Gaijin teacher.

The class gathered to about fifty students. It was quite a large group, and they were all young girls. Hardly any of them spoke any English except for one small girl who seemed to be something of an outcast: Miko-san. She could speak English fluently and had lived in America for two years. Miko quickly placed herself beside Angela and didn't leave her side and acted as a translator. Angela's Japanese was non-existent at this time. The day went relatively smoothly. The students weren't really concerned with studying English but merely wanted to be entertained with English. They didn't care to write notes or read books. They just wanted to have fun with a Gaijin. They believed that if they were bright enough, a little bit would rub off and they'd be able to speak English, without any effort. Of course, that wouldn't happen, but many Japanese people in that sense seemed somewhat lazy.

Ono-san paid the correct money and put Angela back on the train. "I'll call you this week. We'll go out to the nightclub just as we did last time," Ono-san stated confidently.

"I don't think so. I just want to remain business friends."

"Is that what you want, friends only? All right but I still want to take you out. It's a condition of our contract, being nice to me, remember?" Ono-san stated with a smirk.

Angela politely nodded in agreement. As long as it was friends only; then, she would be happy. However, that seemed improbable.

Over the next few days, Angela realized that the ichi-man-en (¥10,000, A$100) was very little indeed. If one were to live regularly in Tokyo, it would cost at least that much per day, only for rent and food. Tokyo was exceedingly expensive, but Angela managed to get by, going out with men for lunch and dinner helped stretch the money a little further. All she needed to do was pay the rent, which was go-sen-en (¥5,000, A$50.00) per day.

Angela returned to a couple of places where she'd been offered to the position of a hostess. Under close examination, it was found that they couldn't employ her as she only possessed a tourist visa and not a working holiday visa. Angela was refused a working holiday visa because the Japanese Embassy in Australia considered her too old. The cut-off visa age was twenty-eight years of age, she was twenty-nine. The Japanese are particularly firm when it comes to regulations. One minute over the deadline and it's too late. So, all those hostess positions quickly vanished, as if they'd never been there in the first place.

There didn't really seem to be any possibility of staying in Tokyo now. Angela began to pack her bags and prepared to leave for Australia. Most of the things were no packed ready, and only clothes for the next few days were left out.

It was impossible to survive on the mere ichi-man-en (¥10,000, A$100) a week from Ono-san. Surprisingly, a couple of days later Ono-san arrived at the ryokan. Angela told Ono-san of her problem with money and how returning to Australia seemed inevitable.

"Don't worry! You don't have to worry in Tokyo, I'll take care of you, it's all right," Ono-san said and quickly pushed yon-man-en (¥40,000, A$400) into her hand.

"Thank you, but what do you expect for this?" Angela asked with uncertainty.

"I expect nothing. I'm just giving it to you because I like you and I don't want to see you leave Japan," Ono-san said sincerely.

For a moment, Ono-san seemed like a decent person. That evening, they went out, and he didn't push himself on to Angela. He looked happy, just dancing, talking, and dining with her. When the evening ended, there was simply a kiss at the door to say good night. Angela was content now, for there was enough money to survive on for a short while, without any special requests for 'niceties.'

As the days passed, the frequency of Ono-san's visits increased. So much so, he'd become very demanding. When Angela refused to go out with him one night, he became very furious.

"But you must go out with me - you are *mine*!" Ono-san shouted.

Ono-san believed he had ownership, of this dependant Gaijin. While Angela felt a sense of obligation towards Ono-san for his financial donations. The thing that concerned her the most wasn't the want of sexual favours, but rather the feeling of responsibility. She felt committed to Ono-san in such a way she'd never thought possible. It seemed the Japanese custom of obligation had invisibly permeated her persona. Ono-san wanted her as his permanent date. Even if Angela refused to have sex, he still possessed her as a social partner.

He loved to say to people, "Look! This is my date - isn't she beautiful?"

Angela detested this situation. Ono-san paraded her around like a model, and everyone knew what he was doing. She cried inside and thought, "How humiliating this is? To be with a man I have no feelings for, to go to places I don't like and talk to people, I don't want to know. There must be an easier way, for this situation is rather distressing, and in a sense is a kind of prostitution."

Angela began to see herself as a freelance hostess. She was paid money to be amicable, or at least pretend to, but inside disliked everything Ono-san stood for. He was merely concerned with his own appearance. He even started dictating what Angela what type of clothes she must wear and how she must do her hair. Indeed, this Japanese man had become very demanding and pushed Angela's obligation to its limit. Each time he saw Angela, money was given as a 'gift.' The payment was always much needed as the rent was so expensive and seemed like a bottomless pit.

Ono-san rang the following day again.

"I'm very sick today. I have to go to the doctor. I have some type of contagious flu," Angela uttered while holding her nose.

Ono-san seemed a little concerned but said that he'd ring back again in a few days. Apparently, he didn't want to catch the flu. It was a pleasing escape for Angela, and the excuse gave her three days of grace from the clutches of the permanent date.

CHAPTER TWO
'The last dance.'

~~

THAT NIGHT ANGELA wandered around Roppongi - a newer part of Tokyo nicknamed, 'Gaijin City'. All the Gaijins went there, particularly the models and entertainment personalities. Although there weren't many foreign people in Tokyo, most were Japanese people who wanted to look and dress like Gaijins. It seemed like the perfect place, but Angela didn't like it. She found it to be pretentious.

The few Gaijins that lived there evidently were indifferent to the Japanese people and were only there for the money, anyone could see that. Some Japanese people hated being Japanese. Some had eyelid surgery to obtain the Gaijin style eyes, for the double bond eye was the fashionable trend. While others had their hair permed into 'afro' hairstyles, very trendy, and from a distance, one wouldn't know the person was Japanese. One may think that these Japanese people had a cultural conflict, identifying with Western culture and rejecting their own. All the while, the Western culture, Gaijins on a working holiday visa, were there for financial security and little else.

Angela walked amongst these people as they hurriedly crowded the streets. It was a very trendy place with people standing in the street talking to one another. Still, it was just a fashion parade, a facade. There were a few female Gaijin models, although they never seemed to *actually* smile. Only giving a fake grin at best. Angela didn't want to be like them, following people around, being friendly and being a paid hostess. She believed there must be a better way.

In the corner of Roppongi Square, the most famous area in all Roppongi, Angela found a little coffee shop, and sat inside and looked out while listening to music and gazing into the night. She barely noticed anyone, yet there were thousands of people bustling about. She wasn't really looking at anybody or anything, just looking for an answer.

Sitting across from Angela was an elderly businessman. He was fidgeting and shaking his coffee cup on the table in an apparent attempt to gain her attention. Finally, he managed to catch Angela's eye by spilling a glass of water. She turned to see his embarrassed face. Then he laughed and waved his hand as he started to speak. He was spirited and not at all pretentious. Angela removed the headphones.

"Hello! Komban wa (Good evening)! Pleased to meet you." He was a friendly type.

Oh, sure he was a businessman, and Angela knew straight away the score. She knew the questions and what he wanted, but at least it was an honest encounter, unlike the guise outside. This was something Angela could understand, so she talked with the man. He was quite an exciting person. A businessman who was mainly, shall we say, excited to see such a Gaijin. Crossing his leg and bending over his knee to prevent anyone from seeing his crotch. The man then quickly requested that they go to a hotel together.

"I don't do things like that - I'm a dancer," Angela proclaimed happily.

The man seemed surprised at the refusal but expected negotiations concerning money.

"It's very unusual to find a person like you here. Most of the girls I meet, all they want is money," the man stated. "So, you're a dancer! Would you like to dance for me?"

"I don't think it's dancing you want," Angela replied with a sarcastic grin.

"Yes, that's true. But if I can't get that, then I'd be quite happy with your dancing. How long is one of your performances?"

"This is ridiculously funny! In any case, twenty minutes is the longest performance I do. Other than that, I can do a short performance for three minutes, but I like to do a ten-minute performance most of all. It's just enough time for a dancer to give all that she has. Of course, my first love is Egyptian Belly Dance. It's the most ancient of all dance forms, the purest of dance. It's also the best form of exercise and the most sensual dance there is," Angela smiled as she spoke about dancing with loving tenderness.

The man became more excited as he listened to Angela's dissertation about the Asian art form. He'd never seen a Dancer before; in fact, not many Japanese had.

"I would like to take you to a hotel room, just to see you dance. I'll pay whatever money you ask. Then, if you don't wish to do anything else, that's okay. I really just want to see your stomach dance," the man exclaimed proudly.

Angela laughed out aloud and remarked, "It's not a stomach dance. It's a Belly Dance!"

She wanted to do a performance, for strangely it would be the first dance job in Japan. But would it be her last dance?

"If I were to appear on television, I'd expect four or five hundred dollars."

The man laughed, fell back in his chair, and stated, "That's a lot of money, even in Japan, especially for a dancer!"

"But I am a professional and the best. If you want me to give an intimate performance, I'm not going to do it cheaply. It would cost the same price, whether it was for a million people or only one because I put the same spirit, effort and physical strength into the dance."

"Well, that's fair; I suppose if you are professional. If you are that good, then, you deserve a reasonable fee." The man smiled while searching in his wallet, then added, "I can afford yon-man-en (¥40,000, A$400) as I must also pay for the hotel room. For a ten-minute dance, even though I'm a rather rich man, it is quite a lot of money!"

Angela, with butterflies and a trembling hand, happily agreed.

The man paid both table checks, and together they left the coffee shop. He then hailed a taxi, and they went to one of the love hotels in Akasaka. It was a great hotel room, huge, richly decorated and quite expensive.

The room had a large television screen and a giant bath that would accommodate six people. The centre was a round-shaped rotating and vibrating bed with a mirror mounted overhead and a built-in stereo system with coloured lights. It had everything except wheels! In fact, if one looked carefully, perhaps it had those as well. The room cost san-man-en (¥30,000, A$300), for the entire evening, but they only needed it for a short while. Angela believed after a little bit of talking, some drinking, and ten minutes of dancing, they'd be on their way. The man wasn't really concerned about the cost, for he looked forward to seeing something extraordinary. But he wasn't in a hurry.

"Of course, this is a private dance. Therefore, you must be more revealing than with a big audience. If you understand my meaning," the man uttered while closing the door.

"Do you want a strip show or a Belly Dance?" Angela asked, raising her eyebrow.

"A bit of both actually but I promise I won't touch you, just as we agreed. You only dance, okay?"

The man seemed respectable, and in a way, he was sort of attractive and had a welcoming smile. He didn't look like the men that haunted the strip clubs of Kings Cross whom Angela had so often encountered. But instead appeared like someone who ran a large corporation.

So, Angela agreed, "Okay, I will do a dance, and then at the very end of it I'll take my clothes off briefly, and that's all. Is that all right with you?"

The man laughed, clapped his hands, then rubbed his fingers into one another and uttered, "Yes! That's just what I want. Thank you." Immediately afterwards, placing the money on the table in a perfect fan, the four notes were visible.

Angela looked at the money and thought, "It's a lot for a ten-minute private show."

Then she put the headphones on and took most of her clothes off except for her bra and panties. The man loosened his tie. Angela began to Belly Dance around the room. There was plenty of space, yet she didn't use the same energy as a real performance. The man lay on the bed with his jacket draped over the edge, shoes off and hair all scrunched up. He seemed hypnotized and gazed endlessly at Angela's movements. He was impressed, there was no doubt about that, in fact, astonished. As he lay there, his eyes glistened with delight.

Angela wondered, "What is it about a woman's body that mesmerizes men?"

The man watched the motion of her stomach, navel, hips, and buttocks; then gazed at that sublime white face.

Angela felt as if she was being caressed without hands. It was a strange sensation - like being handled in a dream. One knows they're being touched but can't feel it. Nonetheless, she continued to dance. Then as the music ended, she looked at the clock on the wall. It was almost ten minutes.

The man ripped off his tie then crawled to the end of the bed, squatted there, resting his head upon his hands, and exclaimed, "Now! It's time now, please!"

The blonde Gaijin stood there as he dimmed the light in the room, leaving only the bed light on. Angela slowly removed her panties and bra, to then stand naked in the silhouette of a darkened love hotel room.

The man cheered and clapped, "Fantastic! Fantastic! Incredible!" As he came close, Angela quickly covered her naked body.

"But you said no touching!"

"I am not going to touch," he said, "I'm just going to look." And look he did, so carefully, it frightened her. He had penetrated her psychological space, come so close and studied the lily-white skin, so intently that he may as well have touched. She quickly grabbed her clothes, ran into the bathroom, and got dressed. The man became a little upset at the episode's brevity to throw himself onto the bed out of frustration.

"I didn't mean to do anything. I was just looking. We agreed to look only."

Now fully dressed, Angela came back into the bedroom and switched the light back on. The man was a little stunned but seemed satisfied and didn't want any more than that. Angela had the money and couldn't believe how easy it was to earn yon-man-en (¥40,000, A$400). Especially after attending so many interviews and knocking on so many doors. Ironically, a hostess job paid that sort of money for a full week's work. Angela had earned it in ten minutes. It was incredible!

While leaving the room, the man asked, "Would you like to go out to dinner? I'd like to buy you a nice meal and talk to you about your stay in Japan."

It was unexpected, but Angela agreed. For it wasn't a good idea to waste money on food if one could help it. Mostly if someone was prepared to offer a free meal, she wasn't likely to refuse. They went to a rather expensive Korean style restaurant that overlooked Roppongi Square. It was very luxurious. The food was excellent, and it was a pleasant situation. In perfect English, the man spoke quite a lot, mostly about Angela, how Japanese society would perceive her beauty. Angela was very interested in his opinion and listened patiently to the Japanese words used to describe her appearance. They were flattering words, words used to describe her beauty.

The man continued to talk, "You know, you need the money, and I know Japan is an expensive place for a Gaijin. You either have to compromise or leave. Japan is selfish and very ruthless."

Angela picked up her drink, took a sip, looked the man in the eye and replied, "I don't believe in compromise."

"Well then, let me put it another way. Let's say a bit of give and take, for a short time."

That didn't seem to rub Angela the wrong way. Compromise appeared to be a forever permanent state of existence. She never wanted to get involved in anything that would substantially alter her dreams and evitable destiny.

The man was drinking heavily due to the excitement of the evening's entertainment. Drinking was a means of controlling that emotion, yet the more he drank, the more he spoke. He was frank and talked openly, but not offensively. He was determined to convince Angela of the thing he'd been thinking of all night. After finishing the fourth glass of beer, he raised another glass to drink the foam then placed it on the table, laughed a little bit and gazed at Angela.

"Let me put it this way. If you were to go to bed with men for money, do you realize how much money you could make in Japan? Someone, so beautiful as you, in *Tokyo*?"

Angela automatically shook her head and replied without pausing, "But you just paid for dancing. Why can't I do that?"

The man laughed. "I'm a little more generous than the average Japanese businessman. There are very few Japanese men who will pay a beautiful girl just to dance!."

Angela stared out the window across the street to Roppongi Square, to see a couple of Gaijins strolling up the road, looking for the latest nightclub with their Japanese friends. It was a real beehive activity out there. At one o'clock in the morning, it was becoming a very charming place. Gaijin City was an appropriate nickname. The man looked at Angela as she stared out at the street, captivated by the visual curiosity, that was Tokyo.

"You love Tokyo, don't you?" he asked.

"Yes, I do. But I don't know why," Angela confessed.

"Then you have to stay here. You must think seriously about my proposal and about your future. It only has to be while you're in Japan. I'm not suggesting you should change your profession."

This time Angela heard the words, but she didn't fully understand the meaning. All the while, she was mentally preoccupied with all those nightclubs out there. She wondered if any of them had dance shows. The man then pulled her hand across the table and began to speak once again.

"I want to see you again in two days. Can we encounter a similar experience together?"

Angela thought for a moment, then looked into his eyes. "But no touching, okay?"

"Well, how about just cuddling, is that okay? We'll just cuddle and no sex," he said.

Pausing for a moment, enticed, Angela replied, "Well I suppose so, seeing my money situation is so bad. Perhaps cuddling is okay."

They made a date in two days, to meet at the corner coffee shop on Roppongi Square. They shook hands, parted, and slightly bowed their heads to each other, a typical Japanese farewell. As they parted, Angela went her way and the man his.

It was a cold and dark night. Angela walked down the street to absorb the atmosphere of Roppongi. She looked high in the sky to see small raindrops falling and beginning to turn into tiny flakes of snow. It was the middle of winter, and Tokyo's streets were bitterly cold. It was only three degrees and a real contrast to the summer weather of Sydney.

Angela noticed that most of the Gaijins were dressed rather poorly. The Japanese wore leather jackets, fur coats and costly designer clothes. Yet, the Gaijins seemed to wear nothing more than jeans and jumpers. Obviously, they were on a limited expense account, and it showed in their attire.

Angela went to the subway station after spending some time looking around and caught the 'Yamanote Line,' the city circle. Travelling around Tokyo on the train was an excellent way to see exactly how large the metropolis was, and it was warm. It took about an hour to do the city circle. The city, even gazing through the train window, had a unique charm.

Afterwards, walking down Shinjuku's streets, Angela noticed the differences between the two areas, Shinjuku was definitely sleazy and cheap. At the same time, Roppongi was very stylized and quite eloquent.

Shinjuku was a fascinating place, but it wasn't the proper place for Angela to be seen. She quickly returned to the ryokan, bathed in a soothing hot bath, and went to bed. As she snuggled under the quilt, the snow gently fell on the windowsill. Angela's heart began to pound in a steady rhythm, producing a sense that couldn't be put into words. Perhaps it was ambition. Her desire pulsed in time with the heartbeat. Drifted into a profound sleep, she dreamt of performing on a golden stage covered with snowflakes.

Then Angela awoke abruptly, the next morning, to the cleaning lady tapping on the door. That was the first perfect night's sleep since arriving in Tokyo. For once, there hadn't been any stress about money. It had been a profound and relaxed sleep. The anxiety that she'd been feeling had suddenly disappeared. That day, the rent of san-man-en (¥30,000, A$300) in advance for the following week.

That didn't leave much money left over, but at least there was another week's stay, and a lot could happen in seven days in a city like Tokyo.

That day, everywhere Angela went, businessmen stopped on the street, wanting to chat. She began to replay the previous night's dinner conversation over, whispering softly, "If I were to do what he suggested, there would be no shortage of clients." Then she quickly pushed the obscene idea away. It was ridiculous to even think about doing such a thing. It was terrible, degrading, and most definitely not the appropriate behaviour for a girl like Angela.

That evening, the plan was to return to Roppongi and continue approaching nightclubs. Gogo style dancers had been widespread, well at least a few years ago. Perhaps there was still a need for that kind of dancer? Anyway, it was worth a try. The clubs didn't open until 8.00 p.m., so there was plenty of time to fill in.

Angela loved window shopping in the big department stores, for there were so many beautiful things: paintings, clothing, and jewellery. The Japanese seemed to have the best of everything in their stores, the most expensive brands, and labels. Things that Angela believed she could never afford. The prices were astronomical. A pair of 'Christian Dior' sunglasses was marked, Ju-man-en (¥100,000, A$1,000). Yet the Japanese loved these expensive things.

Angela wasn't interested in materialism, only stardom. Although it was apparent that the Japanese were obsessed with the quality of consumer products. It meant they only paid decent money for something they considered to be of a very high standard. She kept thinking of the encounter with the man from the previous evening.

She was intrigued that he had paid so much just for a private show. It was flattering to think that perhaps Angela was considered as stylish as some of the beautiful things in the most exclusive department stores. It was seductive to be appreciated, even though it was in a slightly perverse manner.

After the department stores, Angela went to the art galleries, scattered all through Tokyo, from Shinjuku to Ginza. It was easy taking the subway back to Shinjuku, then on to Aoyama, and onto Ginza. All the art was quite exquisite, but the prices were high and utterly out of the question. In fact, everything in Tokyo was unreasonably overpriced. Angela began to realise that Japan was indeed an entirely different place compared to Australia. Yet, what was it about this city, in a foreign land, that a country girl found so intoxicating?

Money to Japanese society was the vital thing, appearing almost like a social icon or a *demigod*. Angela had seen the positive side of the Japanese people in their politeness and manners. Now she was noticing the negative side of Japanese society. It was money, the characterization of it, the obsession with it and the worship of materialism. Nonetheless, if Angela wanted to stay; then it would require a regular stream of income, one that may not come through dancing alone.

Angela would try one more time to find that elusive dance booking, targeting now the Roppongi clubs. For she had inquired everywhere else and was beginning to think that perhaps it was not the clubs after all, as there were various scenarios to consider. One was that dance shows were not fashionable, possibly. The second was that they didn't like Gaijins, but that seemed unlikely. The third was that perhaps they just didn't want her dance act. Lastly, as the club managers had said, it was purely a visa problem. This seemed the most valid reason.

It was now 8:30 p.m. and time to visit the first nightclub. The manager was amicable and offered this Australian Gaijin a cocktail. They talked together while he glanced at her publicity and show photos. Flipping through the pages, he gazed deeply into Angela's deep blue eyes with an air of nonchalance. The manager didn't see the pictures, only those delightful, glistening, hopeful eyes. Then he asked more personal questions. Why was she in Japan? How long would she stay? And, as he leaned closer, asked if she had any friends and mostly if there was a boyfriend? No answer was given to the last question. The meeting was about a dance booking, but the manager was more interested in a date. Angela realised that this was the same situation as before, the promise drained away.

Angela quickly closed the album, stood up and stated boldly, "Well if you don't want my act, then I'm leaving." The man suggested she stay for another drink and perhaps something to eat. She politely refused and walked out of the club and down the road to the next one.

Roppongi had seemed so vast the night before, but it was quickly becoming less so. Nightclub after nightclub was followed by refusal upon refusal. Suddenly, Gaijin city seemed tiny, devoid of opportunity and somewhat unfriendly.

Intriguingly, it was always men who ran the nightclubs, never women. The only things women did was to serve drinks and greet customers or work as hostesses. It was absolutely fascinating that the country was so sexist. Australia was a land of equality, where both men and women were in influential positions. Japan was different. It was divergent.

Then Angela found a small club that was a little hidden away. The manager seemed to respond very quickly; he didn't ask about the show but stated in broken English that he would employ her regardless of position. It was a strange response. Looking around the room, one could see a few Filipino hostesses, but there were no western Gaijins, only Asian girls. The manager called another man, who in turn called yet another person, who called another manager.

All seven men gathered around a small table while glancing at Angela. They looked her up and down then muttered to one another. The reaction seemed optimistic, and they all liked her very much. It appeared they were interested in her act. The manager asked how much it would cost.

Angela thought for a moment, then exclaimed, "Two dance

acts per day, at ichi-man-en (¥10,000, A$100) per show, sounds reasonable."

The head manager rubbed his hands together and nodded at the other men, displaying a pleased grin as if they had a bargain on their hands. Then he quickly called for a younger man who could speak reasonable English. The young translator was obviously new. He introduced himself politely, presented his business card, and stated that the men at the table were the nightclub's managing directors. Angela started to get excited, her heartbeat quickening as he continued. Then he talked to the other men in Japanese and turned to Angela once more.

"We, the nightclub, that is, would like to employ you, but we are not permitted to change our routine of entertainment."

Angela looked at the men, whose expressions seemed fixed.

The young man added, "You can work three hours as a hostess and get the money you asked. All you have to do is serve drinks and talk."

It was a tempting offer, and Angela thought about it for a whole ten seconds. Then remembering the previous night, how she'd been paid so much money in a short space of time and automatically refused the offer. It had to be dance work. Otherwise, she'd take her chances. The men were dismayed and couldn't understand why. They believed the offer was fair and in terms of the hostess market it certainly was. It may have been an excellent offer, but Angela wasn't prepared to compromise.

Angela left the club and descended the stairs to the elevator, then went to the station. It was time to put the dancing things away, for all the more prominent nightclubs had been exhausted. Only little hostess bars remained. Angela placed her photographs, videos, and posters into the station locker and just wandered around Roppongi. A short time later she arrived at the favourite little coffee shop. It was time for hot chocolate. Then Angela prayed for help as she had done as a child. She remembered the prayers of her childhood. Then she felt the presence.

The Voice echoed, "Don't worry, everything will be all right. Let opportunity seek you. The real *yeses* will seek you."

Angela felt a soft pleasurable calmness cover her, feeling relaxed and at ease, mixed with a certain sense of security. She knew the Voice would guide her and that everything would, in fact, be okay. Sure, most people with, so-called, common sense would see the situation as impossible to resolve. Still, Angela's inner essence had told her otherwise. All that was required was to trust the truth inside, the *Voice* and forget the realities that seemingly existed.

Angela was tired. It had been a hectic period since arriving in Japan. It was time to return to the inn and get an early night. As she entered the station, for a train back to Shinjuku, she looked out across the street. It was now snowing quite heavily. There were five centimetres of snow on the ground, and all the cars had chains on their wheels as they whisked past. People carried snowflake laden umbrellas while parts of their clothing were sprinkled with the icy white flakes.

Back at the ryokan, Angela sat on the bed under the heater and read a Japanese newspaper for Gaijins, in English. It became evident that there was a tiny Gaijin sub-culture that existed in Tokyo. Gaijins had their own books, places to go, movie theatre, department store, and locations where they lived. There weren't many foreigners but the few that lived there stuck together, they were an insecure group. Angela thought it was a rather pointless thing to do, to move to a city in Japan and associate with only people who were of one's own nationality. Why bother coming to Japan at all? If you didn't live like a Japanese person, didn't mix with Japanese people and didn't go where Japanese people went, then it would be futile. Clearly, the motivation was money. Nonetheless, Angela found the literature very informative.

Angela lay on the bed, then slowly slid into the sheets, and turned out the light. The snow was settling on the roof as the night drew to a close. She fell into a deep, delicate sleep, just like the night before. To awake early the next morning with a knocking on the door.

"Telephone for Miss Angela. Please hurry."

Angela scampered down the stairs to the phone. It was the same man from the evening before, ringing to confirm their date for that night. She'd almost forgotten.

"Yes, sure, 8:00 p.m., okay."

Then remembering that there was some mention of touching, she started to have reservations. However, there was now confidence in herself, for it was others that weren't trustworthy. Angela would never do anything morally wrong because the Voice would guide the way.

In the meantime, Angela wanted to get her life organized. There were lots of chores to be done. The stay in Tokyo would be a little longer than initially planned. It was just a feeling. After living in Kings Cross, there was a street smartness there. She sometimes sensed the safety of a place in words, at other times, it was in emotions. It didn't matter how her instinct operated. All that mattered was she possessed a keen ability to determine if the situation was *safe*. Angela could virtually stake her life on this intuition, which manifested internally as spoken words. Even if her feelings were doubtful, the Voice could be trusted. So much so, she would risk everything.

Shinjuku wasn't an appropriate place to live. So, hurriedly, Angela packed one bag with things that weren't needed and left a second ready to be filled. The rent was paid for a week in advance. Now the plan was to relocate to a more appropriate sub-city at the end of the week. Image is paramount. People in Japan judged each other by their dress, style, and residence. It's very superficial, but nonetheless, that was the reality of modern life in Japan. Angela spent the day packing, washing, and grooming.

The night came quickly. Angela went to the coffee shop early so as not to be late for the engagement. The man showed up dressed in an expensive suit and tie with his hair wetted back at the appropriate time. He was delighted to see her again. Anyone could see his excitement in his hand movements and the way he shook her hand. The man was trembling, for it wasn't her who was nervous.

Angela remembered the words that the Voice had said the night before.

"Remember, the true 'yeses' seek you!"

"Shall we go to dinner first? Then perhaps a little drink?" the man uttered softly.

"Sure, whatever you like."

He took her to an expensive restaurant, this time it was a Japanese one. The ladies who worked there wore kimonos as they served food. The rooms were made of rice paper and wood, and there was a tiny garden in the centre of the restaurant with Bonsai trees. The menu had prices that ranged from san-zen-en (¥3,000, A$30.00) to ni-man-en (¥20,000, A$200), for various dishes. But Angela only glanced at the cost of different meals. The man ordered for them both - that is the Japanese way. Traditionally the man decided everything yet the woman rarely decided anything, in public anyway. Even in the '80s, women were still subordinate. But outside public view, women had a small say. Angela quickly understood she'd have to behave like a Japanese woman to survive in Tokyo but think like a Gaijin.

The ordered dishes were in the middle of the range. It was very costly, but the man didn't mind, all he cared about was Angela. He was transfixed by every feature of her face. While she gazed at everything but the man, the beautiful kimonos, the Japanese garden, and rice paper screens. With a sense of familiarly, they chatted as she talked about Australia and her dance ambitions. He appeared to understand this Gaijin quite well, yet this was only their second encounter. Angela felt comfortable enough to allow the holding of hands across the table. It was only holding hands. What harm could there possibly be?

The man looked into Angela's blue eyes and announced, "Tonight we must cuddle, remember? You don't have to dance. I just want to hold you."

Angela blushed. "Can I trust you?"

"You believed me last time, and I didn't break my promise. So, trust me tonight."

For some reason, Angela believed him. It was a curious situation. Here was a Gaijin sitting in an expensive restaurant with an older Japanese businessman. He would pay her to go to dinner, then to a hotel to simply cuddle.

Most Australian people believed that there wasn't any middle ground between being a prostitute and a dancer. You were either one or the other, primarily. Angela felt as if she were in a transit zone, an area where she was neither. The most important thing was the money and not the category. The only thing that mattered was that there was no sex involved in this enterprise.

After dinner, the man asked, in a whisper, "Shall we go now?"

They caught a taxi to a different part of Tokyo. It was Shibuya, a trendy place frequented by young people. High on a hill in central Shibuya, there were many love hotels nestled together. Together they walked hand in hand up that hill. The man chose the most expensive hotel and, of course, the most expensive room. He prided himself on his excellent taste and always paid a high price for everything.

As they entered the room, it was Angela who was trembling while the man was relaxed. He now had her just where he wanted - a love hotel room. Angela started feeling apprehensive, worrying if there was any *sin* in this transaction. It appeared that to explore this situation would be the best way to find out. The Voice would tell her if it was right or wrong. In the meantime, this was unknown territory. The man loosened his tie as he slid down on the lounge. There was a huge bed, a sizable television with a vast collection of pornographic videos and a roomy transparent bathtub, viewable from the bed.

"Okay, I will pay you what we agreed, and we will cuddle, but you must take off most of your clothes," the man exclaimed.

Angela quickly stood up. "But you said cuddling only!"

"It's true, but you must be in your underwear. Don't forget I've seen your naked body, it's pointless for me to hold you clothed. What does it matter?"

He had a point. It did seem to make sense, for he'd seen everything. What difference would it make to the client whether she wore underwear or clothing? Then the man presented yon-man-en (¥40,000, A$400), the same amount as before. Angela didn't have to think too long about it. That money was much needed. And so, the clothing started to be removed.

"Please, yukkuri, slowly," the man begged softly.

Piece by piece, Angela slowly discarded each garment. The man took them from her hands and smelt each precious piece; then fondled them close to his face and caressed them as if they were somehow part of her. He found her garments sensually erotic.

This ritual continued until she stood there just in her bra, panties, and stockings. Then the man removed part of his clothing but left his trousers on, at Angela's request. He asked her to lie on the bed as he gazed on. He applauded loudly. Then walked around the bed, staring from every angle as if looking at a diamond on a pedestal. It was bizarre.

Angela was embarrassed and somewhat anxious. "Would this man be trustworthy?" she pondered silently, "Would he force me to have sex, or at least try?"

Then, like an animal, he slowly crawled onto the bed and rested directly next to Angela, barely touching. She trembled at the idea of a strange man actually caressing her almost naked body. It was daunting. Angela had only been truly intimate with one man willingly. She kept focusing on the money, which made it, all right. The situation seemed acceptable, as long as there was no sex. What harm could there be? The man slowly ran his hand up Angela's leg, down into her waist and around her back. He then pulled her in tightly. It was only touching, but he treated it extraordinarily. For a very brief moment, Angela felt a sense of arousal. She hadn't anticipated that a stranger may actually stimulate her in some way. Angela assumed it would only be she who created arousal. It was now the man who was affecting her.

Then he tugged the small Gaijin waist closer still, tightly, buried his head in her breasts and uttered, "I want you; I need you," repeated over and over again.

Angela felt a little empathy for this stranger, for he seemed lonely and so desirous. "How can a man in a society such as this, be so lonely?" she wondered, forgetting herself.

"May I kiss your hand?" he politely asked.

"Of course."

While trembling, he kissed the soft white hand as if it were a rose petal, so delicately. That physical act seemed to touch Angela's heart. The man was more than polite, he was exceptionally tender. They embraced for a full fifteen minutes.

"I think that's enough touching, don't you?" she announced.

The man's eyes began to water, uttering, "Whatever you say, but I could lie here forever with you."

"But I don't wish to do it any longer. It's been longer than last time."

"Please just another five minutes, nothing more, just the same for five more minutes."

She agreed, so they continued for a little longer, but it was a long five minutes for Angela. The man seemed to live hours in those few minutes, entrapping her.

Angela felt transfixed. The man had owned her body for those twenty minutes, possessing her physically, wholly. To leave the bed would be to lose the money, for the stranger had hired her body for twenty minutes.

She contemplated this situation, considering where it fitted into the scheme of things. Perhaps it was a mild form of prostitution, even though there hadn't been any physical touching. For the man possessed her body for a given amount of money. No matter how subtle the physical activity was involved, Angela, for the first time in her life had become the thing that was feared most, a prostitute.

CHAPTER THREE
'The Dream Price'

BY NOW THE snow was beginning to melt and so the temperature dropping, making it icy cold. Angela stayed in bed the next morning, listened to soft music and read her small pocket Bible. A million thoughts ran through her mind as she reflected on the things that had happened since arriving in Tokyo, and of what may lie ahead. Angela had ambition and was extremely passionate about dance and music. More than anything, she wanted those aspirations to be realised. As a single girl alone in Tokyo, Angela was prepared to do whatever was necessary to fulfil an unknown destiny and achieve those dreams. The words of the Voice had continued to echo in her mind.

"The true yeses will seek you!"

Angela remembered all the Japanese men who had taken an interest in her, they all seemed to find her. It was ironic that the Voice should imply that those men were opportunities. This Australian girl had always believed that it was sinful for a woman to be paid for sex. It was that excellent Catholic school upbringing. Her aspirations were pure, without sin. However, life was more complex than the dream of dance. Angela didn't understand many things, especially the world she was entering into.

The ryokan offered two kinds of breakfasts. The first was a traditional Japanese meal with seaweed, dried fish, noodles, rice and Ocha (Japanese tea). And a Western-style breakfast of scrambled eggs, bacon, toast and tea or coffee was also offered, for the Gaijins. That morning Angela was hungry and so ordered a sizeable Western-style breakfast, without the meat. As she sat in the ryokan's little cafe dining area, images of the night's experiences before were replayed vividly. She opened the purse to pay for the breakfast and noticed the money from last night, yon-man-en (¥40,000, A$400). That cash had been so easily obtained, with barely any compromise. It was a lot of money, in Australian terms, and appeared to be a solution to the present situation.

Angela pondered. "I can just be a freelance hostess. I can meet men and offer to be with them, not sexually, of course, at a high price and for a given time."

Despite this rationalisation, it still went against the grain. Angela knew deep inside if a man paid money for her time. Regardless of the real situation, it was indeed prostitution. However, she consciously ignored that single fact. Naïve as it sounds, Angela wanted to believe that the world really was as perfect as the dreams that enveloped each night's sleep. She wanted the world to be nothing more than a big stage, the people in it were the audience. At the same time, she danced on the dancefloor of perfection, without compromise. Be that as it may, rarely is life what we want it to be.

The next step in the plan was to find a favourable ryokan in a quainter area of Tokyo. Angela went out that day with this single purpose in mind. Along the way, many men gazed endlessly at the tall blonde Gaijin, and sometimes she'd smile. They were always genuinely surprised yet rarely smiled back, being a little put off by her openness, especially in public. It was evident that Japanese people were reticent and not prone to public displays of emotions. It wasn't acceptable to express oneself openly; a public facade had to be maintained. The public face was a mask. Looking into the men's eyes, Angela knew their desires, but the 'tatemae' (mask) told a different story.

It said, "I'm a businessman. I do not express my feelings."

Yet Angela sensed a burning desire underneath, passionate.

Without too much trouble, Angela found a quaint little ryokan in a sub-city 'Asakusa.' It was old-style downtown Tokyo and closer to Ginza and Akasaka. It was far less sleazy than Shinjuku but around the same price. This would be the new place of residence - Angela's new home.

On the way back to Shinjuku to collect her bags, Angela was asked out for coffee by a man in the street. She agreed and over coffee they chatted. The man expressed that he'd very much like to make love.

"I'm a freelance hostess. You can talk with me for a fee," Angela stated proudly.

"But we're talking now, and it does not cost me anything," the man replied with a grin.

"Yes, but this is only briefly and over coffee."

"I'm sorry it's all or nothing. I must have all of you or nothing," the man nervously uttered as Angela politely left the restaurant.

The next few days followed rather uneventfully. Angela had met many men, having encounters similar to the one over coffee the first day in Asakusa. Living at the new Ryokan allowed her to enjoy a traditional style Japanese room. The whole area was old-style Japan, and the cultural change was refreshing.

Around sunset, Angela walked through the streets, looking around and absorbing the new atmosphere. Then she noticed something very fanciful. Many of the ladies wore Kimono, walking in 'geta' (blocked wooden thongs) just like the traditional Geishas of a long-lost era. They were carrying purses that could've been as old. Everything about them was so elegantly time-honoured. It was really quite a thrill to see a piece of history unfold itself.

"The way they dress, they're so delicate, just like dolls. I'd love to be like that, so beautiful and exquisite," Angela thought silently as the women slowly passed by.

These women were not Geishas, for these days there were very few Geisha in modern Japan. Real traditional 'Geisha' was an art form, a little bit like 'Kabuki' (a type of Japanese play, where men play all the roles). Geisha was dying out, and there were only a few individual schools that kept the spirit of Geisha alive. The ladies that Angela saw were merely hostesses going to work dressed in traditional Kimono. To a Gaijin, they appeared the same. Geisha is an expert, a professional at entertaining men. At the same time, hostesses are merely women who serve drinks and talk with businessmen. Geisha was the epitome of that, and very few real Geisha existed anymore. Japan was quickly becoming modernised and internationalised.

Many of the hostess bars employed Asian or Japanese women, and some chose traditional attire. Asakusa was such a place; there were many small drinking houses with a classic theme. There were also many love hotels, wherever there was entertainment, then those would be nearby. In fact, Angela's little ryokan was nestled among several love hotels. There were also restaurants and shops, selling traditional items of all kinds.

That evening while exploring Asakusa, Angela found a quaint restaurant that served only udon noodles, a traditional dish originally from the Kansai region. They were delicious and inexpensive. If she only ate cheap food, then that yon-man-en (¥40,000, A$400) would indeed last a long time. It may even be possible to save a little money, mainly if more freelance hostess work could be found.

Angela's thinking was beginning to change. While eating those noodles, she saw another lady wearing Kimono walk past, and it gave her an exciting idea.

"No, I won't be a hostess. I'll become Geisha. I'll become the perfect Gaijin Geisha!"

The future would soon reveal a rather unusual chain of events. Now Angela began to see herself as a Geisha and not a hostess. Before travelling to Japan, she'd read a couple of books about Japan and its history. In them was information about the role of Geisha. A Geisha had to be a dancer and entertainer; she had to be intelligent, witty, and charming. A Geisha had to do many things and do them correctly. Angela wanted to be able to entertain a man and fulfil his every need, except one. Traditionally, Geisha never engaged in sex with the men who paid for their services. However, sometimes a Geisha may choose to have a sexual relationship with a client, of her choosing, but it was never expected.

Angela pondered, "How exquisitely beautiful, to be a Geisha, without compromise."

However, Angela didn't understand one crucial thing: real Geisha was almost extinct. The modern world of Japan had required Geisha to become something else, something more than tradition required. That was something Angela would eventually learn, personally.

The next couple of days passed by rather quickly. Angela had met many men, but it was difficult to find anyone who wanted the Gaijin Geisha service. She had given them her telephone number, but alas they wanted something else. They expected an intimate encounter with a Gaijin. That was their fantasy, and they were prepared to pay well for it. Clearly, most Japanese men were rather promiscuous. All the men Angela had met, although amiable and polite, desired casual sex with a stranger.

The next morning while changing hotels, Angela suddenly realised that she'd forgotten to notify the gentleman. The man who had paid to see the Belly Dance. Quickly scrambling through the bag, she found his name card and made a phone call. The man was delighted and requested that they meet that evening. He suggested having dinner together as there was something he wanted to discuss.

That evening they met at the corner coffee shop in Roppongi Square. Angela felt at ease with this man. Together they went to a traditional 'tempura' restaurant. The man ordered 'sashimi' (raw fish) and 'tempura' (deep-fried vegetables and seafood). It was delicious. They also drank 'o-sake' (Japanese rice wine). As it was wintertime, the o-sake was served hot, and it warmed her insides. It also made Angela quite drunk, thimble after thimble. She liked it, the taste was delicious, but she didn't realise exactly how potent the clear liquid was. As they left the restaurant to go to the love hotel, she became slightly dizzy and somewhat disorientated.

"Oh well, it's not as if I don't know you. I can trust you, can't I?" Angela implored.

The man smiled back at her as they entered the same love hotel as before. They took the same room. It felt familiar, and so had a sense of security about it.

"Of course, it's business first," Angela stated boldly.

"It's a business now? Has it become your new business?" the man asked, smirking.

"Oh, you know what I mean. I now think of myself as a Gaijin Geisha. You want me to entertain you, talk with you, dance for you and perhaps even cuddle you."

"Tonight, I want you!" the man softly replied as he placed the money on the table.

Angela laughed and replied, "Oh, no, no! I don't do that, remember?"

"Each time a little more, till I get you. Sukoshizutsu (little by little). It's you that I want, not the dancing nor your conversation, not even the cuddling, but you, your body."

Angela was very drunk and confused. Looking at the money on the table, it became difficult for her to think clearly. That money was badly needed. She needed time to consider, but the man was incredibly persuasive.

"Tonight, we will cuddle again, but this time you must be naked. I won't do anything you don't want me to do, but you must be naked."

With a trembling voice, Angela replied, "No touching, okay?"

"I must touch you, a little bit, but there'll be no sex, just touching."

Intoxicated and in need of money Angela reluctantly agreed, whispering all the while, "It's kind of like Geisha, isn't it?"

They laid on the bed together. Angela was naked, except for the stay-up stockings, while the man was half-naked. He stroked her back, legs and then her breasts. She stared at the man and felt a strange sadness, for he'd so easily persuaded her to do such a thing. An odd emotion overwhelmed her.

The man sensed the sadness and asked, "What is the matter?"

Angela shook her head and replied, "Nothing!" But inwardly, she felt that part of her innocence was slowly slipping away.

"There's something I want to show you," the man stated.

"What is it?"

"Look," he exclaimed, pointing to an enormous mirror in the

ceiling over the bed. Angela gazed up, to see her own naked body lying on the satin sheets.

"Look at yourself, you are so beautiful," he exclaimed.

For the first time, Angela came close to seeing her own beauty, the image of an attractive Gaijin with blonde hair and a voluptuous body. At that moment, she understood how the Japanese men perceived her as a sexual creature.

Twenty minutes elapsed, and Angela wanted to leave. The man begged to stay another five minutes. Angela agreed as she didn't wish to hurt his feelings. This man had touched her in a rather intimate fashion, and now he was taking advantage. She had done far more on this occasion than at any other time. The alcohol had worn off, and the realisation was setting in, that she'd virtually had sex with the man, without penetration. Touching the naked body of a Gaijin, the man had become highly aroused. Unexpectedly, Angela too had become a little turned on as well. It was difficult not to feel a thrill from the power, the insatiable desire men had for her.

The man adored her body and gazed endlessly at every part of her skin. He would crawl to the end of the bed and just stare at her for minutes on end as if she were some precious jewel. He'd done it several times, and with each prowl, up and down the bed it held a newfound passion. Angela could see that each time they came closer to the actual act of sex, the more passionate the man became. His real personality was slowly making an appearance.

A short time later, they left the love hotel together. Once again, Angela had the promised money, and the man had a little bit more of the beautiful Gaijin. But this time, she felt as if something has been lost, like losing one's virginity. It was as if she'd been touched inside. It was a strange feeling, and it was challenging coming to terms with this new unidentified awareness. There was a kind of dirty vulgarness about the encounter. Angela could feel the lingering impression of the man's hands. Even though it had been some time since the episode, she could again feel his sweaty palms stroking her breasts. They said good-bye and both went their separate ways.

Up until this time, Angela had only known the touch of one man. Thinking of Theo, she started to cry and ran down the street.

It was raining yet the umbrella remained closed. Frantically, she threw the umbrella into the gutter and kept running while tears rolled endlessly. Apparently, she was trying to elude an inescapable reality.

Then she found a public telephone, grabbed the handset and called her best friend. Angela had spoken to Barb on many occasions since arriving in Tokyo. They had always been like sisters, and this night she was in desperate need of a friend as if the crisis were at hand. Barb was still there for her, and this instance was no exception.

"Don't worry Angela. It's okay. It's not as bad as you think. It's just for a little while, I'm sure God will not punish you for doing something you have no choice in. You can always go home if things get bad."

Angela's sobbing turned into weeping and then slowly ceased. Looking at the humorous side of the situation, she started to laugh a little.

"Of course, Barb you're right. I can always go home. I can leave, can't I?"

"Of course, you can, Angela," Barb warmly replied.

"I love you. Thank you!" Angela closed the telephone conversation with a new tear, a tear of love for a real friend who'd helped her through many awkward moments.

A still somewhat emotional Angela caught the train back to Asakusa. Upon entering the room at the inn, she sat on the bed and listened to music. Angela then began to pray to God for understanding.

Moments later, she ran to the bathroom and showered. But she still felt unclean and began to re-wash with thick soap. The more she cleaned, the more the sensation of a man's hands remained. Looking down, Angela noticed a scrubbing brush that was used for cleaning the bathroom. She frantically grabbed the brush and began to scrub her entire body. After a short while, it was clear that the stiff bristle brush was merely scratching her beautiful white skin and not diluting the dirty feeling in any way. Angela threw the old brush into the corner, weeping she slid into the o-furo. She thought of the encounter and how the naive idea of Gaijin Geisha had so quickly vanished. Angela sat in the bath and sobbed to herself, contemplating how impossible life had become. It was clear that it was time to either return home or compromise. The choice was there, either to be a prostitute or a failure.

Angela vowed that day in the bath not to return home as a failure. She did not want to fail. She had come so far and worked so hard and couldn't give up now. Dance may have to wait, for Angela needed a life, here in this place and at this time.

In the calm of the misty bathroom, the Voice began to speak audibly. "My child, fear not, for it is not your sin, it is the world's sin. The world demands it of you. You do not choose it, but it chooses you. Therefore, the sin is not yours. Do not be ashamed and do not be frightened, I am with you. I will protect you always."

A soft peacefulness overcame her; she felt so close to the Voice. Those words would linger and echo in her mind and heart, into her very soul. The steam from the o-furo rose to the ceiling. It was as if there was a spirit amidst the mist. Somehow the spirit had permeated everything in that room, especially Angela. It appeared to be a mystical experience. There was a presence - undoubtedly that of the Voice. Instantly, the weeping ceased, for Angela now understood. It was apparent that the world was sometimes a dangerous place, and people often demanded morally wrong things. However, to survive, she'd need to do what the world required, without becoming spiritually corrupt. She had to be resilient.

After bathing, Angela went to bed and slept deeply. During the evening, she dreamt of the many men. The faces of strangers all were wanting to touch and hurt her while offering money. It wasn't a frightening or sad vision, but neither was it a happy one. It was a visualisation of recognition. Upon waking the next morning, Angela felt as if a transformation had taken place in her thinking, and indeed it had.

Talking with Barb on the phone that morning, Angela revealed the experience in the bathroom. Barb believed in her best friend and understood how difficult her life had been, the problems with Theo, and the poverty she'd experienced. They'd known each other for twenty years - a very long time. They'd been friends since school, but now they were much more than that, they'd become spiritual sisters.

"It may not be what you want, but it's certainly going to help financially, at least until you get what you want. The main thing is to believe in yourself and be strong. Remember Angela, be very careful, it's dangerous out there and you're far too precious," Barb uttered tenderly.

A joyful year formed in Angela's eye. The significant part was that she experienced love from her friend, and also the Voice. It was somewhat ironic, being in a foreign country far from family and home that Angela sensed love. Strangely there was newfound security and confidence in accepting the path that lay ahead. It was time to make plans. The plan was to work and save money, travelling to places that would eventually advance her career. To do these things, Angela needed money, which meant embracing the new opportunities and becoming a modern Gaijin Geisha that catered to a man's *every* need.

Angela hadn't engaged in sex with anyone since arriving in Tokyo, but soon would. She believed that the touch of a hand and the sexual act weren't so different. The principle was the same, yet the thought of having sex with a stranger was disconcerting. For despite Angela's pleasing appearance, she'd never done that before. But with this new attitude, there was a belief that she could do anything. It was merely a matter of keeping herself closed off inside.

CHAPTER FOUR
'The first time.'

~

Angela knew what it was she must do and so made plans to go to Ginza. After much contemplating, it was also clear that the fee must be high if this new occupation was to be taken on. There was no point in giving away such a service. If there was a compromise; then, it would only be for a generous sum of money and very little return. Ginza was the most expensive and exclusive place in Tokyo, in fact, in all of Japan. Therefore, Ginza would be her place, until such time, the circumstances changed for the better.

It was freezing, cold and raining the following evening. Angela rugged herself up with three pairs of stockings, two miniskirts, the imitation fur coat, and a jumper. The final thirty minutes were spent on her hair. After studying the subway map, the best route from Ginza to Asakusa was found. Unsurprisingly, it was the Ginza line. That evening she sat on the train and watched the men as they stared back at her and talked amongst themselves.

"Sugoi Gaijin desu nair!"

Many men used that familiar word, 'Sugoi.' Everywhere Angela went, they all used that unique word to describe this Gaijin's appearance. It was time to become immersed in this image, this new identity. Angela was just a Geisha, a modern Gaijin Geisha, and the word 'prostitute' never entered her mind. The idea of prostitution reminded Angela of the streets of Kings Cross. It created images of junkies who'd have sex with anybody for as little as twenty dollars just so they could get a fix. And so, those girls would have sex with many men each night merely to satisfy an insatiable habit. That's what prostitution was all about in Angela's eyes. She believed that being a Gaijin Geisha was something nobler.

Angela wanted to sell fantasy more than sexual favours - they would pay for an image. She tried to epitomise the Western Gaijin beauty to the Japanese businessmen. Sure, there were a few Gaijin hostesses and call girls in Tokyo, but they didn't compete with Angela. Most people were shocked to see a Gaijin woman alone in Tokyo. It was so rare that when a Japanese businessman saw Angela, the immediate reaction was curiosity.

Upon arriving at Ginza, Angela went to a little shop, near the subway and purchased a very colourful umbrella. It will hide her blonde hair and bright clothing if need be, apart from being excellent at stopping the rain. Angela was down to her last san-zen-en (¥3,000, A$30), yet the rent was paid, and there was enough food money for the next couple of days.

That night Angela strolled down Ginza's Chuo-Dori or main street. The lights glistened on the rain covered footpath, shining like a beautifully lit stage. The act of attracting a client was a kind of performance, except she wasn't doing much dancing. Still, the feeling was similar. Strutting down the street, Angela held her head and umbrella high in the sky, so everyone could see her long blonde hair. There were many designer boutiques in this area. Everything was so costly, so it was essential to adjust her price to suit the Japanese men who frequented Ginza.

"A thousand dollars sounds about right," Angela uttered aloud. "I wouldn't want to do it for a cent less." A thousand dollars was an enormous amount of money to this country girl from Australia. Dancing in Australia paid about $30 per show, while only three to five shows per week were performed. It was inconceivable that she could charge such a sum of money. At that rate, working just for a short time, it would provide enough funds to finance a big show that could be booked anywhere in the world. This job wasn't the end, but merely a means to an end. There was a lingering fear that she may get caught up in something impossible to walk away from. However, the words spoken by the Voice in the bathroom stayed at the forefront of her mind, so she believed everything would be all right. Just then, a car's headlights flashed around the corner, and a man walked close by Angela.

"Hello! What is a beautiful girl like you doing in Ginza, alone?" the man asked.

"Sex business," Angela replied.

"Sex business? Good Heavens! That's a surprise! (Pausing) How much is it?"

"A thousand dollars."

"Oh, so very expensive," the man replied. "But I think you're probably worth it. I'm sorry. I have no money but good luck."

Angela smiled and felt reassured by his interest.

The lights of Ginza seemed to represent something to Angela, but it was unclear what. There were many larger clubs - places she could've danced, yet this naïve dancer was out on the street in the rain and cold. Crowds of people walked by. Some stood and stared as if she were a mannequin that had come to life. Women, men, boys, and girls all noticed the white-skinned Gaijin. Many of them would talk about Angela, right in front of her, but it was impossible to tell what they'd said. All she knew was that this was a show, and so she had to smile and look exquisite. Angela believed that the right person would eventually find her, with whom to make that first inevitable compromise.

Angela wandered around for about an hour or so. The response was overwhelming, in fact, too much so. It was complicated to see how a man could approach a woman, about an intimate proposition, with crowds of people looking on. It was as if a movie was being filmed in the street. A less conspicuous place had to be found, a little spot where she could linger away from the crowds. Single men passing by might then have a chance to talk without being seen. But would it be only by chance? Angela believed that everything was in the hands of *God*. Angela thought that if anyone did meet her that evening, it was intended to be and had nothing to do with a random event. Fate had become the operative word, but Angela prayed that life in Tokyo wouldn't become fatal!

AIDS had become such an enormous problem in Australia. Many dancers and working girls in the clubs of Kings Cross were all terrified. The newspapers had said that scientists weren't even sure how HIV and AIDS were transmitted. Angela pushed all that aside mentally yet remained consciously aware that every possible precaution must be taken. She'd also dared not to think about the final act of sex. Inwardly, Angela hoped to merely entertain men rather than be used by them. But the time for compromise was at hand, and that would occur this very evening. Angela felt as much as her fingers trembled while walking in the rain at Ginza.

Almost at once, Angela found a lovely flower shop. It had lots of colourful flowers, orchids, daffodils, roses and even tulips. Tulips were significant to Angela, being born in a country town where 'tulip time' was the most popular event of the year.

Angela whispered, "Ah, this is my place. I will stand here near the flowers. The flowers look so beautiful, perhaps they'll make me look prettier."

Standing in the doorway's recess to the flower shop, Angela perfectly matched the pink and purple tulips. Some people walked by and would just stand there and gaze at the Gaijin. Then one person uttered something in English.

"Are you a doll? Are you real?"

A blushing Angela replied, "Yes, I'm real."

Realising what was actually said, they became embarrassed and continued on their way. From time to time, men would walk past and see Angela. Shocked, they would soon return for a second look and then perhaps even a third.

"Perhaps this is how it happens. I stand here, and men go past, then come back and keep looking. Is it up to me? Is it up to them? I don't know," thinking to herself.

Angela suddenly moved a little farther out of the doorway just as a man walked by on his fifth pass. It was time to say something, nothing indecent, but it was difficult to know what to say.

"Good evening, Komban wa, komban wa!" Angela stated happily as the man walked past for the sixth time.

Surprisingly, the man turned his head and asked, "Why are you standing here?" He could speak English very well, apparently a businessman about thirty-five years old, reasonably handsome and very interested in Angela.

"Sex business," Angela replied openly.

The man was thoroughly shocked. "It's such a sad thing. Why is such a beautiful girl like you, doing something like that?"

"I need the money," Angela exclaimed. "Tokyo is expensive."

"Mmm, how much?"

"A thousand dollars."

"What! It's too much. Mmm. It's far too much. I'd never pay that much for anyone. I'm sorry," he muttered and walked away with his head down.

"Well, that wasn't the right person," Angela said to reassure herself.

Looking up, Angela could see the raindrops falling from the sky with the neon lights shining through them. Then a gigantic laser light flashes across the street. The laser light was shooting through the raindrops and refracting into rainbow colours. It was like a massive stage show. Angela stood in the shadow of those lights as they reflected into many colours as her golden hair stood out, once again, people began to crowd around. They wondered why she was standing there in the middle of Ginza. It wasn't customary, and so many people were curious. Angela went inside the flower shop and out the back door, walked around for a little while, and then returned. By that time, the crowd had moved on.

If she stayed in one place too long, it would attract considerable attention and perhaps eventually draw the attention of the police. If the cops saw a crowd gathering, surely they'd want to know why? Angela instinctively knew that it may not be wise to use the term, 'sex business,' as it inevitably would also come to the police's attention. After all, she didn't know what the laws were relating to that kind of activity in Japan. Angela needed to change the method of approach and only use the word, 'Geisha.' In any case, Angela believed with more experience, she'd learn the appropriate manner to behave.

About twenty minutes later, the same man returned. He had walked past six times, and now this was the seventh.

"A thousand dollars is too much, but I want you. How about half - five hundred dollars?" The man offered with confidence.

"For five hundred dollars, all I can do is entertain you, not have sex with you."

"That's so expensive! But I want you, all right, let's go!"

Angela was more surprised than the man, she could hardly believe it. Here was a man agreeing to pay her $500, merely to be entertained. But it wasn't clear just how much entertainment was actually required. They talked politely as the man hailed the taxi at the corner of the street. Moments later, they got inside, and the cab drove off.

"I'll take you to a love hotel near here. Do you know Akasaka?" the man asked.

"Yes, I've been to Akasaka before, but I don't know of any love hotels there."

"Taxi drivers always know. How long have you been doing sex business?"

"This is my first night," Angela naively replied.

The man laughed happily, at the same time, rubbing his hands together. Evidently, he felt very privileged, being the first to stumble across an untouched Gaijin in Ginza.

"I must be the luckiest man in all of Japan!" The man chuckled to himself. Suddenly he embraced Angela and kissed her on the cheek.

Arriving at the love hotel, the man chose the most expensive room. It was apparent that Japanese men never negotiated over price when it came to their comfort and style. Angela couldn't understand how the *client* had negotiated a lower fee yet was prepared to pay san-man-en (¥30,000, A$300) for a hotel room.

"Are you going to stay with me all night?" he asked.

"If that's what you require," she replied.

"We will see."

They entered the hotel room. Apparently, it was customary for the woman to shower and bathe a Japanese man in this kind of business. In fact, it was expected. However, Angela didn't like the idea of climbing into a bath with a strange man. Who knows what diseases one could catch? But she agreed to shower with the man as that appeared harmless. Afterwards, she requested that the man bathe alone. When the cleaning ritual was complete, they both dressed in yukata (kimono-style dressing gown) and climbed onto the western-style bed.

"You won't have sex for five hundred dollars. How about 'half sex'?" the man asked.

"Half sex? What do you mean?"

"You want a thousand dollars for sex. I'll provide half that money, so you must provide half of your services."

Angela was inexperienced; then, suddenly realised what the man was talking about.

"Ah, you mean, like in France?" Angela whispered.

The man laughed and replied, "Yes, like in France."

Angela was reluctant but understood accepting this kind of work meant performing sexual acts which were unpleasant. In any case, it was bound to happen sooner or later. This man represented the time of compromise.

"All right, we will do as you wish, but you must wear protection." Angela agreed.

"That's okay," the man decided. Then he embraced and kissed Angela passionately, ripping off her kimono and rolling on top of her. "I'm stronger than you. What makes you think that I can't just take you?" he asked confidently.

"Because I won't let you. You are not buying me - you are just hiring my services. I'm a dancer, not a prostitute and the only reason I'm prepared to do this is that I have too," Angela stated boldly.

The man frowned and suddenly felt guilty about his actions.

"Do what you must do," the man uttered while relaxing back into the bed.

Angela removed the latex condom from the plastic cover and placed it on that particular part of his anatomy. The man so earnestly desired to be pleasured and groaned with desire. Angela performed the physical act of oral sex slowly but found it quite repulsive.

Then with a loud, passionate voice, the man exclaimed, "Your red lips are so beautiful, it is so wonderful."

It didn't last very long - just over a minute, in fact. Then it was all over. Then a moment later, the man glanced at Angela and began to speak.

"It's a sad thing what you must do, but you seem capable. You'll be alright."

He seemed to be a reasonably pleasant sort, but he could also be ruthless. Then the man got dressed quietly, all the while gazing at Angela.

"All night is not required, that's all. I must go home to my wife. You can't stay either because I only paid for one hour." Pausing for a moment, he added, "As this is your first night there was no agreement on who should pay for the hotel room, so you must pay half!" Then the man began to laugh coldly.

Angela was shocked. It seemed like she'd forgotten one small detail, to negotiate payment for the hotel room. The first client had tricked her.

The man laughed, "There are many things you must learn about Japanese business, one of them is you must agree on everything before a transaction is made."

"All right then," Angela reluctantly agreed.

The man was very pleased with himself. It didn't cost that much, but it was the principle of the matter. This type of situation was terribly ruthless, as far as Angela was concerned. The man was nice one minute and unrelenting the next, such a changeable personality.

Angela would learn that Japanese men never mix their emotions with business. This man was just the tip of the iceberg. It cost Angela ichi-man-go-zen-en (¥15,000, A$150). That meant she'd only made san-man-go-zen-en (¥35,000, A$350). Angela felt used and left the hotel with a determination to never be tricked again.

As the man signalled farewell, she whispered under her breath. "I hope they're not all as ruthless as you."

Angela caught a taxi to the nearest railway station. Taxi fares were far too expensive, and she'd had to be careful using them if money were to be saved.

After some difficulty communicating with the station master, Angela managed to find the best route back to Asakusa. Arriving home, she sat down on the 'tatami' (traditional grass matting) in the little ryokan bedroom. Angela began to write, recording her feelings about what had transpired. Shortly afterwards, she showered and washed tirelessly, and cleaned those gorgeous teeth, quite earnestly. Several times, in actual fact.

Curled up in bed, Angela listened to music as tears began to form. Was it just the music? Perhaps it was many things. She visualised dancing on a silver stage, high in the sky, with an audience like the one that had gathered in the street earlier that night at Ginza. They all gazed and adored her as she spun like an ice skater in a circle, pirouette upon pirouette. Little pieces of starlight shone from the transparent dance costume. It was such an incredible fantasy as she fell deeply asleep amidst the dream of the dance. The rhythm of the music was in time with her heartbeat, as she sank deeper into what would momentarily become, a dreamless sleep.

Suddenly, the wind blew wildly, and noisily the ryokan window flew open. Apparently, the maid had left the window unlatched, and now it was banging loudly. Angela awoke abruptly and glanced up only to see the room's darkness with glimmers of the cold rain blowing in. She quickly scrambled to the windowsill and shut the latch. Just then she noticed the moon, grey rain clouds were covering it. It was scary and eerie. Although half asleep, a feeling of pending precipitous danger enveloped her. It was as if something were lurking in the shadows. Then the memory of the physical act, that had been performed earlier that evening returned. All of a sudden, she felt tingling up her spine as if something was waiting in the darkness. Angela knew what the danger was - the haunting fear of AIDS. This was the first-night terror, related to the new business, and it was fearful indeed.

The dancing vision on the silver stage seemed so frivolous now as the realisation began to form just how dangerous the new business's activities were. Those clouds completely covered the moon and blackened the sky entirely. It was cold and pitch-black. Angela sat there waiting for the stars to shine through, but they didn't. She felt a cold shiver go through her body. Then she ran back to the 'futon' (traditional bed) and slipped inside with only her eyes peering out. Angela waited for ages, looking through the window to see when the moonlight would shine through. It was a strange interpretation, for she believed if the light from the moon shone through everything would be alright, but if it didn't, then it would an evil omen. If that precious light didn't shine through, it would be terrible. Angela waited for an hour, and only tiny slithers of light shone, but no moonlight. She began to cry.

"That is my hope. In the moonlight, there is hope. Without it, I have nothing. Please, let it shine!" Angela prayed as tears formed in her eyes.

The moonlight didn't shine through but looking higher in the sky, into a little pocket of clouds, a bright star shone through that reached Angela's eyes. With it, a sense of hope and joy emerged. Her tears turned into a nervous smile.

"The moonlight isn't there, but better still, the starlight is!"

It had been an exhausting night, but it was now eight o'clock in the morning. Sometimes people advertised things in the street with loudspeakers, usually some future event or the promises of a political party. It was always early in the morning, in residential areas, when these announcements were blasted loudly. As if they had exclusive privilege to enter people's houses any time they felt like it.

"Invasion of privacy and certainly noise pollution," Angela stated aloud in the room. All she could hear was the clamouring rumblings of distorted Japanese language coming from loudspeakers in the street. It put her in an atrocious mood.

"They have no right, disturbing me at all hours. What kind of people are they? Don't they have noise pollution control? Their customs are utterly barbaric compared to our society." Angela murmured to herself as she reluctantly began to dress and wash her face for the day ahead.

Angela didn't like many things about Japan, but there were also so many lovely things about the culture. It was a love-hate relationship. She loved the people and attention, and, of course, many of the customs, but some traditions were appalling. Her perception of Japan had been a subtle one, up until now. However, that was changing, for she was no longer a tourist.

When Angela went down for breakfast, the innkeeper presented a message from Ono-san. It read, "I will pick you up at eight o'clock for dinner."

Angela was irritable and unconsciously uttered, "Who does he think he is, assuming that I will be available whenever he wants?" She was furious and ripped up the paper into little pieces and threw them in the garbage bin.

The innkeeper smiled and asked, "Is there a problem, Miss Angela?"

"No, no problem. I'm sorry," Angela replied and marched back up to the room to sit on the tatami in a state of dismay.

Angela considered how to respond to that message. "I'll ring Ono-san. He has no right to control my life. I was planning to go to Ginza again tonight. I must save money. I can't waste time sitting around talking to Ono."

After taking a long deep breath, Angela sighed and reflected on how kind Ono-san had been. Perhaps this was an adverse reaction, and so she had second thoughts, "Perhaps it's for the best. He does seem to care." She ventured downstairs and phoned Ono-san's office. A few moments later, he came to the telephone.

"I received your message," Angela said. "Tonight will be okay."

"I like to take you to dinner. There is a business proposition I'd like to present to you."

Angela agreed. Afterwards, the rest of the day was spent studying Japanese language books. After all her reading, she was so tired that later that afternoon, she fell asleep. Then, suddenly, she spied at the clock to see it was already seven o'clock. It was very late. Angela put on a long black dress and her much-adored imitation fur coat which was now very worn. She looked sexy but not too much so. After all, it was best to avoid too much attention. That was something she'd learnt from the first excursion to Ginza.

Then the house intercom sounded. "Miss Angela, there is somebody here for you."

"Thank you."

Angela went downstairs to greet Ono-san. He wasn't polite and appeared to be a little annoyed that he had to wait so long. Yet it was only five minutes or so.

"Are there that many stairs to walk down, that it takes so long?" Ono-san asked sternly.

Angela smiled and replied, "Yes, I live on the third floor, and there is no elevator."

"Oh, never mind. There's a taxi waiting for us. Let's go."

Ono-san was in an awful mood, and Angela was beginning to feel the same way. As they rode in a taxi to a Sukiyaki restaurant in Asakusa, Ono-san started his dissertation.

"Well, I want you to teach English once again, but this time there won't be as many students. I don't know why, but many pupils aren't interested in learning English or don't have time. If things go well this time, we can get you regularly, say once a fortnight."

Angela pondered at the proposal. A couple of hours per fortnight was barely a job - more like a hobby. It was still a work offer, and so she agreed.

"What have you been doing? And how is your money going?" asked Ono-san.

Angela told him that she had just been out sightseeing and had been on dates with other men. Ono-san became furious.

"You mean you have been dating other men?" he shouted.

"Yes. Why is that a problem?"

"But what about you and me?" Ono-san interrogated.

Angela didn't quite understand the implication, for Angela believed Ono-san was far too old. Besides, he wasn't her boyfriend, but rather just a friend. It was apparent that Ono-san's interpretation of their relationship was vastly different from her own. Angela let that statement go, changed the subject, and started talking about Ginza, what a fantastic place it was at night. But now Ono-san was in an appalling mood and became somewhat aggressive.

"I don't have much time, so we'll just have dinner, and then I must go," Ono-san stated.

Angela nodded her head in agreement as they arrived at the restaurant. They entered the dining area of what was obviously a very traditional establishment. He demanded that Angela serve him. This included preparing the food at the table and serving the o-sake in his cup. It was also customary for a man to serve o-sake in the woman's bowl too, but he didn't return the gesture. Ono-san looked at Angela and grunted from time to time as he drank. After a few drinks, his mood changed as a smile emerged.

He studied Angela's face and narrated, "I have some plans for you, and I think you'll like them. It will mean you'll be able to earn money and stay in Japan."

Angela didn't know what plans Ono-san was cooking up. She just hoped that he didn't assume anything; wanting to be consulted instead of being commanded.

Ono-san chuckled to himself, nodded his head as he drank and said, "Yes, I do have something in store for you..."

CHAPTER FIVE
'Sex versus English.'

~

Angela soon realised that there was one word in the Japanese language that sounded similar in English and that perhaps men worldwide understood. That word was 'sex.' In fact, the Japanese form was 'sekkusu,' but it was close enough. Angela firmly believed that she'd have to compromise for only a short period.

Her rationalisation went something like this, "It's not what one does, but rather the reason why one does something which determines the moral content." If she compromised correctly, there would be no long-term effect, or so she believed.

Ginza was a busy place in the daytime, hustling and bustling. Many businessmen and housewives were shopping in the department stores of Mitsukoshi, Matsuya, and the Wako. There were literally tens of thousands of people shopping at Ginza during the day. Although, most seemed to be looking rather than buying as everything was so expensive. Ginza was hugely overpriced, even for the Japanese, but Angela was drawn to the crowds. Attracted to the excitement, the energy of the ocean of people seemed to stir something deep within her. She loved Ginza and wanted to be in the middle of it all. It was like being on the catwalk.

"Being a foreigner, people appreciate me better than back home,"

Sex Business Tokyo

Angela scribbled on a postcard at the corner of Ginza Square. Moments later, Angela attracted the attention of television cameras that filmed the beautiful blonde Gaijin as if she were a famous movie star. Ginza Square is a bustling place and considered the most expensive real estate in the world. One Japanese businessman remarked that the land there was valued at one million dollars, per square foot. As she stood on the corner, literally one foot squared, this Australian dancer dared to believe that she may be worth that sort of value as well.

It was getting towards the end of winter but still somewhat cold. It had stopped snowing and only rained infrequently. Angela would never get lost in a Japanese crowd with that bright blonde hair visible within the sea of black hair. Looking in the reflection of the department store windows, she could see herself clearly amidst the Japanese people - the image was that of an albino. Gaijins were occasionally seen at Ginza, usually with cameras strapped around their necks and the Tokyo guidebook slashed in their hands. However, they always dressed like tourists and looked nothing like Angela. Most were of an ordinary appearance and went unnoticed. Angela appeared larger than life, being taller than most Gaijins. Moreover, her hair was very blonde, and the skin was porcelain white. And so, every Japanese person noticed this Gaijin.

One obstacle was beginning to emerge from the encounters with men. It was a language problem. Angela didn't understand Japanese, virtually none at all, except for the fundamental things, such as, 'konnichiwa' and 'konbanwa.' Men would ask something, and she wouldn't know how to respond. Very few Japanese people spoke English. After much deliberation, it was decided it would be wise to study the Japanese language, to communicate better with potential clients. Angela wasn't interested in reading or writing 'Kanji' (Chinese characters), 'Hiragana' or 'Katakana' (Japanese writing systems). She only wanted to communicate verbally on a fundamental level.

One evening a man began talking to Angela at Ginza Square. He was Japanese but spoke with a strong American accent.

"So, you're Australian, are you?"

"Yes," Angela replied.

"Good die," the man replied.

"Good die? I don't understand." Angela was quite taken aback by this remark, for it sounded as if he wished her a good death.

"Well, in Australia you don't say day, you say die. Good die mate."

Somewhat shocked, Angela replied, "We say, ga-day."

It seemed that most Japanese peoples' general impression of Australia was slightly off. Some had been there for holidays, however infrequently. Others had the idea portrayed by media alone while others only read about the culture and customs.

Angela filled in the hours walking around Ginza, familiarising herself with the streets and the general location. Strolling down the footpath, she walked past a flower shop - the same one from a couple of nights before. It didn't look the same in the daytime. The lights were out, it wasn't raining, and there weren't as many people around. It looked like any other part of Ginza.

Nonetheless, she continued to scout the area as if she were a businesswoman considering the city for a redevelopment of a particular sort, her type. She noticed that all the night clubs and restaurants were away from the central area; nestled in the little side streets. Even during the daytime, many people were meandering around those small back streets, just like an army of ants. The flower shop may have looked pretty at night, but it didn't have the number of Japanese men needed for the new business. And so, she planned to go into the back-street area that evening.

After arriving back at the ryokan, Angela soaked in a long hot bath and prepared for the evening ahead. Meticulously preening her make-up; then putting on a new outfit that had been brought from Australia. It had been saved for special dance engagements. She wanted to look alluring and so curled her beautiful blonde hair till it was thick and full. As the day slipped into night, she caught the subway back to the city.

Walking down the back streets of Ginza, Angela saw lots of men, usually in groups. Most were a little drunk and boisterous.

Suddenly, a man appeared out of nowhere and grabbed her by the arm, leading her away as he began to speak in English.

"Don't go into here, this is Yakuza territory, it's hazardous," the man said sternly.

"What do you mean, Yakuza?" Angela exclaimed with a laugh of disbelief, "There's no such thing as Yakuza anymore, is there?"

The man was solemn. Although he'd been drinking, he wasn't very drunk at all.

"This area is Yakuza, Japanese Mafia, you know? It's very dangerous, and you're alone. I think it is best you stick to the central area," the man reiterated with a certainty in his voice.

Angela was a little frightened, but still determined, and continued down the same street to a dark area. As she wandered past groups of men, that familiar phrase sounded again, "Sugoi nair!" It seemed to echo through to her heart. She smiled, for it really was as if the streets were calling her name.

Just then another man approached, "Hello! I speak English. Would you like to talk to me in English? Perhaps we could have a drink together?"

Angela responded automatically, "How about a little more than a drink?"

"What do you mean?"

"How about, well, you know..." Angela murmured in a husky voice.

The man laughed a little, blushed from the o-sake he'd been drinking and replied, "Oh, I see. Is it like that is it? Yes well, then how much is it?"

"Well, it's fifty thousand yen to go to France, and it's a hundred thousand to go around the world." The words just seem to come out so quickly.

The man laughed and added, "You're almost as expensive as a plane ticket, probably even more so because a plane ride lasts a lot longer, doesn't it?" Chuckling, he held tight to the wallet clasped in one hand and walked off down the street. "Oh yes, far too expensive."

Angela didn't mind the refusal. In fact, she found it flattering to be considered: too expensive, elusive, unobtainable, and so unique. It was a compliment that most men could never afford her services. However, at the same time, she possessed a kind of hidden desperation. Underneath the smile, underneath the certainty, was a feeling of insecurity. She prayed to her God that this new path would be promising. Otherwise, it would be a frivolous waste of ego to even speak to men boldly. To fail at compromise would be pitiful, wretched, mournful abandonment. Indeed, there was shame in chatting to men in this fashion, to lose one's inhibition, and to speak so directly about something men wanted but were too courteous to ask. Angela could discuss anything, now. She'd already been to that place and made a compromise. In her own mind, all that was to happen now would be only business. Her business had now become sex, the sex business of a Japanese kind. Not a Kings Cross sex business, but an elegant, sophisticated, and stylised form. A high-class Tokyo sex business.

Another man approached and affirmed, "No! Please, don't come here. You must go away - it's hazardous as there are many Yakuza here. They will want to catch you. It's dangerous, please leave now." He then began to drag Angela down the street and across the intersection, to the central area. For once, she started to believe that there may be something to all talk of Yakuza. Could it be that ordinary Japanese people in everyday life were unaware of the powers that be, in the back streets of Ginza?

"I believe you," Angela uttered as the man let go of her arm.

"The police aren't a problem, but the Yakuza are. If you are doing what I think you are doing, it's dangerous. Please stay in the central road area. If you go into these streets, it will be sad for you. You're a lovely girl, and I'd hate to see anything bad happen to you," the man uttered in a soft, caring voice. "My name is Kojima. It's because I care about your welfare. I've seen a few Gaijin hostesses before, but you are the most beautiful girl I've ever seen. Are you really doing what I think you're doing?"

"Sex business, Kojima-san" Angela replied.

"In Japan, it's not customary to stand in the street but to work in a parlour."

"But I don't know where the parlours are."

"Just as well, because the Yakuza owns those too, and if they catch you, they will never let you leave. They will make much money from you," Kojima-san exclaimed.

"Is this thing about Yakuza really right?" Angela toyed with the man.

Kojima-san went into the details of how they operated. The Mercedes limousines with the dark tinted windows that were seen driving around Ginza were always Yakuza. That nearly all the high-end imported cars in Tokyo, according to Kojima-san, were usually Yakuza. Apparently, they worked in groups and used two-way radios. They possessed a secret code - 'Jingi,' a promise they kept to each other. They would sacrifice their little fingers in a ritual called 'yubitsume' or even their lives to fulfil the group's commitment. Each Yakuza level had an 'oyabun' (leader) who would determine what the 'kobun' (soldiers) were to do.

The smaller oyabuns would answer to the higher oyabun. This hierarchy operated right to the very top of the organisation. The function of the Yakuza was selfish by nature. So, they never cared about anyone else and would do whatever necessary to obtain money in any way possible. Kojima-san's talk was quite frightening and very vivid, portraying two Japans. The first was a Japan that was seen from the outside as very safe. "Sure, Japan is very safe, isn't it?" he added. "But underneath it all, Japan is possibly the most dangerous country in the world. The underbelly is extremely dangerous because the Yakuza here has no morality at all. They will do anything to obtain money. Even harm a beautiful girl like you."

"But I have to make money. The only way I can do it is through sex," Angela stated.

"I can't afford it anyway. But just out of curiosity how much do you charge?" Kojima-san asked with a smile.

"It's one hundred thousand yen for everything, all night."

"It is so costly."

On this occasion, Angela was wearing a purple hat. She'd spent some of the remaining money on an elegant wide-brimmed hat. She believed a new hat would create a new image, an original style, and with it many new opportunities.

Kojima-san looked at the purple hat against that platinum blonde hair, together with the sparkling blue eyes and expressed softly, "You are so beautiful. You are a princess. It is sad to think that you are involved in the sex business. I'd like to become your friend." He then proceeded to write down his telephone number, handed it to her and added, "Anytime you need to talk to someone or need help with something, please call me. No sex, okay. Not business, just friends. You will need a friend in Tokyo. Don't forget my name, it is Kojima." Then he smiled and walked away with a wave good-bye. Angela pushed the telephone number into her purse, to reside amongst the many other name cards accumulated. However, it was clear that he was different. The others all seemed to want something, yet Kojima-san wanted nothing. Friends were hard to find in Tokyo, and so, his number would be kept handy.

By now, the awareness of Yakuza had produced a cold shiver up Angela's back. After talking at length with Kojima-san, she noticed that all the limousines and many imported cars had dark tinted windows. These vehicles were always chauffeur driven with passengers in the back hidden from view. There were hundreds of those cars in Ginza. Kojima-san talked about the Japanese men's permed hair, how the Yakuza permed their hair in small curls and walked together in groups.

On the other hand, businessmen always had naturally straight hair, wore navy suits and appeared very ordinary. The men with permed hair didn't wear business suits but dressed in either expensive black tight attire or wore casual clothing, and all had a similar look. Kojima-san had stressed that they were real, Yakuza. They apparently liked to be recognised, for it gave them a feeling of power. People in general society were frightened of them. Yakuza represented a large group and to stand against one member was to stand against a group of many hundreds or even thousands. In their enormous numbers, they possessed unbeatable strength. Angela started to notice that, even on the main street of Ginza, many Yakuza men were walking around. It was frightening to realise that there were two Japans. She had fallen in love with superficial Japan.

She now was beginning to perceive the horror of the second, the criminal underworld.

Angela walked down the main street and found a familiar and safe place, the little flower shop. She stood outside the shop as before, smiling at all the men as they walked past. It didn't take very long, about an hour or so and a man came up to chat in English.

"How much?"

"To France, go-man-en, and around the world is ju-man-en."

"Fifty thousand sounds about right. Okay, let's go," the man replied.

He didn't argue about the price and didn't care about what it actually meant. All he knew was that he had to pay go-man-en (¥50,000, A$500) to be with a beautiful Gaijin.

Japanese men weren't concerned about which service was offered but were more worried about the girl's appearance and price. Angela and the man grabbed a taxi at the corner. Same as before. Then drove to a love hotel in Shibuya, some distance from Ginza.

The man asked in the cab, "It's all night, though, isn't it?"

Angela reluctantly nodded her head. "Yes, it is all night."

The man giggled like a schoolboy. "Oh, I'm so lucky," he sung to himself, almost the same as the previous client.

Angela could almost read his thoughts. Then the man mumbled something to the taxi driver in Japanese, as they talked to each other. The taxi driver kept looking in the rearview mirror while agreeing with the businessman as if they were looking over a prized racehorse.

"Shall we have dinner first? Would you like to eat Sushi?" the man asked.

Angela happily agreed. They spent an hour or so at the Sushi salon, drinking o-sake and 'Sencha' (Japanese green tea). It was a quaint restaurant; the Sushi went around in a circle on a conveyor belt.

Angela loved the distinctive aspect of Japan. All the fashion was kitsch while the customs were quaint. Yet, everything seemed from an earlier time, amongst the technology of tomorrow. Japan was a land of extremes, a place of inconsistency, yet they were a reticent people at the same time. This was a real contrast to Angela's capricious nature, but she loved the weird union of traditional and modern. Another unusual combination was emerging, that of Angela and Japanese men.

They walked the hill together to the love hotel. Then the man paid on the street.

"You can trust me, I'm not Yakuza," he informed, yet Angela hadn't asked. He pushed go-man-en (¥50,000, $500) into Angela's hand even before they had reached the love hotel.

On entering, the man asked Angela to choose a room. She went to pick the least expensive, but the man stopped her.

"No, no. Please choose the best room in the hotel."

So, Angela chose the most expensive, and that seemed to make him happy. The suite had a round bed with an overhead mirror, often the case, and a large television with an enormous pornographic movie collection. Then the man quickly locked the door, scrambled to the videos, and put on a highly erotic Japanese lesbian video. Angela followed his lead as he began to undress. He gazed at her, then at the video, looking back and forth. It was as if Angela wasn't real but merely a projected image, just like the women in the video. The man didn't talk but only gazed endlessly at the larger than life, Blonde Gaijin.

Then he gently showered Angela as if washing a ceramic doll. Neither of them spoke. Afterwards, the man dried her body meticulously, even between her little toes. Then he placed her on the bed while staring motionless at the perfect Gaijin body. Moments later, he moved around to look from the other side as if he had found a precious object, taken it home, cleaned it, and was now admiring it. He must have visually devoured Angela's body for at least thirty minutes. Gazing at her through the mirrored roof, he finally uttered his first words.

"You look just like Marilyn Monroe."

It was clear he really meant it. To him, this woman was Marilyn. At that moment, Angela realised something: to these clients, she was 'The Gaijin.' This was the man's first experience with a Gaijin woman, and he was both nervous and excited.

"Yes, just like Marilyn," he uttered.

Then slowly, he began to make love to Marilyn. It was very passionate. His touch was highly erotic as he caressed her with subtlety and caring that was only ever found in the hands of a boyfriend. He then proceeded to softly kiss the body of Marilyn, all over.

"I love you; I want you always, you're mine," he groaned.

Strangely, it sounded as if he really meant it, which was unexpected.

After another twenty minutes of tender caressing, Angela seemed to open up a little. She felt things she believed could never be sensed with someone in purely a business transaction. Perhaps it was inexperience and being worshipped in that fashion, disarming her emotionally. In any case, the man took something from Angela that evening.

This client had two personalities. Publically, he was stern and unemotional, but he became incredibly erotic and seemingly very passionate in private. Passion was something Angela understood well, possessing a devotion to dance. Her beauty concept was filled with love, seeing such emotion in another person was like meeting a kindred spirit. But what she saw wasn't desire but mere lust - a Japanese man's lustful yearning for the Gaijin body and sexuality. Angela's unworldliness misinterpreted the man's emotions, failing to distinguish lust from passion. It would take time before experience would reveal the subtle visual difference between the two.

That night a stranger possessed Angela in a very intimate manner, yet she didn't realise it until the following day. This was something that a novice would need to learn. As time passed, she would learn to control her emotions and not *feel* certain things with clients.

In the morning, the man became a different person. The seemingly passionate, caring and rather sophisticated attitude had disappeared. When he dressed in his suit, the businessman returned. The business suit was a *mask* that represented all the official mundane and day to day trivia of Japan, which had become so crucial to the process of making a living. In that new identity, Angela lost heart. The image she had of this man was now clearly an illusion, those phantom emotions evaporated in the daylight.

The client was only concerned with two things, hurrying Angela to dress as he didn't want to pay extra for the hotel room and he had to be at work in twenty minutes.

Upon leaving the love hotel, Angela went left, and the man went right. She looked back to wave farewell, but the man just continued walking as if it was all in a day's stride.

Angela had learnt many things that night. Most importantly, clients saw her as being the perfect Gaijin. Perhaps many Japanese eyes would see her in this way and, in time, she'd learn this to be true. To use this fantasy, in the sex business, would inevitably mean success.

It was about nine o'clock when Angela arrived back at the ryokan. However, she was disconcerted, for shortly afterwards she'd have to leave the room again. The ryokan rule was that no one was allowed in the room between 11:00 am and 4:00 pm. This meant Angela had to be out of the inn most of the day. This made life difficult for someone who worked nights and made it impossible to catch any sleep during the day.

The ryokan might have been a good stepping stone, but now Angela had to work hard to get her own place. It didn't have to be fantastic, but somewhere that could be called home.

That day, Angela was in an awful mood. How the man had changed personality had left a sour taste in her mouth. He had just toyed with her emotions. There was no doubt she missed Theo and was lonely, despite the fact he was a lunatic. The experience affected her and had done the very thing she was afraid of, it had produced unwanted emotions. Images of Theo took the place of the client as tears of sadness formed.

Angela began to converse with the Voice as if it were a person standing in the next room. They seemed to be separated by an opaque barrier, referred to as reality. She'd ask for guidance just as a small child would ask a father.

"Is everything all right? Will I be okay?" pleaded Angela.

The Voice's reply was always a positive one.

"Yes, my child, do not worry, everything is fine. It may be best to write our talks down, for your life is about to become complicated. I want you to remember some important rules!"

Angela was delighted that the Voice had taken such an interest without judgement. Soon afterwards, she purchased a hardbound exercise book and started to write the things that the Voice had said. She entitled the book, "Conversations with the Voice."

The first thing the Voice said was totally unexpected. "We have to protect you from three things, AIDS, the Yakuza, and capture by the police."

Angela had almost forgotten about the police, for they seemed so ineffectual in Japan, riding around on bicycles. They seemed powerless, but like everything in Japan, things are not as they seem. One day soon, Angela would learn that the police were exceptionally well organised and quite frightening.

However, the most prominent current fear was that of HIV and AIDS. That worried Angela deeply, haunting her dreams each night, like a creature from some black lagoon, standing in the darkness just waiting to pounce at any moment. If an accident occurred, it would be there, waiting ready. The Voice outlined several ways of avoiding contracting the virus. The first was to accept only Japanese men as clients. Japanese people had fewer reported HIV cases than in other countries. Secondly, was that Angela must always, under all circumstances, use protection. And never under any conditions become involved in deep kissing or any activity where the exchange of body fluids could occur.

The Voice was prolific and quite profound in all the conversations, speaking to Angela genuinely and practically. It was amazing beyond belief. This was definitely enigmatic and outwardly would appear totally insane. Angela had always been a spiritual person, but now it was difficult to distinguish between her *God* and her higher self. Strangely, and in some way, the Voice and her superego had become one. It was captivating to feel such closeness; like the touch of two fingers in the darkness. The *fingertips* were difficult to define, more like a sense of knowing, acceptance. Perhaps one could even describe it as a feeling of *love*.

Angela believed wholeheartedly that the Voice was indeed God because of this sense of love. She concluded that there was nothing wrong with her mind, with no alter-ego or split personality at work. She affirmed that the Voice was a being, a supreme being, who chose to speak to her in this particular fashion. And so, Angela felt exceptionally gifted with this presence. It was a very unique situation, making her an extraordinary person indeed.

The next instruction the Voice gave was unambiguous. "Use only the highest standards," the Voice added, "These are your three commandments of protection. I will always protect you, provided that you keep to these rules."

A sigh of relief echoed from Angela's lips as she put the precious little book into the handbag. It was certainly more than merely a diary. It was something very personal - a spiritual letter from a spiritual protector, and maybe even a deity.

There was a small café that sold Western-style food, and so Angela went there for breakfast. Afterwards, hours were spent browsing through the markets outside Asakusa Shrine, known as Sanja-sama. In the afternoon, she returned to the room at the ryokan. There was a message waiting from Ono-san. It read, "I will visit you this afternoon. Signed Ono-san." Angela was a little surprised that he'd taken so long to make contact. Tomorrow was Sunday, the day that she'd been booked to teach English.

Upon arriving, Ono-san said, "I want you to come with me tonight to Machiya and stay the night there. Then in the morning, you will teach English to the students."

Part of Angela still wanted to have a legitimate job. Ono-san had agreed to pay ¥10,000 for each lesson, plus all the expenses and food. However, she didn't like the idea of staying the night but reluctantly agreed, nonetheless. Ono-san had brought his car, and so after dinner, he insisted they go to a nightclub for some dancing.

Despite feeling uncomfortable at him extending her employment into the personal realm, she wanted to keep the threads to any legitimate job and wouldn't refuse any opportunity. Whether it be through Ono-san, whose intentions and motivations were never clear or if it were through some client, whom she'd met on the street. She accepted every opportunity in her stride and tried to be discreet and honest in all business dealings. After dancing at the club, Angela felt weary.

"Now we will drive to Machiya. It's only about an hour or so. Please rest in the car, put the seat back, relax and in no time at all we shall be there," Ono-san said with confidence.

It was a pleasant drive while the lights of Tokyo flickered past. As they speedily pursued the route of the freeway to Machiya, darkness enveloped them. For the first time, in many days, Angela could see the stars shining through the clouds. Tokyo produced so much light; it was impossible to see the stars at night. Sometimes glimmers could be seen, but only briefly. In any case, away from Tokyo, the stars and moon were clearly visible. It was delightful to let her mind wander to distant places, far distant dreams away in time.

Sometime later, they arrived at the apartment building. Ono-san and Angela entered one of the mansions, being a small Japanese unit. It was Ono-san's business to provide students with accommodation. The students were mostly young girls between the ages of sixteen and twenty-two. Ono-san was very proud of his collection of pupils, so much so he tried to remember them by their first names, which was highly irregular in Japan. The mansion at the front, on the ground floor, was the information room and it was Ono-san's unit. It was also his task to supervise the building, arrange maintenance and so forth.

Ono-san's unit looked more like an office than a home, with papers and telephones everywhere. There was one single bed with just a quilt covering it. Angela sat down on the bed, as it was the only place one could sit. There was an office chair, which had already been occupied by Ono-san the moment he walked into the room. Japanese men were like that. The man always walked through the door first, sat down first and ate first. It wasn't like Australia. Western society exhibited a polite etiquette that made it customary to wait for a woman. However, Japanese custom held the male as superior, and it was he that went first. So too, it was the man who decided virtually everything that happened in a relationship. Angela disliked this inequality and hated sexism. She had tried to avoid it at all costs, only to find it rampant in Japan and particularly prevalent in Ono-san.

"Would you like some ramen noodles? Or we can have Sushi," Ono-san said.

As they had eaten sushi previously. Angela replied, "Yes, I would like some noodles."

Ono-san promptly telephoned the nearest restaurant. Within ten minutes, two bowls of ramen noodles were delivered to the door. They were delicious.

Then, he turned the television on to a romantic movie. It wasn't clear what Ono-san's intentions were, but one could guess. He had always been so formal and business-like; Angela never for a moment considered romance with Ono-san. Besides, he was an employer and not a friend or boyfriend. All this aside, this Japanese man certainly wasn't someone she would be interested in romantically. After Ono-san had put the television on, he turned the volume low and dimmed the lights in the room, loosened his tie and removed his jacket. Then he sat down next to Angela and put his arm around her.

"Yes, it will be very nice having you working here. I'm sure that everything's going to be just right now," Ono-san uttered with a sense of surety.

Angela lifted off the bed and walked around; then, began to examine objects in the room. Picking them up to gaze in detail. Ono-san became cross, for it's not like a woman, in a Japanese man's eyes, to oppose his will.

"Yes, I'm an English teacher, that's what I am, and we are just friends, aren't we Ono-san?" Angela said sternly, glaring back at him.

Ono-san grabbed her by the arm and dragged her onto the bed, while affirming, "We are more than friends. There are things you must do for me, and in return, I'll provide you with work, but you must be nice to me." He repeated, "Be nice to me."

Those words echoed in Angela's mind. It was a cold, dispassionate statement that merely meant, "Obey my will and do as I say." Angela was beginning to dislike Ono-san intensely. Then Ono-san smiled, realising he'd stepped over the line, and sat down to watch television.

"Would you like some ice cream, some chocolate or some sweets? Asked Ono-san in a pleasant voice, as if nothing had transpired.

"Yes, I'd like anything that will keep us occupied."

There was some German ice cream in the refrigerator. Ono-san took it out and started to serve it into two small bowls. Angela asked if it would be all right if she rang a friend who lived in the Mie prefecture, about four hours away. It was Barb.

"Most certainly, as long as it's not overseas."

Angela babbled so fast on the phone that Ono-san could not keep up. His English was merely functional. Barb had missed Angela and was a little apprehensive about Ono-san's intentions. Barb advised that under no circumstances were she to give in to his will, for Barb understood Japanese thinking very well. Barb knew that if Angela gave an inch, Ono-san would take a mile. If she said 'yes' once, he would take from her a thousand times. Angela put down the phone with a certainty of what she must do. Ono-san must be refused on all counts. Even though sex was becoming a business to Angela, it was the principle of the matter. In this situation, Angela wasn't employed as a prostitute but as an English teacher. So, she resolved to be only that with Ono-san.

After the ice cream, as Angela had anticipated, Ono-san moved his body closer. Then Ono-san grabbed her arm and pushed her back on the bed and climbed on top. He had managed to remove his pants within the first twenty seconds before she'd even realised what was happening. Angela immediately started to cry, knowing that physical force could not overcome his strength. Her only defence was to appeal to his emotions. Angela tried to push him off, but he was too powerful. Instead, she cried more loudly. Eventually, that struck a compassionate part in Ono-san's heart, or perhaps it was guilt. In any case, he stopped, climbed off, slowly pulled up his pants, and zipped them back into position.

"I used to be in a relationship a short time ago. I'm not ready to be romantically involved with someone else," Angela wept softly. He believed this to be some kind of promise of future romance. Securing his belt shut, he smiled with delight, thinking it was only a matter of time. That night, Ono-san slept on a futon on the floor while Angela slept in the only bed. In the morning, they were both very private about their dressing and showering habits, at her personal privacy request. Angela didn't want Ono-san to know anything, except how well she taught English.

That morning, at about 10:00 a.m., in the upstairs dormitory, around thirty students gathered. Angela walked into the room to the sound of enthusiastic clapping. It was if they were welcoming a performer, rather than an English teacher. And indeed, they were but without their knowledge. The Japanese girls were genuinely happy to see the lovely Australia woman. Many of the girls would touch and caress the Gaijin's golden hair. They were enchanted by her appearance and personality. It didn't take long to realise that the girls didn't really want to study English. They were too busy with their university courses, in fact too much so, around seventy hours per week. The workload at Japanese universities is hefty, and the last thing these students wanted was to do more study in their free time. What these girls actually wanted was to be entertained by an English-speaking person. Hopefully, and purely by accident, some of the English would rub off. However, when it came to writing or reading English, they weren't at all interested. English study was just a fun thing, a little bit like watching television and not taken seriously. This made Angela's job very difficult, not being a professional teacher; she was unaware of many techniques to overcome this disinterest. Angela was a dancer, an entertainer, so that's what she had to do, entertain them with English. That would mean telling little jokes, singing songs, and getting them all to sing along, in the language of English. They learnt the words to 'Waltzing Matilda.' It was the most popular song, and they loved it. The two-hour class ended very quickly. At the end of the course, each student came to Angela, to say good-bye as if she were a friend. Most shook her hand and politely bowed their heads in appreciation.

The students left the room, Angela noticed that Ono-san was

slumped in a chair in the corner of the room. He'd been watching the whole time intently. Then he walked over, congratulated her on an excellent job and pushed ichi-man-en (¥10,000, A$100) into her hand.

"Get your things together, and I'll take you to the station now," Ono-san stated.

Angela was glad that she didn't have to ride back to Tokyo in the car with Ono-san. She wanted to be left alone and didn't wish to bear Ono-san's advances any longer. Ono-san was, to say the least, an obnoxious and a very selfish person. 'Ichi-man-en' wasn't much money, considering all the trouble she'd been through the previous evening. For that money it meant having to peel his hands off consistently and spending all night there, then teaching English the next morning, only to spend two hours riding back on the train. However, Angela wanted to hold on to legitimate work, but now it seemed like a waste of time. All she knew was that it was possible to make go-man-en (¥50,000, A$500) doing something else, very quickly.

The train ride back to Tokyo was rather pleasant. It was a long trip, and there were lots of people, mostly from the country areas, and they were quite startled to see Angela. Outside the city, most Japanese only saw Gaijins on television. Occasionally, a traveller was spotted carrying a knapsack on their back, hiking their way through a working holiday. These people had never seen someone so glamorous as her before. During the trip, she read a small book called 'Teach yourself practical Japanese.' It was interesting. It was undoubtedly the best way to communicate with the men Angela was beginning to meet, namely the sex business clients.

The book was quite illuminating and revealed something quite strange. The Japanese placed honorific classification on certain words, such as 'Otosan,' meaning 'father' and 'Okasan,' meaning 'mother.' The 'O' signified honorary notification. Then she noticed the bizarre part; they referred to money as, 'Okane.' They classified cash and people with the same degree of honour. This was a disgusting thing, and she hated it.

Angela threw the book into the bottom of the bag and said aloud,

"What a stupid book! Anyway, who wants to learn a language that considers money of equal importance to people?"

Just then, Angela looked up to see a Japanese gentleman with a huge beard and glasses. It was a rarity to see a Japanese man wear such a beard. He had a very characteristic face, that of a typical old man. He smiled at Angela with fond eyes, evidently full of wisdom.

The old man walked over and asked, "May I sit next to you?" The words were spoken in perfect English.

"Certainly, please do," Angela replied.

The man sat down, introduced himself and presented his card. "My name is Doctor Nomoto. I am a psychiatrist at Tokyo University Hospital. I have lived in America for ten years, so I am delighted to meet someone who speaks English. I rarely get a chance to speak English these days, so if you don't mind, I'd like to spend the rest of the trip chatting with you."

"That's fine. After all, I am an English teacher," Angela replied, believing that a single class qualified her as one.

The man talked at random about various subjects, not leaving room for Angela to respond. He was more interested in telling her about Japan, about the things to be aware of and avoid. He seemed concerned, and so asked several questions.

"Are you married? Are you in Japan alone? Are you working in a full-time job?"

"No. I'm alone, not married, and I'm not in full-time employment." She replied.

"In that case, you have to be very careful. For one, Tokyo is a dangerous place. Believe me, as I know, there are many sick people out there. They always seem to gather in the big cities and so Tokyo is no exception. It looks safe on the surface, but do not let that false sense of security lull you into an uncaring attitude. Tokyo underneath has many dangerously sick people. Secondly, there is an enormous Mafia in Japan. They are extremely dangerous, and if they see you, they will probably want you," the man said with a caring smile. He was a genuine sort and didn't want anything. In fact, he wanted to give Angela something, merely advice. He wanted her to treat this visit to Japan with a particular kind of prudence. One that up till now she didn't possess.

Arriving back at Akihabara Station, being the station where one changes trains, the man and Angela said farewell. He was slightly teary-eyed. In the short trip together, he'd become very fond of this Australian Gaijin.

As he started to walk off, he cautioned Angela once more. "Remember, there are lots of sick people out there."

While slowly walking through the railway station, his words echoed in Angela's mind. It was always the last thing that someone had said that stayed with her. She always pushed words of warning into the forefront of her mind. When there were encounters with certain people, these crucial words could easily be recalled. It was sad that the last thing a person said was often the most important, but it usually wasn't the most beautiful.

It was Sunday and a day of rest. That day, Angela wouldn't be concerned with going to Ginza. Just for a change, it was time to have some fun, go out to see a movie and forget about worrying about money. It was a great day, sunny and warm for winter. Angela went to Yurakucho and saw a Hollywood movie. It was entitled "Black Rain," not an appealing name, but it was a good movie and ironically rather frightening. It seemed like everything was now leading to one thing. The film was about the Yakuza. It painted a very violent picture about bloodthirsty, money-hungry, gangs of hoodlums, who would kill or do anything just to obtain their precious pot of gold. Angela was daunted by the violence but enjoyed the film, nonetheless.

Angela thought to herself, "This Yakuza thing sounds like an overreaction to a small minority." Yet she was to learn the truth the hard way. You see, soon she'd enter the danger zone.

The next day passed relatively uneventfully, and in the evening, Angela went to Ginza. It wasn't raining, but it still looked beautiful. She stood outside the flower shop for about three hours. It was such a challenging task, standing in one place for so long and smiling at so many people.

Occasionally a man would ask, "Ikura desu ka? How much?"

Angela would reply with an almost automated response, "go-man-en!"

"Far too expensive," they'd usually respond, only to would walk off in dismay.

Nonetheless, people were delighted to see a beautiful Gaijin standing there. Even the people who worked in the flower shop loved to stand near a window and gaze at her. Angela was exhausted after standing for so long in the cold. Yet the flower shop people continued to stand there. It was arduous smiling so much. She wanted to smile naturally, but it was becoming contrived. Neither did she want to look cheap and tarty. She aimed to beam with a fresh newness that the Japanese women who worked in the night club area no longer possessed. Japanese people never smiled at strangers but may if someone smiled first. Angela always had to present a big open smile and make the first advance. The Japanese were 'hazukashi', meaning shy or embarrassed and would never reveal their emotions publically, particularly with a Gaijin. For foreigners were 'those people' out there, the rest of the world — the non-Japanese. There was a 'us and them' mentality, meaning, 'us Japanese' and 'them,' being all the Gaijins in the rest of the world. Japanese people were culturally separated. Angela felt a kind of sorrow for that alienation. She wondered what kind of people they really were deep down, what they thought, and what they believed. However, as time passed, the answers to those question would be realised in extreme detail. Still, it would take a long time before she'd understand the implications of that knowledge.

Angela stood outside the flower shop for another two hours. It was now 11:30 p.m., and the subway closed at midnight. If she didn't get someone soon, it would mean having to catch a taxi after midnight, from Ginza to Asakusa, which would cost an enormous amount of money. Angela waited until 11:50 p.m., but there was no success. The men liked her, but that evening it seemed that most didn't have quite enough money.

Angela ran to the railway station and caught the subway train back to Asakusa. She met many men on the train, but of course, it was inappropriate to talk about such things in close quarters. Such negotiations were only possible in the privacy of a street corner, cafe or even a bar. In those places, Angela could utter words related to sex business. However, on the train, she could only smile, or at the most wink, hoping the men who were interested could read her thoughts. When Angela arrived back at Asakusa, she was a little depressed. There was a sense of failure that evening. She took it as a personal reflection on her desirability.

"I'm not pretty enough," she thought. "I'm too tall for the Japanese men, or I'm too fat." However, it just wasn't possible to succeed every time. Angela would have to learn to live with this reality. Even an expensive call girl in Tokyo didn't have bookings every day.

That night, Angela had slept peacefully and didn't worry about money. After all, she still had that go-man-en (¥50,000, A$500) and some English teaching funds. It was a blissful night's sleep. Quite early, Ono-san telephoned again. He was becoming a real pain. It was now almost 11:00 a.m., and Ono-san rang a second time. Angela didn't want to see him and made excuses when he phoned back.

"I have to leave the room now. I have to see my friends tonight. I'll call you soon. When do you want me to teach English again?" Angela uttered.

"Every Sunday."

"Well, let's leave it till then, shall we? Because there are lots of other things, I must do."

Ono-san was slightly annoyed but agreed.

"Thank God for that," Angela said to the Innkeeper after hanging up the telephone. Ono-san was unpleasant. He was selfish. It was like throwing scraps to a dog, providing a job which consisted of one hour per week and little money, and in return, expecting her to be on call. What kind of man does that? Angela didn't even know if he was married, had children or was divorced. She knew nothing about him, but he knew everything about her. It was an unpleasant situation she'd found herself in, the position of obligation, simply because he'd made gifts of money. That feeling of 'Giri' or social responsibility was something Angela would learn not to become involved with again.

"Never take money for nothing, because later someone will expect something from you!" Angela murmured, climbing the stairs. Slowly this Gaijin was beginning to understand the first principle of business in Japan. That it's not wise to be obligated to anybody, for one day they will call on that obligation. It may be in a manner and at a time that they choose, and in a fashion that they desire. It was better to be financially independent and not rely on anyone except herself and, of course, the *Voice*.

CHAPTER SIX
'The Danger Zone.'

~~

As often as possible, Angela phoned Barb. In Japan, this existence was like being stranded on a life raft, floating on an ocean of strange customs. The only link to the 'real' world was a telephone call to a close friend. Barb was that confidant. Everything Angela thought and did was shared with this splendid accomplice. At length, they talked about Angela's experiences, dealings with Japanese businessmen, and daily life in Japan. Barb had lived in Japan for five years, and so, she understood the Japanese mentality exceptionally well. This knowledge helped Angela adjust to the almost godlessness of the country. Japanese society didn't believe in the God of the western world. They were Shinto and Buddhist. Although many people were undoubtedly Buddhists, while others didn't believe in anything at all, which, at first sight, seemed neither good nor bad. The general society possessed no apparent morality, and that was just merely the way it was. This society was based on laws and honour, not character, then Western societies based on a combination of both elements. She found this fact hard to come to terms with. It goes without saying that Barb was primarily instrumental in helping Angela keep spiritually stable, especially during the first few months.

Angela also called Lynn a few times a week. Still, she wasn't as forthcoming about her activities with her beloved sister. Angela did not want to worry about an already concerned friend and sibling who was so far away.

Of course, Angela's daily conversations with the Voice were of prime importance. The Voice stated that her presence in Japan wasn't only for personal reasons. It was also to directly influence the lives of all the people in her world, particularly Japanese men. She was instructed to always remember that she was in Tokyo to find work and teach people about faith through example. Even those she'd meet in the most precarious situations, such as the sex business clients. Angela did, in fact, have a full-time job now. It was also a fact that she'd created this unusual position, with the guidance of the Voice.

Except for Sundays, each day, Angela would go to Ginza and wait outside the flower shop between six and nine in the evenings. Usually, if she met someone, it would be within that period. However, there were many days when she didn't get any business. That was a cause for concern. To live in Tokyo, one needed a stable income; financial security was crucial. Having never had it, it had now become of paramount importance. That stability would enable Angela to concentrate on the dance career that, hopefully, would develop later.

The best nights were Mondays and Fridays, oddly enough. Angela looked forward to Friday evenings. People who frequented Ginza, on Friday evening, were happier. Everyone was relieved that the week was ending and they could relax. Although most Japanese worked six days per week, as some put in time on Saturdays. So, Friday night was rather significant to Angela. The spirit in Ginza on those evenings was alive with optimism. At the same time, the rest of the week seemed rather dull, drab and somewhat pessimistic.

That particular Friday night, Angela was in a good mood and hoped to meet someone nice. So far, she'd been with about five different men and had spent quite a lot of time with each of them. It was always the same situation, 'French style.' It was never her choice; it was theirs, and ever due to financial considerations. All of their personalities were basically the same, and each encounter was too. Angela stuck to a particular business formula, making everything clear before even embarking on such a situation. Secondly, she collected money upfront. It wasn't very prudent to engage in sex business on credit. She was to learn that, as well as many other things, in the future. Anyway, that evening, she was in a happy mood and chatted to many men generously. They all seemed to cringe when the price was mentioned.

"Oh, so expensive! So expensive!" The reply was nearly always the same.

One man who knew Ginza reasonably said, "You're in the wrong place. You should be right over there, where all the night clubs are. I'm sure you'll meet lots of rich men there."

"Yes, but aren't there Yakuza over there?" Angela asked.

"Ah, but there's Yakuza everywhere in Japan. I don't think it'll make much difference to you. Just be careful wherever you go. Remember if you have any trouble, run to a police station."

There was a strange kind of irony about that statement. The two powers Angela feared most were the Yakuza and the Police. How could she run from one to the other for protection, when she needed to safeguard against the one she was running too? It was a precarious situation, and the solution was unclear. All she knew was that the Voice would warn of any trouble.

That night changed Angela's thinking. People were always delighted to see the blonde Gaijin, standing in Ginza's main street, night after night. They were usually businesspeople returning home. They passed by the flower shop around the same time every evening, and they'd looked out for the beautiful foreigner. Angela had become a Ginza curio and a well-known personality in the area.

Every night as they passed by, they'd say, "Komban wa, Gaijin san." Angela was a familiar and friendly face to them all.

This popularity was making it difficult to get clients near the flower shop. Angela knew it was time for a change of business address. That evening Angela went home alone and somewhat disappointed because it had been so busy. There was something wrong if she didn't meet a client on such an occasion.

The following day, Angela thought very carefully about the reasons for this and the fact that she'd made very little money. After all, she'd compromised to make money, not to make friends. She decided it was time to enter, 'The Danger Zone'. Several men had warned her to stay clear of that area, at all costs.

Oddly enough, the man of the previous evening had said, "That's where all the rich men are. That's where you'll meet someone, without any trouble at all."

Sure, the Yakuza were there, but Angela wasn't Japanese. She believed that being a Gaijin made her unique, and so exempt from Yakuza persecution. This Gaijin didn't have to become involved in Japanese situations with the Japanese Mafia. She was different, and could go into the danger zone and not be affected by it. Only time would tell if this thinking was correct.

After a somewhat subdued Saturday, the plan was to go into danger zone the following Monday evening. However, it was Sunday and time to catch a train to Machiya and teach English. Ono-san met Angela at Machida station. He was quite annoyed and relatively short with his words. Upon arrival at the apartment building, the dormitory had already been prepared, and the girls were eagerly waiting. Angela taught a tiresome two hours of English. The girls were lovely and enjoyed her company. However, Ono-san projected a very displeasing attitude, and everyone sensed it. The girls didn't like Ono-san either. During the class, he noisily fidgeted and was somewhat distracting. Angela ignored him and continued the lesson. After the lesson had ended, everyone came over to say farewell.

"Jar nair, Angela-san! Sayonara Angela-san!"

It was touching that the girls had become fond of Angela so quickly. It was quite flattering. She had never taught anything before and now felt she could do virtually anything in this country. Japan seemed to be a land where anything was possible, and it could be a place that she might be able to call home. It was ironic that a foreign country, particularly an Asian country such as Japan, could be home to this Gaijin. After class, Ono-san walked over to Angela, looked at her sternly for a moment and then began to speak.

"Let's go. I'll drive you back. There's something I want to talk to you about."

It was difficult to argue with Ono-san. If Angela were to interrupt his conversation, he'd just speak louder. He was rude, impolite and not exactly one's favourite person. On the way back to Asakusa, Ono-san talked about how he expected Angela to do certain things if the English classes were to continue.

Angela was very annoyed. After a long enough pause in Ono-san's dialogue, she stated, "Well, if you expect so much for so little, then maybe this job is not for me."

Ono-san reacted with a surprised expression, for he hadn't expected any display of independence. Angela was not so concerned with money now and believed that the job would be a merely good experience, but it wasn't worth the money.

Ono-san replied, "Well it's, it's not that I... just, it's just..." He was confused and didn't know what to say.

Angela interrupted one more time. "If I'm expected to do lots of other things, then maybe this job is not for me."

Ono-san was very displeased. Trying to cover up the obviously failed approach, he began to smile and act more friendly. "How about I take you out this evening, and we talk about it over dinner?"

After a little persuasion, Angela reluctantly agreed. She didn't want to lose this job, simply because it was legitimate employment. Although this Gaijin English teacher had other work, one made from pure necessity and not by choice. She had tried to avoid sex business as much as possible. But had it chosen her? Perhaps compromising a little with Ono-san, may result in full-time employment as an English teacher. Then there would be no need for sex business until the dance career got underway.

"Where would you like to go?" Ono-san asked politely.

"Ginza. Do you know Ginza very well Ono-san?"

He prided himself on his knowledge of Ginza and of inner-city Tokyo. "Yes, I know Ginza better than most. I've spent a lot of time there."

On arriving at Asakusa, Ono-san waited in the lobby of the ryokan while Angela changed. Shortly afterwards, they caught a train to Ginza to go for dinner. Ono-san found a typical Japanese style steakhouse, where people would sit wearing aprons, looking like overgrown children. They usually were so messy and had to cover their whole bodies with a rather large napkin. It was funny to see grown adults sitting around tables, wearing giant bibs. Angela found it very amusing. Ono-san misinterpreted her laughter, thinking she was laughing at him. That made the situation even more hilarious. Ono-san looked more like a child than the others, sitting there with a grumpy look on his face. After a short time, Ono-san queried Angela as to what she'd been doing.

Angela thought for a moment, then discreetly and tactfully replied, "I have another job but don't worry, it won't interfere with my teaching. It is a freelance job. I choose my hours and my days. It's very flexible and won't interfere with our arrangement."

Suddenly, Ono-san became very curious. "Is it English teaching?"

"It's similar, a bit like English conversation, but a little more involved." The statement was rather funny and unexpected.

"English conversation, hmm, sounds like you're doing a little bit more than that," Ono-san stated. Apparently getting close to the right conclusion. Then he added, "Ah, I know. I know what it is."

Angela started to feel a little apprehensive, thinking Ono-san had perceived what she was really up too.

"You're a hostess, aren't you?"

Angela smiled with delight, realising Ono-san hadn't uncovered her secret life. "Yes, I'm a freelance hostess that's right."

Ono-san commended himself on his intelligence, smiled and nodded. Then said, "Yes, there's very little that I don't know about Japan, and there is even less that I don't know about women." He went on to suggest that if Angela wanted to stay in Japan for any length of time; then, she'd need sponsorship.

Ono-san had prepared a little piece of paper that was folded into eight pieces. He took the small document out on removing his wallet from the suit jacket and unfolded it delicately. Then he pushed the plate aside and placed the paper down in front. It was written in English, and he was delighted that he'd done it himself. After pausing for a moment, he then began to explain. It was a business proposition. Angela was very curious and somewhat flattered that Ono-san had spent so much time preparing something, especially for this Gaijin.

"Well, let me see. You will need the correct working visa, and so, therefore, you will need sponsorship. I am prepared to sponsor you." He smiled and looked at Angela.

Angela looked straight into his eyes and pondered for a moment. "There's something sneaky about you, but I don't know what it is." It was uncanny, but this instinct would prove to be correct.

Then Ono-san continued. "First, there are documents that must be completed." Reaching into the coat pocket, he pulled out an envelope. He opened it to reveal half a dozen papers all typed in Japanese Kanji. All the documents had very official-looking seals. He presented these to Angela then added, "This is a declaration of my income tax, this is a sponsorship application, and this is our contract."

Angela was confused yet suspicious. Why did Ono-san go to such lengths? What was the purpose of the contract? Lastly, to whom was she to present these illegible documents too? Apparently, it was possible to lodge an application with the immigration department for a working visa for a reasonable time. All one needed was the correct documentation and most importantly, a sponsor.

"All the documents are for the immigration department, except the contract. The contract will be talked about a little later," Ono-san added. Then he pulled out something else from the suit pocket. It was a bank book, which he presented to Angela and added, "This is for you."

Angela glanced at it. There was a name printed on it in Kanji. Angela asked, "Is that my name?"

"Well, well no, it isn't. It's my name, but it's all right, I'll explain later."

By now, Angela was growing increasingly confused. There was something fishy going on here, but it wasn't clear precisely what it was. Then Ono-san looked at the little piece of paper that had been unfolded so delicately and resumed reading.

"Now if you want to work in Japan legally, without any issue, then you must lodge an official application for a working visa. I am prepared to take a big chance with you, on one condition. I don't think my condition is unreasonable and I'm sure you will agree." He then smiled and folded up the little piece of paper.

"Just before we go any further, please tell me what the one condition is?" Angela asked.

"Well, this contract is an agreement between you and me, with one important condition. It's in Japanese, so I'll try to explain as best I can in English. However, it's important to keep all these documents in Japanese. You can trust me!" Ono-san seemed to be quite the opposite.

Angela knew something was going on. "Please tell me straight. What is the one condition?"

"Well, it's not really a condition, it's just a... well... um, it's security. I need security."

"What kind of security?"

"Well, it's best if I explain it like this. This bank book is my bank. Your money goes in there, and when you want money, you ask me, and I will give it to you."

"But I already have my own bank account," Angela replied.

That statement didn't seem to register with Ono-san, he continued. "No! No. I want security. I don't wish to take responsibility for sponsoring you unless I have security."

"Well, please tell me what you mean."

Ono-san sighed intensely and realised that he needed to tell Angela directly. "Well," he said. "All the money you earn will go into my account, which is mine and when it comes time for you to leave Japan, I will give it to you. But if something happens then, I will keep it because I'm taking a huge chance, sponsoring a foreign person in Tokyo."

"You will give me back all my money when I leave?"

Looking down at the floor, he added, "Well, not all of it, I will keep 20% for my services."

Angela scoffed. "Your services?"

"Well, it is a big thing to sponsor a Gaijin. I am Japanese, and if you want to live in Japan, then you will have to do it the Japanese way."

In a sarcastic tone, Angela replied, "Listen here, Ono-san, here is your contract and your sponsorship. You can take all of that and put them back into the little envelope and back into your suit pocket where they came from because I won't be needing them."

"This is Japan, you know! You must do things our way!"

"I know this is Japan, but I don't need that kind of assistance. I don't need you Ono-san. If you want me to teach English, I will, but if you want me to give you all the money I earn, then we better just forget all about it."

"If you don't let me sponsor you, I won't let you teach English," he whined.

"Well, we are agreed then. I won't teach English!"

"No, no. I didn't mean it that way. I still need you to teach English, but... but." Then he tried to smooth things over and make it sound like it wasn't such an important thing.

"All right then. Let's just forget the whole thing happened and continue the way we were before."

Ono-san seemed to go along with that. Then he added, "Can you please let me make it up to you by taking you out for a drink?"

Prudently Angela agreed. After all, she was used to complying with men's needs and didn't like to disrupt things unless absolutely necessary. She wanted to be popular and preferred to be easy to get along with. However, in Ono-san's case, time would prove that she'd been a little too compliant. Perhaps it was wise to reconsider this relationship.

They went to a bar of Ono-san choosing, not so far from the restaurant. He ordered French liqueur, Angela's favourite. After one sip, then another, she started to relax. Ono-san became very curious as to what Angela had been doing and persistently queried. He was particularly interested in how much money she was earning. After a third drink, she was ready to tell Ono-san anything. She believed that no matter how shocking the truth, it would never hurt one.

"Well if you're going to push Ono-san, I'll tell you what I've been doing, but it's got nothing to do with my work with you."

Ono-san rubbed his hands together, intrigued. "Please tell me. What is it?"

Angela responded with a very proud speech-like tone. "Sex business."

Indeed, Ono-san was most delighted. His eyes flickered, and his cupped hands opened like a blooming flower. "Oh, how interesting, most interesting." Moving closer to Angela, he gazed into her eyes. "This is very promising," he replied once more after thinking about it for a moment, as he raised his glass to finish the drink. Angela realised that perhaps it had been a mistake to reveal this fact; it may have been better to keep it confidential. In any case, Ono-san had pushed so hard, perhaps it was time he experienced a verbal slap in the face. After all, ichi-man-en (¥10,000, A$100) per week wasn't a lot of money. Perhaps the reality of this situation would motivate Ono-san in helping her gain some other work, rather than having resort to such desperate means of survival. However, on the contrary, Ono-san was inquisitive. "I would like to experience you, myself," he said, his face flushed and glowing.

After nearly choking on the drink, Angela put the glass down, nodded her head from side to side and replied, "No, no! We have a business relationship. It's not wise to mix that relationship with this other kind of business." She then remembered the lousy week and how little money had been made. Even Friday night was uneventful. Now here was somebody interested, but she had to refuse because it may interfere with the other job. It was a delicate situation, and besides, she didn't like Ono-san. "But business is business," Angela thought. "Personalities shouldn't enter into it. If Ono-san fits into the category of a prospective client, then I must consider him just as other men." It was a question of equality and made business sense to take every opportunity. Ono-san pressured her even further and ordered more drinks, to which she politely refused. He was such an odd fellow and persisted all the while. At this particular point in time, the situation seemed to accentuate Ono-san's personality's negative aspects, irritating Angela.

"All right then, if you must know, I do certain things for certain amounts of money."

He nodded. "Yes, yes. How much does it cost?"

"Fifty thousand to one hundred thousand."

"Yes. Can I please have the fifty thousand one?"

Angela laughed while almost knocking Ono-san's drink over. It was such a funny situation. The man didn't even know what he was buying yet wanted it anyway. He didn't even know what Angela was prepared to do but wanted the cheapest service. It reflected Ono-san's personality, and it was quite amusing. Especially after all the other clients had shown such class and style.

He said once more, "Please, let's go now."

Angela disagreed and refused to engage in sex business with an employer.

"All right then, I will take you home. It's late," Ono-san said rudely.

Together they walked to the street, and Ono-san hailed a taxi. He hadn't been drinking that much yet had still managed to change personality. Then, almost at once, he became quite pleasant.

In the taxi, Ono-san was polite and extremely courteous, much more than usual. It was as if he were another person. "Please, please. I want your business. It's important to me and, perhaps, I think this will make our relationship even more honest."

Angela thought about that, then a moment later answered. "Yes, I can understand that. Perhaps that would make our relationship honest," she said. "Yes, then I agree."

Excitedly, Ono-san directed the taxi to Shinjuku. Angela didn't like Shinjuku, yet Ono-san did. That was quite evident in his personality. Shinjuku was reputed to have more Yakuza than anywhere else in Tokyo. They drove to the love hotel area in Shinjuku, 'Yon-chome,' area four. No sooner had they gotten the room and entered than Ono-san had his clothes off and was sitting on the futon in the Japanese style room, waiting eagerly like a spoilt child.

Angela said, "Well, it's business first, even though I know you."

Ono-san quickly reached for his wallet and slowly pulled out go-man-en. He looked at the money, then at Angela, looked back at the cash, then gazed at Angela's legs. Then he placed the banknotes in Angela's hands, closed them and uttered, "All right, just as you say." He was so excited.

Angela thought it was an odd situation but wasn't surprised. There were many things about Japanese men that were often difficult for her to understand. It was impossible to tell if this was a good or bad thing. Only time would soon tell.

Angela performed the routine, it was something like a dance routine. "Let's shower first. Issho ni shawā? Shower together?"

Ono-san scrubbed Angela meticulously, particularly her breast area. It was not such a delicate situation, for he was rough and treated her like a rubber doll. Angela disliked Ono-san's personality and detested everything he did. However, the business was business, and Ono-san was just like any other man. Then they got on top of the futon, Ono-san expected everything. Angela reaffirmed, for such payment, only certain things would happen. He was surprised at Angela's good business sense. As he'd previously believed, she thought ichi-man-en (¥10,000, A$100) was a lot of money. Yet here was Angela saying that go-man-en (¥50,000, A$500) wasn't much money at all and that if he actually wanted everything, it would cost twice that amount. However, Ono-san refused to pay the top price.

"So, then you must do whatever it is you do for go-man-en, but please, do it slowly and do it very well." He murmured.

"But I do everything well, Ono-san. You won't have to take my word for it." Angela removed the latex from the plastic cover and placed it on Ono-san. Strangely he was much larger than she'd expected. That disturbed Angela a little bit. She had believed that most Japanese men had small genitalia, but Ono-san proved that theory incorrect. He was a rather stocky built Japanese man but in one way of rather a large stature. After a short time, he arrived at some kind of physical release, without a sound. Angela showered once more. After the shower, Ono-san became silent. He'd changed back into the other man, which she disliked intensely except for one variation, he said nothing, nothing at all.

"Are you all right, Ono-san? Is everything okay?" Angela asked with a smile.

Ono-san did not answer and refused to look at her. He just got dressed and waited for Angela to put on her skirt and jacket. Then he walked out the door, down to the lobby and checked out. All the while saying nothing. It was strange, and it made her feel apprehensive. It now appeared as if she'd done the wrong thing. It was true that she needed the money, but perhaps he wasn't such a right choice. After all, he knew all about Angela, where she lived and every detail. If he wanted to inform the police or do something similarly dangerous, he was in an excellent position to do so. Ono-san was the type of man who liked to manipulate someone. Realising this, Angela became a little concerned. Ono-san, continuing the silence, hailed a taxi, got in, and drove off, without even looking back. It was so weird.

The Voice said to her, "An unsuitable choice. Never mind he will not hurt you. He is a sad person. You must just feel pity for him."

The next day Angela rang Ono-san. Concerned that something may have changed.

Ono-san came to the telephone. "If you don't pay me the twenty per cent I ask, then you won't have a job, and there's a new condition. I also want twenty per cent of your new business. I am a Yakuza. If you do not pay me, then you will not stay in Japan, I guarantee that." He slammed the phone down, not even waiting for a reply.

Angela became frightened. "Ono-san is Yakuza?" The words unconsciously came out, perhaps for reconfirmation. She didn't understand the implication. "What does 'Yakuza' mean? What does it mean that he is Yakuza?" Angela was confused and rang Ono-san back again to clarify the situation, only to speak to his secretary. Angela said, "Please can I talk with Ono-san? It's crucial, it's about money."

Quickly the secretary transferred the call directly to Ono-san.

Ono-san asked, "Do you now agree with my new condition?"

"No! There is no way on this planet that I'm going to agree to that. I don't care who you are. You don't frighten me Ono-san, and you won't get twenty per cent of anything and as far as your English teaching job goes, you can put that in your little brown envelope too! I don't want it, and I don't want anything to do with you, especially if you're Yakuza." As soon as Angela put the phone down, Ono-san rang back.

"I'm serious. Are you going to pay me twenty per cent or not?"

"No! Good-bye, Ono-san. Sayonara." Then she put the phone down and walked away from Ono-san forever. Instinct told her that he was one person she should forget and never to regret that decision. Ono-san was out to use Angela, as much as he could. He'd showed his true colours. In a short time, Angela had become better at business than he and had earned money honestly with sex business. Ono-san wasn't worthy of this Gaijin, that was certain. Angela had made the right decision for many reasons. Mainly, because of principle, of equality, and most of all because he was Yakuza.

CHAPTER SEVEN
'A Perfect Client.'

WHEN ONE THINKS about this situation, the irony can be seen. Here was Angela frightened of entering the danger zone for fear of Yakuza, yet the very person who she was working for happened to be a part of that same organisation. She'd now seen the forest for the trees, and it appeared safe to enter the danger zone, providing Ono-san was avoided at all costs.

That night Angela went into the danger zone, right in the centre of all the activity. It was a delightful place, the real heart of Ginza, 'nana-chome' (area seven). There were literally thousands of clubs and bars. She found the busiest street corner and stood there for all the world to see. People were utterly shocked at the boldness of this Gaijin. They couldn't believe it! Men gathered in groups to gaze from a distance.

"Sugoi! Sugoi!" They actually were calling Angela's name.

It was raining a little, and there were umbrellas everywhere. Angela had bought a rather beautiful French-style umbrella with yellow fringes. It was characteristical of her. It stuck out amid grey and navy businessman style brollies, or as the Japanese called them, 'Kasas.' Even in the rain, her presence projected out just as stars do. Men walked by uttering broken English.

"Hello! What is your name? Where are you from?"

Many could speak just a little English. It seemed many Ginza businessmen had some necessary English skills. Most were dealing with international companies and so had to learn to communicate. Angela had first noticed this standing near the flower shop. People in this area were indeed far wealthier. They dressed more exquisitely and generally behaved in a more sophisticated manner. She felt there was nothing to be afraid of here. The people all appeared to be refined, and none of them looked dangerous. In actual fact, they seemed quite the opposite.

Strangely Angela now felt secure and looked up into the sky to see a couple of stars shining brightly. Looking at the brightest star, she smiled and reflected for a moment.

"Please protect me and thank you for helping me. I know that you understand and forgive me. Please don't ever forget me!" Oddly enough, just when she'd forgotten about trying to meet a client, she looked down only to see a man standing there.

"You're beautiful. I must have you. You're the most beautiful thing I've ever seen."

He was handsome and very well dressed, the perfect client.

"May we go?" the man asked.

"But don't you want to know how much?"

"No, I don't. All I know is I want you, and that's all that matters."

This man was more refined and focused than many of the other men she'd encountered. He signalled a hire car, which was waiting on the corner. They drove to a rather large hotel in Ginza. It was 'The Imperial', perhaps the most expensive hotel in all of Ginza. The man tipped the driver ichi-man-en (¥10,000, A$100).

Angela was bewildered. "What kind of person tips the driver one hundred dollars to drive three blocks?."

They entered the hotel room, which had already been reserved.

"Is this suite, okay? Would you like something more expensive?" the man asked.

As the door swung open, Angela examined the room; it was a deluxe suite on the second floor. She could hardly believe her eyes. It was so elegant and beautiful.

"No, this is great, just right. I don't need anything more than this."

"Are you sure?"

"No, this is perfect, please come in and shut the door." The man did as she requested.

He strolled into the room and sat next to Angela. Turning his head gently, then gazed into her eyes, speechless for moments at a time. She'd almost forgotten why they were there. He was hypnotised by her presence and said nothing, but just like a caring puppy, stared deep into the Gaijin's blue eyes. Remembering why they were there, Angela stood up to break eye contact and walked to the window that overlooked Ginza. It had an excellent view. The building was high enough to see Ginza and many other parts of Tokyo. The lights were magical. They seemed to mesmerise Angela, as she had done the man. It was a strange situation, she gazed at the lights, and he looked at the lights in her eyes. Remembering once more precisely why they were there, Angela thought to herself.

"I'm here to have sex, not to sightsee. Remember, Angela, you're working."

"Business first," she uttered out loud, almost as if talking to herself, forgetting that she'd already been in the room for ten minutes and they hadn't even talked about money. The man pulled out his wallet, smiled and started to pull bills out.

"How much do you want?" he asked eagerly.

Angela said, with almost, by now, robotic repetition in her voice, "It starts from fifty thousand and goes to a hundred thousand."

"What is fifty thousand?"

"That's French style, a hundred thousand is everything, and it's for all night."

"What if I don't want to have sex with you?"

Angela was surprised at this rather unusual situation. Thinking for a moment, she replied, "But if you want me to stay with you and not have sex, it's no difference to me, you must still pay the same."

"Of course, must I pay five? Is that what you require?"

She thought for a moment, "That's fairly good, isn't it? I can get go-man-en just to stay with a man. Obviously, he's lonely and wealthy." Then replied, "All right then."

The man took out the go-man-en (¥50,000, $500), then added another ni-man-en (¥20,000, $200) and gave it to her. A smile came over Angela's face, she couldn't believe it as if it were a dream. This man was giving her seven bills just to spend time with her. The room was beautiful, she could order anything her heart desired. It was like she'd won first prize at a beauty pageant. As he was about to put away his wallet, the man pulled out another ichi-man-en (¥10,000, A$100) and gave it to her. That made eight bills.

"Is that enough?" he asked. "Do you feel comfortable about that?"

Angela smiled and replied, "Oh, yes, very comfortable."

The man put his wallet away, and the conversation of money ended.

"Of course, I would like to see you, but I don't wish to have sex."

"I understand," Angela replied. The man wasn't interested in anything other than admiring her beauty. He found her profoundly beautiful, and his eyes never left her.

Angela stood in the silhouette of the window, in the lights of Ginza and removed her clothing, piece by piece, slowly. Without moving his gaze, he leant over and switched the music on near the bedside. It was slow, soft jazz music and Angela slowly removed one piece of clothing with each new part. It was perfectly timed. The man loosened his tie and relaxed back on the bed, as he gazed endlessly. He was entirely encapsulated. It was a slow, but superb performance, to the very last piece of clothing, her underwear.

"Shall I take it off now or later?"

"Please, leave it on. I prefer to see you like that."

Angela stood in the silhouette, wearing her bra and panties. "And what would you like me to do now?"

"I'd like you to sit next to me and talk."

Angela sat down, and they talked, mostly about her life, why she was there, where she was going and where she hoped to go. The man looked at her teeth as she talked, then her lips, then at her neck, which quivered as she spoke. He surveyed every precious part of her body as if he were making love to her with his eyes. Then he came close and gently touched her arm, caressing it. The touch was enchanting and felt pleasing. Angela didn't think it was a sexual touch but more like an affectionate one. It made her feel relaxed and comfortable. It was as if he wanted her, but he didn't want her. She found it curiously fascinating but didn't mean to push her luck. She was happy with the situation, but, at the same time, there was something unresolved in her mind. "Why would a man do this? Why would a man be happy with so little? Is there something about him that I don't understand?" Angela thought to herself.

After listening to the man muttering about his business, his wife, his mistress and about his life, Angela said, "Excuse me, there's one thing that I'd like to know. Why are we here? Why don't you want to have sex with me?"

The man looked at her, smiled and said, "But, I am having sex with you."

Angela was somewhat confused; it was a strange reply. "Yes, I think you are, I feel the same as if we were having sex, but we physically aren't touching. I'm not saying we should, I'm just curious as to why we're not."

"For one straightforward reason. I'm frightened of getting AIDS. And Gaijins have AIDS."

Angela smiled, "Oh, it's not a funny situation. I know better than you, but why do you say Gaijins have AIDS? All nationalities have AIDS these days."

He refuted the statement and replied, "No, Japanese people don't have AIDS."

"They can catch AIDS, can't they?"

"Yes, from Gaijins, but they don't have AIDS, otherwise."

It was a ridiculous reply. The man was wealthy, intelligent, handsome, but he'd made an absurd and utterly stupid statement. Angela disliked this but quickly changed the subject. She didn't want to query the man any further. However, the frightened Gaijin knew well and understood his paranoia. And she now knew the type of sex that they were having. In his mind, it was sex and just as exciting if not more so, flirting with the unknown danger. The man wanted to pay the same price, in fact, a little more, evidently to feel like he was actually devouring Angela. The man wanted the experience but not the risk. The strangest part was that Angela was purer than the man. She'd known very few men and, as far as penetration had gone, she hadn't had penetration with anybody, since her boyfriend. Theo was the only man who she'd ever known intimately before Japan. The experiences Angela was having in Japan were not of a penetrative kind, thus far. However, this client had obviously had many affairs, together with a mistress, a wife and was a few years older. If anyone was in the high-risk category, it wasn't Angela, but the client.

After about an hour or so, the music dialled down to a slow murmur. Some of the lights in the city started to go out. Angela yawned softly, as the man's eyes began to get tired.

"What shall we do now?" She questioned.

"Now, you must remove your underwear, and we shall lie in bed," the man uttered softly. He kept his underwear on but removed the business suit, neatly folded it, and placed it on the clothes rack in the corner of the room. Angela slid into the pristine sheets, naked, white on white. The man ogled at the white body of the Gaijin and said, "You are like snow. You are my Snow Princess, so pure. If only it could be true." He repeated while peering at her breasts. Then, he slid into bed and positioned himself right next to her, without touching. Staring at her body and then at her blue eyes, the man fell asleep. Angela pretended to sleep, for she found it impossible to go sleep in the presence of a stranger.

"After all, who knows what this guy is really thinking?" she thought. "He could be a psycho or something, I can't go to sleep, I'll just lie here with my eyes closed." Looking up at the clock on the wall, Angela noticed it was 2:00 a.m. and thought to herself, "I must leave as early as possible, 6:00 a.m. will do. I will have to stay here for four hours. I'm really going to earn that money, after all." Suddenly it became apparent that, apart from the sex, this was what this job was all about, being physically restricted for the whole evening by a client's whims and desires. It wasn't so much the sexual aspect that was daunting and frightening now, and Angela was surprised. It was the entrapment, the claustrophobic possession that she hated most. It wasn't the intimacy and businesslike manner in which sex business was performed, it was the imprisonment. The man possessed her body for the entire evening. Angela started to feel anxious, as her palms became sweaty. The Voice came to her in the strangest of situations.

"Don't worry, I'm here with you." The Voice was talking to her, ever-present, even when she was in this compromised situation. "Fear not, I'm with you, always."

That little piece of heaven-sent speech was Angela's comfort. It made the four hours of confinement seem entirely comfortable, and no problem at all. She simply meditated the four hours away, thinking only of how beautiful the Voice was, and how in the most precarious situations, it would come and inwardly release her. It would take her anxiety and fear away. Angela had fallen into a strange waking sleep.

Then, Angela peeked out from the corner of her eye to see the sun rising over the windowsill. The wall clock was at 6:30 a.m. It was clear that she had fallen asleep, yet the man was still snoring. She got out of bed and started to dress.

Angela leant over, gently tapped the man on the shoulder and said, "It's morning now, I'm sorry, but I must leave."

His eyes slowly opened, and he nodded, "I understand. Thank you, thank you very much." He was such a delight, so polite and courteous, so very different from the other men.

As the man returned to his sleep, Angela left the room, then found her way to the hotel lobby, out the door and walked to Ginza Square.

After riding the Ginza line to Asakusa, Angela made her way to the room at the ryokan and scrambled into bed. She had at least three hours to sleep before she'd have to vacate the room. After a night of confinement, a tired Angela slowly drifted into an abyss of three-hour sleep.

Living at an inn wasn't an ideal situation. As time went by, Angela would find that the nightly confinements never allow her to rest. The anxiety of being imprisoned, with a strange man in a strange room, would virtually never let her sleep. She'd have to catch up the next day. Having to leave the ryokan at 11:00 a.m. each morning made this impossible. It was a frustrating situation. She'd have to find an apartment. Knowing the prices of things in Tokyo, an apartment would cost the earth, and she'd have to work very hard to get that freedom.

CHAPTER EIGHT
'Lessons of the Game.'

EVERY DAY WAS an adventure, a learning experience, and a great challenge, which was all a part of a jigsaw puzzle, called Angela's life. She looked for wisdom even in sex business. There are many ways to find understanding if one dares to look.

As the seasons changed, it rained every day. The people at the inn said it would probably rain for about a month, as it usually did. Armed with her umbrella, Angela went to Ginza and stood in her spot. By now, everyone in the area knew her and started calling the Australian dancer, 'Gaijin Geisha.' Some were calling her other names, but most were complimentary. People loved to see the beautiful Gaijin standing in the street.

Many people who walked past said, "Komban wa! (good evening)"

She would give everyone that big beautiful genuine smile of hers. It was as if Angela was a small ray of light in their evening. No other girls were standing in the street, only her. However, as luck would have it, the rain meant that business would be slow. There were many nights when she met no one but just stood in the rain for hours on end, only to smile at those passing by.

Angela's money had held out quite well. She had managed to

buy some new clothes and, of course, new umbrellas. Her room was decorated with Marilyn Monroe's picture and an original woodblock print of a Geisha returning home after a night's work. Angela saw the woodblock print of the Geisha, as herself. She also saw the Monroe picture as a symbol of the likeness she shared with her. The similarity was apparent to many. Both women in the two photos had compromised. Both showed signs, in some way, that they had returned from work.

After braving the rain, Angela realised how lonely she'd become in bed one night with damp feet. Listening to music, she imagined herself on stage, dancing to a beautiful soft melody. The body image was that of subtle undulating movements, as the veils trickled past her face. Twirling endlessly in circles made it magical. She was mesmerised by the dream for she looked like an ancient princess.

Angela appeared, for the first time in her own mind, perfect. The dance was skilful, and so was the music. There was a precision to the beauty that she aspired to. She fell deeper and deeper asleep, to wake the next morning with a feeling of romantic relief and inspiration. Angela believed she could find wholeness in those dreams, but perhaps, could never find it in the waking moments. Her life was a series of unpredictable events, but the dreamscapes were a perfect tapestry. She yearned to make these dreams real and felt that 'sex business' could help realise that destiny. It was merely a matter of trusting hard enough, long enough and doing certain things. There was a tremendous desire to turn the dream of stardom, dance, and music into something beautiful. Angela wanted to express to the world, the beauty that she felt inside. She longed to share that vision, yet the world required something else. It needed her body, not her heart.

The next day, Angela stood in her usual spot for about three hours in the pouring rain. There was a young man in his late twenties, standing across the way. He watched the Gaijin for about ten minutes or so; then, came across the road to talk.

"Would you like to go for coffee with me?" he asked.

"I'm working now. I would be interested in something other than coffee, though."

"Exactly, what is that?"

"Sex, of course," Angela replied quite openly and frankly.

"How much is it?"

"go-man-en."

"Alright, let's go."

They drove some distance away to a new suburb by taxi. Angela had never been there before and didn't know exactly where it was located. He was a strange person, speaking English at first, then afterwards only Japanese. A few minutes later, the young man was not concerned with communication and spent most of the time admiring the beautiful Gaijin.

"Yes, you look like Marilyn Monroe," he uttered many times, but that was all he said in English.

They soon arrived at the man's house. It was a little strange that a young man owned a large two-storey home in Tokyo. He lived alone. Angela thought that he must be very successful in business.

"What kind of business are you in?" Angela asked.

"Oh, I'm um... How do you say? I'm a real estate agent."

Angela was surprised at the young man's success in such a ruthless business, in the world's most expensive city.

They entered the house and went to the loft bedroom. It was very cosy with a heater, a very modern stereo system, and an enormous bed in the centre.

"Business first, if you don't mind," Angela said.

The man quickly grabbed five bills and passed them to her.

"I am hazukashi (shy). Can we turn out the lights?" the man asked timidly.

Angela thought it was a little odd but agreed. He turned out the lights, got undressed, then jumped into bed. Then he pulled the sheets and blankets over his body and switched the lights back on, to watch Angela undress.

"Why didn't you undress with me? There's no one else to see you, and if we're going to have sex with one another, it's going to be a bit difficult not seeing your body," she asked him.

"I'm just shy."

Angela undressed, slowly. The man became aroused while watching.

Angela's instinct was relatively acute. She felt the man was hiding something under those sheets, and it wasn't necessarily his body. However, she didn't know what but wanted to find out. Slipping off the last piece of clothing, she stood naked for the man to see.

"Alright, slide under the covers and join me," the man said with an excited voice.

Angela started to slip under the covers, then grabbed the edge of the sheet and ripped it off the bed, to reveal the full man's naked body. What a surprise! The man lay there with a tattoo, from his ankle all the way up to his neck. It was an enormous dragon, somewhat frightening, as it looked so aggressive. Angela jumped back out of bed.

"Aagh!" Angela shouted. "What a surprise! What is this? Why are you trying to hide it? It's quite incredible, I've never seen anything like it!"

"Don't worry, it's alright, don't worry," the man stated.

Angela then remembered that real Yakuza members were always covered in tattoos.

"Does this mean you are Yakuza?"

"Don't worry, it's alright. I used to be when I was young, but now I'm not."

The man was obviously lying and trying extremely hard to explain away something that hadn't scared Angela, only surprised her.

"He must be telling the truth. Otherwise, there'd be some other sign of Mafia in this house," Angela thought as she gazed around the room.

There was no sign of anything unusual. It was quite a stylish house, a modern style dwelling. There didn't seem to be any guns or drugs, nor anything lying around that shouldn't be. So, Angela believed the man was telling the truth. She got back into bed but pulled the sheets entirely off.

"It's alright, now that I've seen it. What difference does it make?" Angela uttered.

"So, you will have sex with me, then? You will trust me?"

"Yes, I will. Business is business, after all."

Then, they began to have sex. It was very slow and quite sensual. The man did everything he could to stimulate Angela. She refused penetration but did many other things. The young man was very imaginative, energetic, and highly excitable. She almost enjoyed his oral stimulation. The light from the bed lamp shone on the dragon, as the man's body moved. It was almost as if he'd became the dragon. His personality suited the tattoo, but something was unsettling about it.

"Do you trust me?" the man asked.

"Yes."

"Then, I wish to insert you. I must have all of you."

"But that is expensive. Can you afford it?" Angela asked.

"How much more must I pay? The same again?"

"Yes, you must."

"Alright, I will pay you in the morning. Now, let's do it and do it right. I have much money. Please trust me," the man pleaded.

A cold feeling was associated with that tattoo that Angela certainly didn't like, but she didn't know what it was. It represented much more than merely a tattoo. What it actually stood for Angela didn't fully understand. It appeared to be just marking on the skin, but it represented a whole tradition and culture. One that dated back five thousand years, comprising many customs a Gaijin, such as her, would never imagine or even try to comprehend. That is what was frightening, the real meaning of the marking. However, Angela had trusted the man just because he'd asked her too.

After the short interval of penetration, which occurred more than once, Angela felt comfortable in bed. She fell asleep from exhaustion, for he had been so physical. At 5:30 a.m., Angela woke up, looked at the clock, and realised it was time to leave. She got out of bed, started getting dressed, then tapped the man on the shoulder and asked for the extra money.

"Don't bother me, I owe you nothing now," the man snapped.

Angela was a little annoyed and said, "You must pay me the money you owe."

"Don't you know who I am? You should leave now. You should forget all about that money, you will never get it."

Angela was very annoyed and started to pull him by the arm. "You must pay me. You promised, remember? I trusted you."

"I am Yakuza. Now, leave or else it will be too late."

Angela let go of the man's arm and realised she'd been cheated. Quickly gathering her things, still half undressed, she scrambled out of the man's room, shut the door, and ran down the stairs. She finished dressing at the bottom of the staircase, picked up her bag and quickly left the house without thinking about the go-man-en that was still owing.

It really wasn't such an important thing. It was unclear what the man meant by 'too late.' All Angela knew was that he was a cheat. She wasn't that upset but just annoyed, being an honest person, she hated liars and cheats. All her life, she'd tried to keep a moral attitude and do the Christian thing, like treating others as she'd have them treat her.

On the train back home, Angela became furious. He'd promised to pay the next morning and hadn't. That was the first time she'd been penetrated, since Theo. In a sense, she'd lost her virginity as a prostitute that night. Ironically, she'd not even been paid, and it had been with a man with two types of personality. One was a very gentle, caring, sensitive person but in the morning, a very rough, ruthless hoodlum, who'd do anything to get his way. She didn't like the other personality yet was easily conned by the first. Angela had been taught her first lesson, 'never trust men with money and sex,' especially, those who were supposedly Yakuza.

Angela wrote it down in the diary. It was a significant event because she'd understood something; the first rule of sex business. The Australian dancer wasn't totally naive but not a woman of the world either. She'd seen a few things but now was beginning to learn new ways, firsthand. She'd never been given instruction by anyone and would learn everything about this business herself.

The next day it rained again. Angela didn't meet anybody, well not until it was quite late. Around 1:00 a.m., a young man came along. Unlike the young man of the previous evening, he dressed very casually in an expensive double-breasted suit. This man wore jeans and a windcheater and a little hat. He asked Angela what she was doing and how much it cost. She robotically repeated her business spiel.

"Sure, no problem, I have much money. Let's go," the man said.

They grabbed a taxi and drove to Ueno, a rather adventurous place. In the cab, the man couldn't keep his hands off her. He was trying to touch her breasts and legs.

"Please don't touch me like that. Please stop it."

But the man ignored Angela's request and continued to maul the Gaijin body. The taxi driver smirked as if it were something funny. She felt degraded and tried to push him back, but he was a big guy.

When they arrived at Ueno, they parked outside the love hotel area, where there are many love hotels on a hill. The place is called 'Yushima,' and is a favourite place for lovers. Ueno love hotels are quite beautiful and not so expensive. The man led Angela up the hill, all the while touching her bottom, pinching, and degrading her a little more. She was annoyed and furious.

"Please stop it, please or I'll leave," Angela said, but she didn't leave. She kept thinking about how she must work hard and save money.

Soon they arrived at a not so sweet love hotel. The man picked the cheapest suite. He was young and apparently not wealthy. After entering the room, the man immediately pushed Angela onto the bed. He tried to have sex with her while fully clothed. Angela managed to get off the mattress and out of his clutches, for a moment.

"Listen here. There're two things you've got to know," Angela uttered.

The man didn't understand, as he didn't speak English very well.

So, she spoke slowly. "First, money. 'O kane.' Second, be nice! Don't treat me disrespectfully. I'm highly expensive, you see! Watashi is a very high-class girl!"

"I no money have, but I want you," the man uttered slowly in English.

Angela was furious. "What do you mean, you have no money?

You agreed to pay my fee. You brought me all this way, mauled me in the taxi, pushed me on the bed, and tried to rape me; then only to tell me you have no money!"

The man laughed as if he had won a contest to trick a Gaijin as if it were some great deed, something pitifully fantastic. Surprisingly, his English became much clearer. "Well, seeing you're here now, we may as well have sex because it's too late, you can't go back. We should stay the night here and have sex because it will cost you too much if you catch a taxi home. You must wait until the subway opens in the morning." Sure of himself, he grabbed Angela, threw her on the bed, and forcefully began kissing her.

Angela pushed the man off and slapped him across the face. Then she grabbed her bag and headed for the door. While leaving, she turned to the man and shouted loudly, "You are the kind of person I detest. I'm beginning to realise that not all the Japanese men in this place are decent. You most certainly are not!" She slammed the door loudly and scampered down the stairs.

It was time for lesson number two: make sure that the man has the money before you go anywhere with him! Angela wrote it down in the trusty diary. It seemed like she was at school again, in the class of sex business. She was learning quickly, day by day, and lesson by lesson. It was sad because trusting people came naturally to Angela. But it was a very different life now. There had never been any adverse situations in Australia when she trusted people. All her family and friends were sincere and never ever let her down. In a foreign country, it was only now engaged in an illicit business that she'd seen the darker side of people; where crime and corruption are prevalent. Now, this sweet Gaijin was being cheated more than even she realised.

The next morning, Angela checked her purse to see how much money was left. It was quickly going down, for the nights had been slow. It rained all week, and very few people accepted her price.

Angela went to work every night that week and for five nights in a row, didn't meet anybody. The money was beginning to run out, and so was her self-esteem. She decided it may be time to consider working during the daytime. If she were to go to Ginza in the daylight hours, it would be impossible to work as the department stores would be open. Ginza was a very different place during the day. Reluctantly, she knew the only place to work during the day was the place she'd first stayed in Tokyo, namely Shinjuku. Although it was sleazy, perhaps her presence alone would add a sense of elegance to the area.

Angela arrived at Shinjuku around lunchtime. Most of the people gathered near the big 'Koma Theatre.' It was a stadium where many rock bands performed. There were also quite a few movie theatres, dance halls, nightclubs, and restaurants. The centre of Shinjuku was called 'Kabuki Cho.' For a while, Angela wandered around, gazing at the movie bill posters, and talking to different men. It was great to be outside. She was trying not to worry about money. The plan was to have fun while working at the same time. She didn't stand in one place like in Ginza but just strolled endlessly. If someone liked her, they would follow.

The rain stopped for a short time, and the sun started to shine on through. The water on the seats, near the Koma Theatre, had evaporated. People were beginning to sit to enjoy the sunshine. Angela decided to soak up the sun, as well. It was delightful sitting there and feeling her soft white skin become so warm. It was like being back in Australia. The sun on her face gave a reminiscent sensation. It was something she'd experienced every day back home, yet only once since living in Tokyo.

Angela sat there, almost asleep with her eyes closed. Then she noticed the shadow of someone sitting next to her. She turned to see a very strange-looking man.

"Konnichi wa, Gaijin san," the man uttered.

He was very traditionally Japanese. Two other men were sitting next to him on his left-hand side. He was dressed in an expensive suit, wore sunglasses and a moustache. As Angela looked closer, it was possible to see little curls in his hair, the 'Yakuza curls.'

Although the man whom she'd slept with the previous week didn't have such curls. Angela knew that he may be Yakuza but wasn't sure. In any case, he was clearly influential. The other two men were quite obviously his bodyguards. He gave one man a large amount of money and instructed him to go do something. Then, he told the other one to stand a little distance away and watch.

It was a curious situation. This man spoke fluent English and began to ask Angela some questions.

"What are you doing here?" he asked.

"I'm just going to the movies." Angela didn't know why she had said that. Usually, she'd say, "Sex business," but her instinct told her, "No, you're at the movies today."

"Are you sure you're not doing some kind of business here?"

"Really, I just want to go to the movies."

"Do you do business in Shinjuku? Angela nodded her head back and forth, then replied, "No, I work in Ginza."

"Ginza is very high class. You must be expensive. I know what kind of business you do because I'm in the same line of work. How much do you get for a night?" He asked.

"Ju-man-en."

"It's expensive, but you're probably worth it."

The man revealed that he had some share in an establishment, in Shinjuku, that offered call girls. So, he granted Angela a job.

"Why don't you come and work for me?" the man asked.

Angela immediately thought, "If he's in the business, then he must be Yakuza."

"Are you Yakuza?" Angela asked naively.

"Yes, I am," the man replied straightforwardly. Then, he removed his sunglasses and looked directly in Angela's eyes. "But you need not fear me. I simply would like you to work for me. I will pay you two million yen per month if you work for me and only me. I will also pay you the same money, guarantee to start, but you must work for me exclusively."

Just then, the bodyguard standing a few feet away, said something to him in Japanese, distracting his attention. Angela became quite apprehensive. She hadn't confronted more than one Yakuza member at a time before and didn't know what she was supposed to do. Of course, it sounded like a great offer. She could make a tremendous amount of money doing, basically, the same thing.

The Voice said, "If you get in, you can never get out. It's better to be patient. Stay alone, and be sure."

After the man had finished talking to his counterpart, he turned to Angela to hear her reply.

Angela said, in a very polite, soft voice, "Thank you very much for your generous offer, but I'm okay the way I am."

The man laughed and added, "That is hard to believe, but you know where to find me. This is my area. Everybody knows me, my name is Toyo. I don't have someone as beautiful as you, and I don't have a Gaijin. If you ever want the job, my offer is there."

"Thank you," Angela replied with a smile.

The man gathered his two counterparts and slowly walked off. As they did, they looked around as if there was something to fear. They were apprehensive. They didn't see Angela anymore, they were too busy looking out for something or someone else, perhaps, another Yakuza. Angela didn't sense the danger. She was a Gaijin, and above it, or so she believed and would be so for a time.

However, something Angela would also learn was that the longer she stayed in Japan, the deeper she became involved in the Japanese tradition, the Japanese way of life. Even if Angela didn't associate with the Yakuza, she became involved in the day to day dealings with people who may be Yakuza. It would probably be just as dangerous or would become just as dangerous, but Angela didn't even think about that.

Angela thought to herself, "Ha! If that's Yakuza and that's what all the fuss is about, what's the big deal? Why are people saying to be careful all the time? "Be careful. If the Yakuza catch you, they will beat you, they will do this, they will do that." He seemed very nice. He didn't hurt me. The only man who hurt me was from the previous week, he cheated me out of five bills. All I have to do is be careful, avoid them and only have sex with them, if they pay me upfront. "

The rain had ceased altogether that day. Angela was about to watch a movie but continued sitting in the sun for a short time. It was pleasant and relaxing. Listening to her headphones, she couldn't hear anything outside and with her eyes closed, it was as if the world had disappeared in the middle of Shinjuku's busiest place.

Then, Angela felt a tap on the shoulder, from the same direction the man had been previously. Thinking he had returned to make a firmer offer, she turned to say, "No, thank you." Then, she noticed it wasn't him, but another man. Angela removed her headphones and saw a slightly plump businessman. He was kind of cute looking, a little older, but positively not frightening and definitely not Yakuza.

"Hello. How do you do?" the man said.

"Hello," Angela replied.

"What are you doing here?"

"Sex business."

The man laughed. "Oh, it's so unusual to find a beautiful, blonde Gaijin, like you, in Shinjuku. It's such a delight. I am so happy to meet you."

"Usually, I work in Ginza, my price is very high. I'm sorry, but I think it's probably too expensive if you're used to coming to Shinjuku. "

The man laughed again, as he said, tilting his head sideways, "Perhaps, then again, perhaps not. How much is it?"

"Fifty thousand is the starting price. "

"Ooh, it is expensive! Is that for all night?"

"Yes, and that is only for half sex if you know what I mean."

The man continued to laugh. "How much is everything?"

"That is a hundred thousand."

His eyebrows raised in surprise. "I think that's the most expensive I've ever heard of, in Japan. It must be the most expensive in all of Japan. It is really the first time for me to meet someone like you." He said, "What about a short time, how much is that?"

"The same price. I don't do short times, nothing less."

The man was extremely surprised, he couldn't believe it. Angela had been so direct and frank with him about her business, yet, had a sense of pride about herself.

"You are very proud, aren't you?" he murmured.

She nodded. "Yes, I am because I have a dream, and sex is only a means to an end."

"Alright, I will pay you fifty thousand yen for one hour. How about that?"

Angela smiled and said, "But, only half sex, remember?"

The man laughed and added, "You are excellent at business, aren't you? You will go a long way, I think, especially in Japan."

"Do you still want it?" she asked.

"Yes, I do."

Together, they walked to a love hotel, not so far away. It wasn't expensive but beautiful, surprisingly enough. The man watched Angela undress, then quickly scrambled out of his clothes. They showered together, then got into bed. He didn't grab hold of her like all the rest of them immediately did, but he lay there and seemed happy.

"I have a dream too. It's not like yours, mine is more of a fantasy. I have a fantasy of my Angel, my special Angel. She's probably not a white angel, but she's an angel to me, nonetheless," the man said softly, looking into Angela's eyes.

"That sounds very interesting. I hope you meet your Angel someday."

"It's quite likely that I've met that Angel today," he said, as he turned to her and started to caress her.

Soon afterwards, the man had been reasonably satisfied, without penetration. He didn't let go of Angela but held her tightly, even as they showered, once more. Most men liked to be washed clean. This man didn't care to shower but just wanted to hold Angela.

After they had washed, the man requested that she lay next to him. He held her hand as he looked in the mirror above the bed.

"My fantasy, I shall now tell you. Forgive me for telling you this, but it is to hurt the one I love. The more I hurt my Angel, the more wonderful it feels. You can probably not understand that. I think many people cannot, but, if I were to hurt you, it would give me great sexual pleasure and satisfaction, as well as peace of mind."

Angela was a little confused. "You mean, you are masochistic?"

"No, I'm a sadist. I'd like to tie up someone perfect, like you, Angela. To make you completely immobile, then, to inflict pain upon you. That gives me total sexual satisfaction and release."

Angela was feeling a little uncomfortable, as she let go of the man's hand and moved to the side of the bed. "But wait a minute. We're finished now."

"Yes, I know. I'm not talking about now. I'm talking about the next time."

"I've never done anything like that, although my boyfriend used to spank me sometimes."

The man became highly excited and said, "Yes, that's what I mean. That's what I mean, only, perhaps a little more forcefully than your boyfriend did."

Angela thought she understood, perfectly well and said, "So, let me see. You want to inflict pain upon me, tie me up and then have sex with me? Is that what you'd like to do?"

"Yes, I would like to do that, and I would also like to whip you."

Angela was overcome with confusion. This man was quite clearly very wealthy. After all, it didn't have to be the real thing, it could be a fantasy.

"I'll have to think about this one. I don't get many requests like this. Can I have your telephone number and I'll get back to you?"

"Most certainly, but remember, it doesn't have to be real, you just have to make it real for me. Do you understand?"

Angela did understand. She knew the difference between reality and fantasy, only too well. She knew this man was intelligent, but; somehow, strangely, was abnormally driven to peculiar sexual behaviour. This type of sexual aberration came out cruelly. Could Angela handle this situation? Could she possibly use this fantasy in such a way, that it wouldn't hurt her, so there was no actual danger to her body? They got dressed, ready to leave the love hotel.

"Tell me one thing. If I were to do this particular thing for you, I would expect my top price. Do you understand? As it is a rather unique situation, I think it would have to be only for a short time.

I couldn't do anything like that all night, it would be too painful. But, perhaps, for a short time, for a hundred thousand yen, I could do it. Can you afford that?"

"That is certainly the most expensive I've ever heard, but I'll pay whatever you ask. Please consider my offer. I really would like to have my fantasy fulfilled with an angel, like you."

"I'll call you tomorrow," Angela said.

The businessman's name, who was a sadist, was 'Mr Tako.' Angela would be thinking of him a lot within the next twenty-four hours. He seemed to be a rather peculiar fish from the ocean. If only his scales weren't painful, it would be alright. Angela would have to talk to the Voice about this one, a very tricky customer. Sooner or later, Angela would have to decide. Just now, it appeared the decision would be 'no.' She wouldn't like to do such a thing. But this girl didn't know herself that well. Perhaps the answer would be, yes.

Angela spent the next day in a state of introspection. She knew that this man had a lot of money and knew she'd only waste a relatively short time being with him. Could she do what he requested? Mr Tako and others like him were successful businessmen. They lived ordinary lives under a lot of pressure and developed abnormal behaviour. Angela would meet many men whose sexuality weren't average. Still, to understand them, she had to know what really satisfied them. The Voice said that He would protect her in all circumstances, as long as the rules were kept. The rules didn't say anything about S & M, so Angela believed that she could handle it being relatively big and strong.

The next morning, Angela got up early. She went to Harajuku, a fun place, where lots of young people brought rock and roll accessories and punk-wear. Some of the punk-wear consisted of leather and chains, even handcuffs. Angela grabbed a pair of handcuffs off the shelf and quickly paid for them. They looked so real and worked just like real ones, with a key and everything. Angela thought, "This is ideal for my Mr Tako." She went home and put the key on a unique necklace that she hung around her neck.

"Only that key can open these handcuffs," she would tell Mr Tako, but the handcuffs could be opened if one knew the mechanism very well. They weren't real ones, they only looked authentic. Angela said to herself, "These would be great for his fantasy. He would think I'm really handcuffed, but actually, I can escape at any moment."

Then, Angela went to a sex shop in Asakusa. She was on the hunt for all kinds of gimmicky, but not expensive things, to make the fantasy seem as real as possible. She found a bondage rope made of soft cotton, which wouldn't hurt but looked brutal. The man could tie her up and do whatever he liked. Angela also bought an imitation, leather whip. It seemed very realistic, but it was totally painless. For the game of pain, Angela had bought all this new equipment.

Angela rang Mr Tako and said, "I have lots of material for our particular event. How about this evening, at six o'clock? Is that alright?"

Mr Tako was overwhelmed with excitement. "Yes, most definitely! Shall we meet at 'Asakusa View Hotel' lobby?"

At 6:00 p.m. sharp, Angela walked into the lobby. Mr Tako was waiting eagerly, rubbing his hands together and hungrily looking her up and down. She was dressed in a black skirt with a floral jacket. Her make-up was very dark, and her legs were covered in black fishnet stockings. Mr Tako was delighted with her appearance. He quickly whisked her out of the door and down the street to an exquisite love hotel.

When they entered the love hotel, Mr Tako said, "Are you sure that you can do this? Can you satisfy me? After all, you're not very experienced. Perhaps, you should charge me a cheaper rate. If you're very experienced, I wouldn't mind paying a reasonable price."

Angela blankly refused to enter the room and said, "I am a professional. You will be satisfied, but you must pay the full price."

Mr Tako entered the room, dragging her in behind him. He shut and locked the door. They entered the living room, and Angela sat on the bed, with her little bag of tricks next to her.

Mr Tako asked, "And how much do you want for two hours of this kind of entertainment? I know we talked about money before, but, considering..."

Angela stopped him. "Considering nothing, Mr Tako. I want ju-man-en, a thousand American dollars. Whether it's one hour or two hours, it's still the same price."

Mr Tako walked around the room for a minute, scratched his head, then looked back at Angela and saw how she was dressed.

"Mmm... I'm not so sure about this now."

Then, Angela unzipped her little bag and pulled out the handcuffs, bondage rope, and the whip prepared for the occasion.

Mr Tako's eyes nearly popped out of his head. "Oh well, yes, in that case, most definitely!" He then reached into his pocket, pulled out his wallet and presented Angela with one hundred thousand yen.

Angela was happy, as it was the most she had been paid. She then put the money in a special hiding place in her bag. "After all, you can never be too sure," Angela thought.

Her experiences in Tokyo were becoming varied, and her lessons were, almost always, practical experience. She didn't want to take chances with money that was very hard to obtain. Mr Tako requested Angela to strip to just underwear. Angela was wearing very sexy, French-style lingerie, black suspenders, a black bra, and panties. Mr Tako was exceedingly excited at the beautiful Gaijin's appearance.

"Please stay like that. Don't change completely, I like, a little bit of mystery," Mr Tako said, as he got the bondage rope and meticulously tied Angela's legs together.

"The cuffs are for my hands. Please don't tie my hands, we must use special equipment for them."

Mr Tako excitedly agreed, not realising that they were simply an imitation. Then, as Mr Tako tied Angela's calves together, Angela placed the handcuffs key on the chain around his neck.

"Now, this is the key to the handcuffs. You are in control," Angela said.

"Oh, excellent," he said. "So wonderful. You look so beautiful tied up, it contains your perfect beauty, in a moment in time, just for me."

This man wasn't so interested in sex, but in fantasy and now, his illusion was becoming real. Then, Mr Tako removed Angela's bra. He obviously had some experience with a bondage rope. He tied it in such a way that it held Angela's breasts together without covering her nipples. He pulled it tight. It was a little bit like something you'd see in a pornographic magazine. Angela felt a tiny bit of pain and cringed. That excited Mr Tako even more. Then, he tied the rope back down Angela's stomach and knotted it near her navel. Her whole body, except her arms, was tied together. At the corner of the bed was a bedpost. Mr Tako put the black ribbons that Angela had brought with her, around her wrist. Then he cuffed one hand, placed the cuff chain around the bedpost and cuffed the other. Mr Tako, by now, was sweating with pure excitement. He quickly ripped off his clothes and grabbed the whip. Believing it to be real, he started to lash Angela.

Angela cried out. Inside, she felt nothing. She was now, not a prostitute, but merely, an actress, playing the victim of a sadist, Mr Tako. He whipped and whipped her. It didn't hurt, but Angela cried with pain. Her acting was a magnificent performance. Mr Tako was thoroughly convinced. He was so excited, his heartbeat had increased and, by now, was hyperventilating at times. Then, after whipping Angela for a good fifteen minutes, he threw the whip into the corner and started to cuddle her, like a little, baby doll. Angela felt pity for this man. He had a very passionate, lustful way about him, that was something to be pitied. The man was obviously lonely, sexually frustrated and confused, all at the same time. He couldn't make love to a woman in the usual way but had to instead inflict pain.

Then, Mr Tako pulled at the rope to cause Angela pain and turned her over, on her stomach, while her arms crossed, so the handcuffs would hurt her. Mr Tako slid her panties down and started to spank her, wildly. As he did, he yelled with delight. From time to time, the Voice said to Angela, "Be alert, be ready to escape, but don't worry. I am with you..."

"It's incredible, oh, so wonderful! You are my Angel; you are so perfect! It is so wonderful!" He repeated it and then, said, "If you were to cry, you would make me the happiest man in the world. I've never been able to make a girl cry, and I dream of that every night."

Angela began to weep slowly. It built up and up to a moan, and Mr Tako spanked harder. By now, it wasn't difficult to act, because his spanking was hurting. Angela did feel pain and displeasure. It was effortless for her to perform. Then, she really cried. Tears fell from her eyes, then Mr Tako stopped and masturbated. While Angela whimpered, Mr Tako had his lifelong sexual fantasy fulfilled. It was over before it had begun. Then, Angela, realising the fool's paradise had finished, quickly triggered the lock on the fake handcuffs and they popped open, to Mr Tako's surprise. It now seemed, the key around his neck was purely a gimmick. The cuffs had been released.

Just then, Angela untied the ropes. Mr Tako's fantasy had ended, so Angela packed her things together and started to get dressed. She hadn't even had sex with this man, yet, strangely, perhaps, she had. It was in a unique way that Angela would never quite understand and, maybe, Mr Tako wouldn't, either. It didn't matter. Angela had done what she had set out to do and had done so safely. Mr Tako had thought that Angela was wholly incapacitated, but, all the while, she was ready to escape out of those handcuffs and protect herself, at any moment. Mr Tako then had a sad look on his face, as he realised that the game was only a fantasy and that never, at any moment, was there any reality there.

In any case, he smiled and said, "You have done well. Please give me your telephone number. I must see you again, you are superb."

Angela reached into her bag, passed out a little handwritten name card with her ryokan telephone number. She then shook his hand and said, "Please call me anytime you need to."

Angela grabbed her bag after dressing, walked out of the room and waved goodbye to Mr Tako. As she walked out of the hotel, she realised what a splendid performance the man had received. On this occasion, she was a paid actress, and it felt better than anything she had ever done. It seemed as though the more abnormal the situation, the less sex was involved. Angela liked that idea, but one thing in the back of her mind scared her. This man was sane and didn't lose control. Sure, he hit her a little harder than she'd thought, and there were bruises on her bottom, but he did not lose himself.

Angela thought, in the back of her mind, "What if he was crazy and what if he took that fantasy to be very real, took it to an insane point? What would have happened then? I must remember my next rule from this lesson! Always keep the fantasy and never let fantasy become a reality!"

It was the third lesson. It was also a lesson that Angela didn't want to learn from the mistake. Angela would remember the fear and so, never forget.

CHAPTER NINE
'Monroe Chan.'

EACH NIGHT, ANGELA would go to Ginza to find business. There were very few days when Angela didn't contact anybody. It seemed that her reputation was growing, yet many men still haggled over the price.

Some men said, "That is still a lot of money for Japan, because most Japanese people aren't rich, even though the country is. We're prepared to pay thirty thousand, but fifty thousand, minimum, is too much and nobody, except a wealthy man, can afford a hundred thousand."

Nonetheless, Angela was firm and believed her price range to be reasonable.

One night, a man said, "For that price, I'd expect to sleep with Marilyn Monroe, herself."

That seemed to give Angela a perfect idea. The next day, there was an exhibition of photographs of Marilyn Monroe by Sam Shaw, located at Shibuya. It seemed, Angela's life was always patterned and a complex arrangement of coincidence. Angela knew very well that she must be at that exhibition, regardless of how much it cost or where it was. Fortunately, for Angela, it wasn't expensive, nor was it far away.

Entering the exhibition room, Angela felt some kind of affinity with the Monroe poses, the smile and the sacrifice, like meeting a kindred spirit. To Angela, Monroe had been a kind of virginal sacrifice, as in the days of volcanic eruptions. Angela felt a purposefulness about this exhibition and spent hours walking around, examining each piece.

After a while, she noticed a very peculiar thing. Most of the Japanese people at the exhibition were spending fifty per cent of their time looking at Angela and comparing her to the Monroe photos. Many people remarked in Japanese of the resemblance. Angela didn't have to understand the language to understand the sentiment, what they were saying was quite evident. That struck at the innocent core inside Angela.

After the exhibition, Angela went home and spent some time laying on her bed, oddly enough, listening to a Marilyn Monroe cassette purchased some weeks before.

Angela didn't have to worry about money anymore, as she was doing very well. She had quite a few thousand saved and had regular business. Many men were coming back, time and again. Angela had even bought some new clothes and purchased a little Walkman cassette player to listen to music while working.

Angela's standing was becoming more like dancing. She would stand in the street and casually move her body in time to the music. She listened to Monroe singing and remembered the photographs at Shibuya. She could really relate to this woman wholly.

A few days later, Angela gazed into her mirror for about thirty minutes. Then, she studied a photograph that was bought at the exhibition. It had cost only ¥500, but it was money well spent. Slowly, piece by piece, Angela transformed herself by mimicking the Monroe makeup and curling her hair in a very 'Monroe' like fashion. Yet, there was one thing missing. Angela couldn't figure out what it was. Everything looked perfect, well, almost complete. Angela certainly did look like Monroe, except for one small thing. Even the mole was there, she had it all worked out. Everything looked like it should, except, ah, yes, it was the smile that was missing. Angela had yet to obtain that smile, a very characteristic smile that's difficult to obtain and very difficult to do spontaneously. Angela practised for at least two hours, without success. Then, when she wasn't trying so hard, she began to laugh, thinking how silly the whole thing really was. Then, the smile came naturally.

"So, that's the secret," she thought. "To think about the silliness of it all, that's the smile of Monroe."

That evening, Angela got ready, but in a specialised way. Even her clothes were carefully chosen. Then, she went to Ginza. All along the way, on the train and along the street, people were so surprised.

"Monroe! Monroe!" they called. It echoed everywhere she went.

It seemed Angela had done a very excellent job. A couple of people actually came up to Angela and sincerely, with a simple look on their faces, asked, "Are you, Monroe?"

It was as if some Japanese people believed Marilyn Monroe was still alive, and thirty. They knew very little, except that she was beautiful and very much the epitome of Western beauty. Many Japanese people were ignorant to the point of being laughable.

Many knew very little about Western culture. Some considered it to be, primarily, McDonald's, Marilyn Monroe, and The Beatles. Apart from that, they were very naive. So, Angela had chosen the right character. Perhaps, the Japanese had chosen it, and she just went along with the fantasy. The illusion looked so very real, but this was a different situation from Mr Tako's. The imagination of Mr Tako was that of painful intimacy. This was a public fiction, and so, there was no danger.

On this night, Angela must have stood there for only five minutes. She would often stand for hours on end and virtually pray to get someone. There was a real determination, not because of the love of money, but because of the desire to succeed. However, she didn't want to get caught by the police.

On this night, a man said, "How much? You are so beautiful, you are perfect. You are Monroe Chan."

Then, the man whisked her away to a love hotel. He spent very little time having sex. Most of the time was spent kissing Angela's body from her tiptoes to her neck. She wouldn't let anyone kiss her lips, that was far too intimate.

"That is only for someone you love," Angela said. "That's for your wife or your girlfriend, not for a prostitute."

"But you are not a prostitute, you are special."

"That may be so, but to you and your wife, I am a prostitute."

Then, the man categorically denied the ring on his finger. He was obviously married; anyone could see it. However, this wasn't the first time this had happened. Many of her customers denied their marriage and sometimes hid the amount of money they possessed and their position. In fact, to be quite honest, most men lied.

Angela said to this man, "All men lie about sex and money. They're the most important things in their lives. Take the money and sex away, and there's no reason for a man to tell a lie."

The man laughed, shook his head, and said, "You know men very well, too well, in fact."

After a couple of hours, the man decided he must return home, inevitably, to his wife. As for the lies and trickery to obtain penetration with Angela and to deep kiss her, they didn't work. So, he reluctantly retired, virtually, with his tail between his legs. Angela, with her new nickname, 'Monroe Chan,' decided to go back to Ginza. It was too early to go home, with it being only 11:00 p.m. Naturally, she wouldn't meet anybody before then, anyway. This time, Angela had more confidence and stood closer to the centre of the danger zone. That's where all the lights were. Angela was really bold now.

Angela thought to herself, "There's no Yakuza here. I've been standing here for ages, and nobody's given me a hard time or tried to catch me. It must be a rumour that the Japanese made up, to scare Gaijins away. There can't be any truth in it, at all."

She now stood in the centre of the danger zone, under the lights on the Shimbashi corner. That's where all the well-known night clubs were, Petit Rose, Club 777 and Club Cash. On that corner, people were amazed at Angela's boldness. Almost everyone commented on how beautiful she looked and called her, 'Monroe.' Word spread quickly, and it was only half an hour before a policeman walked past.

Angela thought, "They can't touch me, I'm a Gaijin. I'm free from their law, I'm not Japanese."

The Voice inside, said, "It's good not to be frightened of anyone, but it's not good to be too proud. You should be patient and humble."

Indeed, anyone would've understood Angela's enthusiasm. It was the first recognition of Angela's beauty, even though it was through Monroe's image. Nonetheless, a short time afterwards, a man came up, who didn't care how much it costs nor about what Angela was prepared to do. All he wanted to do was be with that image. Angela had uncovered a secret, had discovered the ultimate fantasy in the minds of the Japanese men. So, she knew just how to use it to create her own success. In Japan, money equals success and success equals the realisation of a dream. To obtain that success, Angela had to first attain financial security. Now, Angela possessed the means to achieve that success, the correct fantasy.

On the way to the love hotel in the taxi, Angela asked the man, "Don't you think I look like somebody else?"

The man laughed and said, "You don't look like her, you are her!" The man knew what Angela was talking about. This Gaijin had done a very excellent job, and it was only the first night. She earned twice her average amount in less time.

As Angela lay on the bed, she thought to herself, "How easy this is? It was simply daunting at first, and now it has become so easy because I understand men's' thinking. I now know the naivety of the Japanese man." It wasn't sex they wanted; it was the fantasy. Men and women weren't so different, after all. "Perhaps, men are more ruthless than women," Angela thought, "In that, they will lie and cheat without feeling anything along the way, or will they? But women also have fantasies, perhaps even more so than men. Everyone says that men only care about a woman's appearance." Angela had, so far, proven that theory correct, only by changing the way she looked.

Angela stayed with the man till morning. Most of the time, they just embraced as he kissed her body, but, never on the lips, of course, that was taboo. They would always try only to fail. Angela was adamant about that.

"That's dangerous," Angela said. "AIDS is dangerous."

"Japanese don't have AIDS," the man replied, adding, "Only Gaijins."

Angela laughed. It wasn't the first time she'd heard such nonsense. The Japanese were very ignorant about many things, not only Western civilisation but also about medical science. Angela was intelligent, witty, and considerably charming, at least, to the Japanese people. "Japanese don't have AIDS. That is a ridiculous statement. It's just that kind of thinking that will get you AIDS," Angela said.

The man retreated and started mumbling in Japanese as if confused about her determination.

In Japan, it's apparent that most prostitutes do whatever men require. Even though Angela was only giving the man French-style sexual entertainment, the man continuously insisted that the condom be removed.

Angela thought about it seriously, then said, "Ninety per cent of all the men I go with want to pay me extra to take that off. That's crazy! That is really crazy! Sure, I don't have AIDS, but what if I did? And what if I had it and didn't about it? That would mean everybody concerned would also get it, not counting the fact that they could have it!"

"But Japanese girls don't use them, only if the man requests."

Angela laughed and replied, "What a foolish society this is! How quickly will AIDS spread through Japan, if the man, just through a physical whim, decides not to have safe sex?" Angela shook her head wildly and added, "Not with me. There is no way in the world, and there is no money on this planet that will make me take that off. If you remove it, I am walking out that door."

The man went along with whatever she said. Still, it was an excellent illustration of just how far men were willing to go to get complete intimacy with their ultimate fantasy. The more real the sexual illusion, the more determined they were to lie and cheat to obtain it. The private desire for the man was deep kissing and unsafe sex. They were undoubtedly dangerous circumstances. However, Angela's new image gave her new power to control a man's desire.

Angela possessed a weapon, the image. It would help keep safe the most important thing she owned, her body.

The next morning, Angela went home. She'd made a hundred thousand yen and done very little. Her money was increasing rapidly, and she'd not seen any Yakuza. Angela was beginning to think that they really didn't exist.

In Australia, Angela had seen many fights in Kings Cross. It was a far more dangerous place. Every Friday and Saturday night, when Angela worked as a dancer, it was common to see two guys virtually beat each other to death in the street. Sometimes, people would be stabbed, either, over drugs or money, or over a girl. Yes, Angela thought Kings Cross was a much more dangerous place. Yet, there were fewer people in Australia, compared to Japan. Ironic, isn't it, that a vast city like Tokyo looks far safer than little Kings Cross, Sydney, Australia? At least, that's what Angela thought. She sometimes had the unfortunate tendency to assume too much. The Voice told her always to be patient and never react purely out of greed or over self-confidence. To respond only by instinct. Angela wasn't perfect and so, sometimes, would not hear the Voice properly, only to misunderstand the true meaning. The Monroe image began to make Angela something of a curiosity, and she was becoming extremely popular. Some people would even take photographs standing next to her. She was quickly becoming one of the sights of Ginza and very much a part of the Ginza nightlife.

Everybody loved to walk past her corner, just to see 'Monroe' up close. Angela's spot was elegant, outside a very modern boutique and contemporary art gallery just so men would know how expensive this Gaijin was. However, she was the only one standing in the street. Nobody else did it, and that seemed curious to Angela.

"Why? I know that in these night clubs are many girls who prostitute themselves. Why do they work inside, instead of out in public?" Angela pondered.

A young man came up to her and started to talk. Then, shortly afterwards, a hand grabbed Angela on the arm, very fiercely and pulled her. It was a policeman. It seemed that he had caught Angela talking to a man about sex.

The young man said, "No, thank you," and walked away, as if Angela had propositioned him, when, in fact, it was he who had propositioned her.

The policeman said, "I know what you're doing. You're under arrest."

Quickly, he called on his two-way radio and shortly afterwards, two more policemen came to his assistance. Angela was instructed to walk between the two assisting policemen, while the head policeman walked in front. They walked Angela to the nearest police station. The police sergeant pushed her inside. He was very rough with her, abused her and then ordered her to go into the back room.

Angela stood up for herself. "Who do you think you are, pushing me around like that? I've done nothing wrong. I've certainly done nothing you can arrest me for! If you want to see my passport, here it is." She slammed it down on the table and walked out of the police station to stand outside.

Angela was proud, and no policeman or any official authoritarian was going to push this girl around. The policeman slid his hand under his hat and started scratching his head. He'd never met a woman like this before, who stood up for herself, especially when they were involved in an illegal act.

Angela turned around, walked back into the police station, and started waving her finger at the sergeant. "You have no evidence to prove that I've done what you think I have. I'm only doing half of what you think I'm doing. So, there! Arrest me for doing half of what you think I'm doing and where's your witness? You're just trying to scare me. Well, it won't work, because I'm going right back to my spot. I'm going to stand there and wait for a friend!"

The policeman sitting in the chair started laughing. All the other policemen in the station looked at each other and burst out laughing, too. They all thought it was a hilarious situation. This Gaijin woman, who looked like Marilyn Monroe, told the police off when she was basically breaking Japanese law. The police were so dumbfounded; they couldn't do anything except laugh. Soon, they let her go and told Angela to go home, not to go there anymore. Otherwise, they'd return.

Angela said, "If you want to find me, just go to the same place you found me before. I'll be there, every night, in fact," as she walked out. The young policemen started clapping their hands and laughing.

Angela went straight back to her spot and stood there. Virtually following her were the same two policemen who had assisted in her arrest. Following the two was the sergeant, still sniggering a little. The others were now containing their laughter, as they were in public and had to set a good example. The police sergeant couldn't help but laugh. Angela stood in her spot, and the sergeant began trying to push her along with his banner.

Angela said, "Alright, then. If you don't want me to stand still, I'll walk up and down this area, so it won't look so conspicuous. Still, you know, and I know that in all these clubs, everybody's doing what you accuse me of doing, yet I'm only doing half of what you accuse."

The sergeant quickly lost his smile and said, "What do you mean, you're only doing half?" He said, "You're selling your body, aren't you?"

"What if I'm not selling my body? What if I'm only selling half of my body?"

The policeman couldn't understand that. Then, the younger policeman explained it to him in Japanese.

"Do you promise that is all that you do?"

"Well, if I could do more, I would, but most people can't afford to do any more than that. So, that's what I really do," Angela said, quite honestly.

The policeman laughed and added with a sigh, "Alright, then. We will leave you alone but be careful. The Yakuza here are very dangerous."

Angela looked at him and said, "Yakuza? I've never seen any Yakuza here."

"We're more concerned about your safety than in arresting you. This is a dangerous area. Please take care." The sergeant walked away, giggling to himself.

Angela walked up, down and around her spot. She didn't stand still because the police didn't like it. It didn't look nice; it was too honest. Angela had to pretend to be only walking down the street, then turn around and walk back again. Nonetheless, people still knew what she was doing, and she still had lots of business.

On that night, it was raining very heavily. Angela didn't get anybody and so, caught a taxi home. For a change, she had an early night. At home, Angela thought about her dancing, her coming to Japan and how so much had changed. It's funny how she never thought she'd be working in Ginza on the streets, in the sex business. And never imagined looking like Marilyn Monroe. She also never thought she'd ever had so much money so quickly. The main thing Angela was concerned about was whether she was succeeding or not. In any case, she was becoming financially independent, which was the most important thing. She didn't have enough to get herself an apartment. It would cost her at least seven to ten thousand dollars to get a lovely little apartment in Tokyo. In Australia, a person could do it for a fraction of that money, but this wasn't Australia. This was Tokyo and, even for Japan, Tokyo was the most expensive.

As time went by, Angela's reputation grew.

People would call to her as they walked past, "Komban wa, Monroe Chan!"

'Monroe Chan' was the name they chose. Angela never told them what her name was, they just called her that. On average, most nights, four out of every five nights, Angela would meet somebody who had the right money and wanted the fantasy. Angela now refused to accept strange requests and stuck to typical, ordinary, straight sexual desires, believing those bondage assignments were now a little too risky.

"Life is too valuable and too important to risk, merely for money," Angela thought.

Then, one night, two young guys came to her. One could speak excellent English, while the other couldn't.

"Hello, Monroe. How are you?"

Obviously, they had heard of her reputation, and the non-English speaking one was interested in her business. The other man was his friend and was acting as an interpreter. They asked if the young man, who couldn't speak English, could go with Angela for the evening. Angela said, "Yes, no problem."

He was very nice looking, in fact, a little too nice looking to be acquiring Angela's services. He could probably find a lovely girl. He had style and class about him, was young, handsome, and obviously had a lot of money. Angela was curious about why he came to her, as he didn't seem quite like the others. He didn't look at her breasts and buttocks nor deep into her eyes, as they usually did. This man was very casual, superficial and wasn't concerned about how long she would stay.

The man said, "He will pay you now. Here are fifty thousand yen. Please come with us, we would like to go for sushi first. Is that alright with you?"

"Of course, it is."

They went to a sushi salon, sat, and talked. The conversation had continued for about half an hour, longer than Angela had imagined. They asked many questions about Angela's business, her previous occupations, and her aspirations and dreams. It seemed like they were asking too many questions.

Angela became very annoyed and said to the one translating, "Just what is all this about? What kind of thing are you guys into?"

"Mmm...We're not into anything, really. We just want to know about you, that's all."

"And what about sex?"

"Well, my friend's changed his mind. He doesn't really want to have sex with you, he just wants to talk. We just have a few more questions if that's alright with you," said the translator.

"Just what kind of business are you guys in?" she demanded.

The man who couldn't speak English understood that question and smiled. Then, he presented his card. "I'm from 'Focus Magazine.' I'm a writer," he said.

Angela became furious, stood up, put his card down on the table and said, "Are you guys going to write a story about me? Is that it? Are you going to get me in trouble with the Immigration department? Is that it?"

They were amiable and peaceful about the matter. One held

Angela's hand and asked her to sit down and be quiet, so they could explain. They said they would change her name and everything, so no one would ever know who she really was. The Japanese people would be curious about an individual such as Angela, a Gaijin. In such a short period, she'd been so successful in the most competitive and expensive place in the world, Ginza.

Angela refused. "I don't wish my story to be published. If I did, I would call you."

"Well, alright, then. We won't publish it, we won't. We'll keep it a secret, and you can keep the fifty thousand yen, it doesn't matter."

"If you publish it, I will sue you."

"Do you have a lawyer in Japan?"

"Just by chance, one of my clients is a lawyer, and I'm sure he'd hate to see me deported out of the country, simply because you guys want to sell a few magazines."

That seemed to disturb them. A solemn, concerned expression came over both men's faces as they spoke to each other in Japanese. Angela had them over the barrel. She knew that they had intentions of publishing, and she believed this would stop them. Hopefully, this would be the last time she ever saw them, but it wasn't.

The following night, Angela was standing in her spot, as usual.

She'd been sick of the game the police had set up to walk up and down the street. It was dishonest, so Angela stood in her spot. If the police had any questions, they could come and ask her. They didn't, but ignored Angela and stayed right away from her, but every night, from time to time, they'd check. A policeman would walk past to check if she was still there. They didn't want to arrest her but just wanted to see if she was still in Ginza.

The next night, the man from 'Focus Magazine,' the one who couldn't speak English, came to Angela and started speaking very fluent English. Obviously, he had been playing a game with Angela. He could speak very well.

"Do you remember, one night, not so long ago, a man came up and took a photo of you? Well, he was from our magazine, too. We now have a story and a photo of you. We're going to run it, and you can't do anything about it, because it's the truth," he said boldly.

"If you publish that story, I'll be arrested. What kind of people are you?" Angela insisted. "If you publish, I will sue you. I have a lot of money, and I have many powerful clients. I'm sure that I can make it very difficult for you and your magazine."

"I will talk to my editor about it. It's not up to me. It's not personal, I actually like you. It's just business."

"That's right, it's business, so I'll have no problem with my conscience. Seeing you lose your job, seeing that the magazine is drawn out into the open, being the kind of people you really are!" Angela exclaimed.

The man went away, came back about half an hour later, looked at Angela for a moment and began to speak.

"I've been talking to my editor on the telephone, and we've dropped the story. We're not going to run it now, at all, so you're safe. Don't worry, that's the last you'll ever hear of the matter." He then walked away as if beaten in a game of chess.

Angela was very pleased with herself. She had won, a victory that had insured her security. Angela would never know the real answer to that. She couldn't read Japanese and, even if she looked at a Focus Magazine from time to time, she'd never really know if they'd published anything about her.

A little while afterwards, another young man came to Angela. He was one of the men who had spoken to her, the very first night that she'd worked in the danger zone.

"Oh. You're still here," the man said. "I'm so surprised to see that you're still alive!"

"Alive?" Angela asked. "What do you mean by that? Do you think I get AIDS?"

"I'm not talking about AIDS; I'm talking about Yakuza. Strangely, they've let you live so long, I can't understand why." He was seriously perturbed about the situation.

"You're just trying to scare me. Go away, please and don't disturb me anymore," Angela uttered, treating the whole thing as a joke.

The Voice said, "There's more reality to that than you'll ever know. Be happy that you are safe and that you are alive."

A silence fell over her as she looked up into the sky and saw the twinkling of stars, cast by dark rain clouds. There was an exquisite excitement about the danger that lurked in those streets. At the same time, she feared the unknown but was pleased with her victory.

"Yakuza, perhaps, do exist," she thought, as she looked at those stars. "I'm just lucky that I've escaped them. How will I know who they are and where they are?"

"I will tell you, My child. Fear not, for, I am always with you," the Voice said.

Sex business was going well and Angela, for the first time, wasn't worried about it. In fact, things were going too well. Angela was becoming popular and perhaps too well known. She wondered what the end could be. Could she save money and get out of this situation without any trouble, or would this be her life? Would Angela be on the streets in Ginza for a long time? Would she be able to stay in Japan for more than six months? These were such incongruous questions that she didn't know the answer to any of them. If it did continue, would this be the total of her existence? Would 'sex business' be the only thing that Angela could do, or could she really fulfil the dream of stardom and glamour? There was only one who knew the answer to that question. It wasn't the people whom Angela talked to in the street, it wasn't even Angela, herself.

It wasn't anybody, except the Voice. He knew all the answers, He told her the solutions to all Angela's questions, piece by piece. As the time suited the occasion, so to, was the correct piece of information given, as if her journey were a staircase, a long, spiralling walkway, ascending into the clouds. The mist covered the stairs, so no one could see each step, but, as sure as Angela knew she was alive, she knew there was another step. The only certainty was when her foot landed on that next platform. The clouds would always cover the next level, but Angela's instinct knew they were there. She also knew that the staircase was long and stretched forth, very high. All she had to do was believe, and she would with every fibre of her being. Day by day, step by step, her faith in the Voice would become secure, more reliable than anything else in her life.

CHAPTER TEN
'Different Kind of Prey.'
~⁓

Each week, Angela averaged from three to six thousand American dollars. She'd never imagined being able to make that kind of money, particularly when she did very little to obtain it. She'd never known anyone making that sort of money before. In no time at all, Angela had rented a beautiful waterfront, penthouse style apartment in Tokyo. She also had many lovely clothes to make her life more comfortable. Financial success had come to her very quickly, but it wasn't what she wanted. The dreams of stardom and dancing hadn't been realised but were in the far, distant future. There was an enormous amount of work to be done before those things could be accomplished. Still, at least Angela could lead a comfortable existence while she waited. It was great not having to leave her room at 11:00 a.m. every morning, to return at 4:00 p.m., as in the ryokan.

The apartment was two storeys and very luxurious. Compared to Australian standards, it was quite incomprehensible how Angela could have attained it. Prostitution in Tokyo, for a start, was extraordinarily lucrative for a stunning Gaijin female and would continue to be so, until something intervened to stop it.

Each night, Angela met a new man. She went home alone very

infrequently these days. Angela's reputation preceded her. Everyone who came to her already knew her name.

"Monroe Chan, isn't it?" they would ask.

Nearly all the clients knew someone who had been intimate with her. Ginza was a prominent place, and there were many thousands of businessmen every evening, but, still, word spread like wildfire. All the hostesses would talk about Angela in a bitchy fashion. When walking home after their evening's hostessing, some would speak about her with a nasty tone. The Gaijin hostesses, mainly, were the worst ones. Some of them would call her all sorts of terrible names.

Angela would stand there, smile back at them, and think, "Oh, well you're lucky to have a straight job, and I suppose, I'm lucky, too to have what I have."

However, every now and then, Angela would meet a nice hostess, whom she would befriend. Then, each evening, they'd talk. Angela didn't have many friends. Most of them were just the people who worked in the location around 'nana-chome' (area seven). Even the guys selling noodles in the street at the little 'Ramen' stand would bring Angela a glass of 'O-sake' every evening and stand with her for a quick chat. Monroe Chan was so popular among the Japanese. It was very unusual because the general trend was not to like Gaijins in Ginza, but they had accepted Angela.

Angela's clients all ranged from salarymen, people with regular jobs, usually office workers, to executive businessmen, wealthy men who managed large companies. The latter had limousines at their disposal and could, on a whim, go or do anything they wished. Sometimes, Angela would meet such a man, a top-level executive. They'd always want her telephone number. Angela refused to have the phone connected because she believed it to be an excellent way of getting caught by the police. Angela wasn't too consciously frightened of the police but felt the telephone was an added risk. So, Angela lost a significant amount of business because she didn't possess a phone. However, the amount of trade that came her way equalled the security attained by remaining somewhat aloof.

"It's good to be famous," she thought, "But it's not good to be too accessible. When I go home, I don't want anybody to know where I live. I don't want anybody to know what I do. If I can live a double life, I'll be safe."

Angela's clients seemed to fit into four categories. First, the 'average' category or the 'affair' category was the most common type. Eighty per cent of all the clients were in this category. An example would be a middle-aged, thirty-five to the forty-year-old businessman, who was, perhaps, in some dominant position, but subordinate to a mandatory level. Most likely married with children and living a reasonably comfortable life, bored with it and felt something of a failure in his career. To compensate for that, he would visit Angela. Almost all would pretend that it wasn't business. Instead, they were having an affair with a Gaijin, who was what any Japanese man wanted: blonde, tall, blue-eyed and white-skinned.

That was the most typical type of client. Angela understood that personality so well. She'd played the image and fantasy, to the point where these men really believed they were simply having an affair, rather than just engaging in sex business.

Then came the second category. It was somewhat amusing, but, in any case, a little disturbing. This group was called 'the mother syndrome.' Angela would be the clients' mother substitute and play that role for them, either subtly or actively, as the man required.

This type of client would like to be nurtured like a baby. Angela would cuddle them as they formed into an embryonic position on the bed. While holding the 'baby' client, Angela would pat them on the head and tell them that everything would be alright; it was okay to be that way. Ironically enough, the people who had that kind of personality in their sexual fantasy were top echelon businessmen, in the most influential positions. Angela found this incongruity laughable, yet sad.

Of course, the third classification was the type like Mr Tako, who wanted to hurt a woman or, even worse, a young girl. They derived pleasure from inflicting pain and were sadists. Mr Tako's weren't so frequent. Angela would always recognise them, ever since her first encounter with the first, Mr Tako. He was, however, the most extreme. But many clients would like to spank Angela, hold her down, and simulate rape. Some men's fantasy was to rape a helpless woman. This did not impress Angela, but, with business as usual, the illusion must be made as real as possible, without going into the danger threshold. These men were emotionally ill and needed a physical release to take the fantasy out of their minds, at least for a time. Angela would give them that release, for a price.

Then there was the fourth type, the masochistic client. Angela relatively infrequently met such a person who needed to feel pain, who needed to be disciplined.

One night in Ginza, while Angela was standing in her spot, a familiar face came along; the very first man who ever asked Angela for sex. It was some time ago now since she'd first come to Tokyo at Shinjuku and had met Mr Sato. He was somewhat surprised and shocked to see her standing there.

"Why are you standing here?" Mr Sato asked.

"Sex business, don't you remember? You were one of the people who helped me choose this profession."

"You mean, I'm responsible for this?" Mr Sato replied, laughing.

"Not directly, but you and many others like you influenced my life to this point."

A smile came across Mr Sato's face. "How much is it to buy you?" Mr Sato asked.

"No money on the earth can buy me, but you may hire my services, for a short time, at a reasonable fee."

Mr Sato found that very humorous and started chuckling, as he looked inside his wallet.

"If you have go-man-en, I'm sure we can work something out," Angela said.

Mr Sato agreed, so they left together and went to a luxurious and expensive hotel, not a love hotel, but a businessman's hotel in Ginza. Mr Sato was an engineer. At first, he seemed quite reasonable but would fit into the masochistic category, that Angela was beginning to define.

Mr Sato spent most of the evening requesting Angela to stand on him, spank him and scold him as if he was a naughty little boy. Then, he had to be tied up. Mr Sato didn't need penetrative sex, merely wanted to experience little bits of pain and discipline. He needed to be scolded and told that he was naughty. He didn't need intercourse. That suited Angela down to the ground. She didn't particularly want sex, unless she could very well avoid it and only in extreme circumstances, would she even consider that. She would prefer to do anything other than sex, yet her profession was that of a prostitute. It seemed that Mr Sato was a perfect catch, as it was all fantasy with very little pain. He didn't like pain that much but just wanted to play the game of pain. However, if Angela scolded him too hard, he became disturbed.

"No, no, please, only pretend," Mr Sato would say.

"He's not really in a masochistic deviate," Angela thought. "He's in an entirely different category altogether, in a confused group."

Mr Sato wanted something but didn't need it. He wanted to feel pain but was too frightened to experience it. This man wanted to be treated badly, but not too severely.

"What would happen if this kind of character went over the edge?" she thought. "Anyway, in that case, I best not fall asleep," she said to herself as she lay down after the evening's game around the hotel room.

The Voice always came to her and said, "Don't worry, I'm here with you." That would give Angela peace and patience to stay till morning and not fear the man she was with.

Mr Sato fell asleep blissfully and remained so, even during Angela's departure. Mr Sato seemed to make an impression upon Angela. She now had all her little classifications for different kinds, except Mr Sato. He didn't quite fit into the 'mother syndrome' nor the 'masochistic syndrome.' She didn't know what group he belonged to. Determined to understand a man's mind, Angela created one more vacant space. The fifth classification for all the clients of whom personalities were unknown.

"We'll call it the 'abnormal' box," Angela thought to herself. "Put all the perverted ones in this class and treat them as if no one knows their true nature, so we can never really predict what they will do next."

Angela was more correct than she could ever imagine, as the next day, she would meet another man. This new man appeared very average. However, he would be the one who fitted into the pinnacle of that recent 'box.' He would scare Angela beyond belief, not with his actions, but with his intentions and thoughts. He was a nice man who introduced himself as Ken. Angela had met him in the street. She wasn't even standing in Ginza, but rather, by accident, met him at Yoyogi station. Angela was changing trains to go shopping in an evening she had off.

"Aren't you so and so?" Ken asked, placing some European name under his breath.

"No, I'm not. My name is Angela."

"How do you do? I suppose it was really just an excuse to talk to you."

Angela was very quick to respond to the man. It was evident that he could be a potential client, as he had all the trimmings, such as a business suit, trench coat, briefcase, gold watch and a fat wallet.

"Typical client," Angela thought and, of course, the look in the eye was there, the look of lust.

That's what Angela called the look in a man's eye, at any rate. However, when she was generous, she'd call it 'passionate lust.' This man disguised his desire that much, it looked as if he really didn't want sex and it seems, he didn't after all but wanted something else entirely. Perhaps, he wanted a piece of Angela. Angela would find Ken hard to understand. She would learn many new things, hopefully, without going into a hazardous region.

"Shall we go for coffee? I want to make a proposition to you," Ken asked.

"Yes, of course, let's go," Angela remarked with a smile.

They went to a coffee shop just around the corner. Ken had obviously been there many times before. He was very educated. He could speak seven languages, was a scientist and an engineer, and now he was the executive manager of a large chemical company. Ken was at the pinnacle of Japanese success, being wealthy, reasonably handsome, and remarkably successful, but was missing something. He wanted to fulfil his fantasy, too.

"I'll be honest with you, I'm a call girl. Do you just want

coffee? Perhaps you'd like something more, isn't that right?" Angela inquired.

Ken laughed. "I admire your honesty. Yes, it's true, but I probably want to do something that you haven't done before, then again, I don't know."

"Perhaps. What would you like?"

Ken reached his hand into his suit pocket and pulled out, very delicately and gently, an unusual, precious, little container.

"I want this," Ken said, quietly.

The container was made of gold and leather. It was small. Ken treated it as if it were sacred, placing it on a handkerchief on top of the table and pushing all the other things aside.

He opened the container slowly. Inside was yet another container of a pouch type with velvet cloth and purple in colour. Ken then opened the bag and inside it was little, plastic, laminated cards.

"How curious, what is this?" Angela asked.

"These are my girls, the ones I have known. I keep them with me, always. I don't want a fleeting experience with someone who I never see again. What I want is to keep you forever, with me."

The man was quite serious about his ludicrous statement. Angela looked at his collection of naked photographs of women, each laminated, in their own unique, little folder.

"This is Diane," Ken stated, "Now before I show you anymore, promise me you won't tell anybody about this."

Angela agreed and looked at the picture of Diane. It was quite an unusual photo, as Diane was standing in a precarious pose. It looked like a very awkward pose, and Diane had a bizarre look on her face. There was something distasteful about it, and Angela didn't like it.

"Then, this is Louise."

He introduced each person with the same feeling given for a person present. The man placed an authenticity on the photographs that disturbed Angela. It wasn't natural, and they weren't photographs to him but living lovers. It was peculiar, and Angela felt a small trembling on her hand as she looked at each one. Oddly enough, every girl in the photos was in the same pose. It was freakish, indeed.

Then, Ken collected the photographs, delicately placed them into their pouches, put the bags into the container and placed it back into his pocket, close to his heart.

"I carry my girlfriends with me wherever I go. They are very special to me, and no one ever sees them, except for me. I would like you to become one of my lovers," Ken uttered to Angela, gazing at her legs.

"It's quite unusual, what you're asking. What does it mean to become one of your girlfriends?" Angela asked curiously.

"Simply, let me take one photograph of you. I will keep it, and I swear on my honour, never to show it to anyone, except another girlfriend, like you."

Angela thought it was quite a reasonable request, although she didn't really like the idea of her photograph being shown.

"I will do it on three conditions," Angela told him.

"Sure. What are the conditions?"

"First, you show the photograph to no one. Secondly, you pay a very high price and, thirdly, if the shot isn't any good, you must destroy it."

"Usually, I pay twenty thousand yen."

Angela laughed. "I don't do anything for that kind of money."

"Yes, I admit you are special. You are magnificent, so I know I must pay a high price. How about fifty thousand?" Ken asked.

Angela paused for a minute and thought, "Perhaps it's too cheap for such a situation. After all, he is going to keep my photograph for a long time. That is incriminating evidence if the police should ever get it."

"No, I think it should be more like seventy thousand. You only keep one photograph, and you keep all my conditions," Angela stated, frankly.

The man agreed without hesitation. It was quite outrageous when you think about it, nana-man-en (¥70,000, A$700) for a small Polaroid. However, Angela was a good businesswoman. She knew exactly how to extract money from rich men, and this man was no exception.

"Tomorrow evening, eight o clock, same place. Is that okay with you?" Ken asked.

Angela agreed. So, at 8:00 p.m. the following day, they met in the same location as they had when they first bumped into each other. Then they went to a love hotel in Shinjuku.

"I use this hotel because it's lovely inside. The room that we shall be using is like a Grecian bath. It's exquisite, and so the photograph can be taken in an elegant setting, and you will look your best," Ken stated.

Angela looked at the man's belongings. He had a suitcase with him.

"Excuse me… umm… what is in the suitcase?" Angela asked.

"My photographic equipment. Don't worry, I'll explain it all to you when we get inside the room."

Angela didn't feel any anxiety and had forgotten about the oddity of the photographs the previous night and felt very relaxed with Ken. At this moment, she didn't really know what category Ken fitted into. Perhaps, she would have to make up a new one, for 'photographic clients.' Little did Angela know, Ken was in the deviant class, the fifth kind, the kind that would scare Angela, so much that she would only take typical clients from this day onward.

"You're not like the other girls, you look perfect. Please don't change anything, just sit down and wait for me. I have to prepare the room," Ken uttered, excitedly.

Ken pushed the tables and chairs aside and turned on the lamps near the bed, to the wall. There was a beautiful, big, Grecian bath with Grecian columns surrounding it. It was of marble with stained glass windows surrounding the whole thing. The room looked very elaborate, and Angela believed it to be an excellent selection for a photograph. Then, the man set up his photography equipment. There was much more film than what Angela had agreed upon. There were three cassettes of twelve photographs, thirty-six in all.

"Excuse me, but you agreed to only one photograph," Angela told him firmly.

Ken smiled and nodded his head as he hurriedly prepared everything. "Yes, yes, I know, but I must take thirty-six then, together, we shall choose the best one and then, I shall destroy the rest, before your eyes."

"Oh, in that case, it's alright."

Angela agreed and felt pleased that the man wasn't trying to cheat her. After all, they were Polaroid's, so there were no negatives. Angela felt comfortable about that. Then, Ken set the camera up on the tripod. There was also a dazzling light to shine onto the wall, where Angela would stand.

First, he took Angela's shots in her underwear in the same pose the other girls made. Ken only liked one particular posture. Then, he requested Angela to remove her bra and took another twelve photographs in the same pose. After which, this odd man asked Angela to take her panties off. Then he took another twelve pictures, once again, in the same pose. Angela thought it was bizarre, but, after all, he was paying enough money.

Angela believed fifteen minutes was fair for the money, and indeed it was, except for one, small thing.

"There, we're finished now," Ken said. "Well, almost. You can get dressed now."

Angela got dressed, and they sat on the bed together. He collected his equipment and placed the thirty-six Polaroid photographs on top of the bed.

"It's peculiar that you choose this particular pose. It makes people look like they're... like they're dead," Angela muttered, unconsciously.

Ken looked at her for a long time and scratched his head. Then, he inspected the thirty-six photographs, one at a time, reached for his bag and pulled out an enormous knife. Angela became extremely apprehensive.

"Oh, don't worry," Ken said. "I'm just going to cut up the other thirty-five of you because you agreed to one photograph, is that not correct?'

Angela slowly nodded, as a suspicious silence overcame her. She was frightened, as Ken became more peculiar as time passed.

Then, Ken pulled a large pair of scissors out. That scared Angela even more. She took two steps back and looked for the door. The door was farther away than she had hoped. The man was placed between Angela and the door. Angela felt that she should just play along with him.

"No need to get anxious," Angela thought. "He is probably harmless."

Then, Ken started to laugh, obsessively and gazed at Angela, then, back at the photographs and commented on how he loved to keep her forever. That really scared her.

The Voice came to Angela then and said, "Don't react violently. Just be nice, but be extremely careful, for he is dangerous, but if you're nice and pretend not to know, he will be alright. Don't fear, I'm here."

Immediately, Angela understood and acted normal again, giggling. Like a young girl, pretending that there was nothing odd about Ken's behaviour. There was something seriously wrong with the man's mind. Ken sat down on the floor like a child, with sprawling photographs around him. The tools and implements by his side. At all times, he rested one hand on the knife.

"And which photograph do you think would be you and which photograph would you like to be?" Ken asked, as his voice changed in tone.

It was an obsessive voice, and there was a change in his personality. Then, Ken became more and more excited. The man was becoming aroused, not by looking at Angela but by looking at the Gaijin photographs he had taken. He began to sweat. Angela noticed the excitement in the man's pants. He was aroused, yet he was fully dressed. Without thinking, Angela pointed to one of the photographs.

"Oh, of course, this one is you," Ken said. "Yes, I think so, too, yes, that will be you, that will be you forever."

The man quickly picked up that photograph and placed it in an exclusive new cardholder prepared in his top, left-hand pocket.

"And now, I must destroy the rest of you."

An enigmatic smile came over Ken's face, as he began to attack the other photographs, violently with the knife. He slashed each, across the breasts, the vagina and the face, almost as if he were actually cutting Angela. She stood back in the corner of the room and watched in terror, observing the man's crazed act.

The Voice said, "Act normal, don't overreact. He will be alright if he doesn't know that you know."

Angela did know. Angela knew the man was psychopathic. He fitted into an entirely different category, 'crazy beyond belief.' The man slashed at each photograph, time and time again, meticulously cut the nipples of the pictures, then the lips, then the eyes. Then he would hold each damaged photo, in turn, up against his cheek and say goodbye to it.

As Angela gazed on, the man very conspicuously reached orgasm in his pants. Angela was shocked. She felt like vomiting but controlled her emotions and quietly edged her way around the wall, towards the door. She wasn't concerned with anything, except getting out of there in one piece. Ken was so frightening to Angela. She had never believed that this would ever happen. She'd always been so careful and always chosen very ordinary-looking men. It seems that the most normal looking and... how shall we say, sociably likeable people, could be the craziest. In this particular instance, it was the case.

All the cutting now seemed to be finished, so he then gathered the pieces, picked them up, one by one and placed them in a paper bag. Angela was, by now, halfway around the room. Ken looked up and noticed that her position had changed. Angela continued smiling and acted normal so as Ken wouldn't sense her fear. Then, when all the pieces had been gathered, he started to burn them. He then placed the bag into the sink. Angela then edged her way far enough to grasp her handbag. Ken reached into his pocket, as Angela shrilled against the wall. Then, he pulled an envelope.

"Here is another twenty thousand yen."

Angela quickly grabbed it, then lurched back against the wall, smiling, but not trusting the man for one moment. Ken bent down to pick up the knife, then Angela ran for the door.

"Please don't go yet. I must speak to you," Ken said.

Then, he placed the knife and scissors back into his bag. As

Angela turned the handle and was prepared to run out the door, he put his camera in and zipped up the case. Then he patted dry the sweat from his head, he seemed to return to normal. It was if there had been two Ken's in the room, and the original had reappeared. Angela's instinct told her that everything was now alright, that the experience had been very close but was over. The man's pants were damp, but he didn't seem to notice. Then, he looked at the single remaining photograph in the cardholder and began to speak.

"Yes, it was a good session. This is a superb shot I have of you. I'll keep it forever. I would like to see you again."

"Yes, yes, whatever you say, any time you like. I don't have a telephone, but I could call you if you give me your business card," Angela articulated, nervously.

The man handed Angela his business card and said, "Call me anytime. I'd like to take more photographs of you."

Angela agreed, politely, but thought to herself, "No way on this planet would I be in the same room with this psycho again."

Then Angela left the room as the man followed. He appeared quite alright now, but she didn't forget the fear that she'd experienced when he was cutting up those photographs. This man was disturbed, and his sexual obsession came out in a very daunting manner. Perhaps, on this occasion, he was in control, but on another circumstance, he may just go too far. Angela imagined that there may be another girl in the future. An unsuspecting girl, who is not so prudent, may overreact and become the victim of Ken's inevitable horror.

Angela's thinking changed. From now on, she resigned herself to only have business with those who only wanted regular sex. Even if intercourse occurred, it couldn't be as dangerous as her experience with Ken. The men who were prepared to have conventional sex were, perhaps, the most predictable. Finding release in a natural way would be less dangerous. Then, the only danger would be that of AIDS. If Angela stuck to the rules, the Voice had given, listen to her instinct and always use safe sex, the danger would be minimised. The risk of men like Ken could never be reduced. Suddenly, Angela knew that her business would have to change. The abnormal category would have to be abandoned. She would only take those clients who she could trust. Even if Angela had penetration every day, it wouldn't be anywhere near as risky as this night had been.

CHAPTER ELEVEN
'Ginza Yakuza.'

Everyone knew that Monroe Chan earned a lot of money. Sometimes a not so prudent, young businessman would ask; "Just how much money do you make, Monroe?"

Angela was always reluctant to tell them, but after she'd known someone for a long time, would reply, "Probably, more than you."

They would laugh, thinking they were in the high-income bracket and add, "But, I earn... so much."

Angela would reply, "But I earn twice that."

It was always a funny situation. Clients could never get an actual figure from her. The fact that Angela made more than many of her younger clients threatened the Japanese idea of class. Men were always supposed to make more than women. Angela gave them something new, an injection of Western equality or, in her case, female superiority. She meticulously kept a note of everything she earned and spent. Angela had become an excellent businesswoman when it came to money and sex. Her concept of sex business meant she must never lose control, never enjoy the experience and, indeed, never climax. To do that would be to lose control and lose a part of herself. That would mean to give too much for the money they paid. Angela didn't have sex with very many men. Yet when she did, she controlled the feeling, the sensation, blocking it off completely, like a machine or computer that had shut down its peripherals. Angela refused to feel the sensations the men tried to create in her body. Sure enough, as time went by, Angela engaged in penetration more often.

The Voice inside told Angela it was alright because it was necessary. It seemed the Voice was all for Angela and wanted the same thing Angela wanted. Angela also wanted what the Voice wanted. The Voice wanted Angela to witness the truth, tell the world, through her art and stardom, of her demise, captivity, and by which means she was eventually freed. Angela believed that she was cleansed from sin. The only transgression would be the act of fornication if she were to enjoy sex with someone with whom she didn't love. If she didn't want sex with someone, then there was no sin imparted, it was merely business. As far as the client was concerned, that was between him and his God. Most of the men were married, all of them had the lustful desire, but Angela was in no position to judge. It was difficult enough to maintain a moralistic and honest life, living as a prostitute in Tokyo, without worrying about other peoples' sins. Sin, to Angela, was to doubt the Voice.

Angela was beginning to think that Yakuza was an overrated legend and that she need not be so afraid. Perhaps, it was just the word that survived, like 'Samurai' or 'Geisha,' yet, the real essence of the symbolism that lived on was, desire.

"Perhaps, Yakuza, Geisha and Samurai are legends, maybe, nothing more than just that," Angela said to one of her clients, one evening.

"I don't know much about stuff like that, but it seems you're pretty smart. I think you will eventually find out the truth, one way or another," one man said.

That man was right, more than he realised. Angela would find out more than she cared about Japanese history, Japanese law, and particularly Japanese Yakuza.

Every night now, Angela would meet someone. Many men would return, so Angela now had a group of regular clientele who were all relatively prosperous.

Sex Business Tokyo

Ginza was like a carnival to Angela, glamorous and exciting. Beautifully dressed people would be going everywhere. Geisha girls or traditional hostesses dressed in traditional kimono attire would walk past, fluttering their fans. It was getting towards Spring. Although it wasn't warm enough to use a fan, the girls always had their hand fans placed in their kimono belts, it was kimono tradition. Usually, the Geisha style ladies still bowed their heads politely to Angela. They respected her, as she was the 'Western Geisha'. It was a sign of respect to one another. Occasionally, a hostess dressed in kimono attire would walk past and ignore her. However, that was now the exception. It was usually a young girl who had some problem with what Angela was doing, jealous of her beauty or, even worse, her money. Strangely enough, all the Japanese, even the ladies, considered Angela to be the most beautiful woman in all of Ginza. Angela never believed that for a moment. Many Western hostesses worked in bars and entertained men; Angela considered many girls to be more beautiful than her, but the Japanese never agreed. Sometimes, one of the hostesses would go home with a gentleman if the price were right, but most infrequently. They weren't professional, but simply hostesses who took advantage of certain situations. Angela was the only professional Gaijin working in that area. That would eventually lead Angela to attract the attention of someone she cared not to know.

Across from Ginza Square was a very exclusive club, and most evenings, two vehicles would arrive outside. A dozen or so men would appear near the cars. Then, one little old man would get out of the Rolls Royce, assisted by two men either side of him, and walk to the elevator. He would always stay there for about two hours. Sometimes, Angela noticed him glaring back. She thought him to be just another wealthy man, but that was not so.

One particular night was enjoyable. It wasn't raining nor cold but the kind of night when many people would like to stroll around and take in the evening air. On this particular occasion, the black Rolls Royce was waiting for its client. However, he chose to walk down the street. Before the man preceded four bodyguards with two-way radios, who walked in front. As they walked past Angela, some smiled, winked and grinned at her, as if they knew all about her. Then came the little old man and two other hefty, rough-looking characters dressed in black suits. They stood on either side of the old man, virtually holding his frail body upright. The old man walked up to Angela and looked at her from head to toe. Then, he muttered something in Japanese to the men who were with him. The little old man didn't speak to Angela directly, but only looked at her, then turned to his guards and said. "Kirei desu nair!" (Beautiful, isn't it?).

Then the little old man turned and walked away. Behind him were another three bodyguards. Angela didn't think much about that at all. However, she noticed that as they walked down the street, all the people who usually worked in the area got out of their way very quickly and bowed deeply. Clearly, they were influential, or at least the old man was. He saw women as merely, objects, adornment, or stimulus or, perhaps, all those things together. Angela had sensed a particular kind of Japanese tradition that she didn't like. She didn't really know what it was but instinctively disliked it. That's what she had sensed in the little old man. He had commented to his guards about her beauty. However, he did not speak directly to her. Angela disliked that, for she was a modern girl who believed in the idea of equality. However, in a place like Ginza, the centre of old Tokyo, tradition lay under the whole city's superficial layer. In a way, Ginza could be said to be the most affluent place in all of Japan. Yet, from the outside, one would never know.

It was business as usual, night after night, client after client. Angela's bank account increased, and the ability to plan a career move improved. Angela's plan was three-phase, designed merely for success. Now, Angela didn't want to dance in a nightclub, but on film. Angela wanted to be able to do a dance routine in such a way she'd never done before. When young, Angela was a musician and a splendid one, too. Now, armed with the past, Angela's dream grew into something greater, something all-encompassing. She wanted to sing, dance, and play music. She tried to combine all three together onto film, a complete artistic, music and dance experience. She passionately believed that if she put all the money into her work, success would be guaranteed, and would never need to return to the street again. It was a good plan but would require plenty of time and money, and so, Angela would need to work hard. Ginza was very profitable. It was nothing for Angela to take three or four thousand dollars home a week. She never had to pay any money to anybody. It was all profit, that was, until one particular night.

It was quite a warm night, and there were more people around than usual. Angela was standing in her spot. At the Ramen noodle stand, across the way, were a group of what looked like Sumo wrestlers eating noodles. They were staring at Angela and talking to themselves. That was nothing unusual. Things like this used to happen all the time, except, Angela had never seen these men before, who didn't smile like most men. Usually, men would talk about her, laugh and giggle about what it would be like to go with her.

All of a sudden, the Voice said, "Tonight will be a little frightening, but don't worry, I am with you. Just be strong."

It was a bizarre time for the Voice to say that. Everything seemed perfect. The business was booming, the people were friendly, the police now left her alone, and everything was just right. The group of men or what appeared to be Sumos finished their Ramen and started walking down the street. As they did, they would yell at people from time to time, who would then get out of their way. There was a large group of them, maybe eight or nine. Some were dressed in Sumo attire while others were in suits. They all looked rough and very nasty, not smiling. Then, they walked up to Angela.

"Business is it?" one man asked.

"Sex business, why?" Angela replied with a nod.

The men then started talking to each other in Japanese. The biggest one stood in the middle. He was huge and looked like a typical Sumo wrestler.

He yelled at Angela in a booming voice, raising his angry hand, "Ginza, get out!"

Angela shrugged her head from side to side and lifted her nose in the air, as she replied, "Who do you think you are, to tell me to get out?"

They began to walk off, then the big one repeated his bland

statement. His English was obviously very limited. "Ginza, get out! Ginza Gaijin, get out!"

As he walked away, another three men in the group wearing suits stood by Angela. They didn't look like businessmen. Their outfits were far more colourful, and they held themselves too proudly, holding confronting poses, their legs wide apart as if ready for anything. One watched the street, meticulously looking for something or someone.

As he tapped another man on the shoulder, he uttered, "Daijobu (no problem), Ima, daijobu (now, no problem)."

One of the other men could speak English. He said, "We are Ginza Yakuza. You are doing business here, so you must pay us money or leave."

Angela became fearful and took one step back. As she did, the men stepped closer. She stepped back into the recess of the shop, towards the elevator, and the men came closer, pinning her against the wall. Angela began to feel nauseous. The people walking past didn't notice any difference but thought she was just doing business, as usual.

"We want ni-ju-man en (two hundred thousand yen), right now or you get out," the man said, loudly.

"I don't carry that sort of money around with me and, even if I did, I wouldn't give it to you. I don't know who you are, and I don't know anything about Yakuza," Angela replied. She then pushed them out of her way, and gracefully walked down the street. The people across the road who were watching knew what was happening. Those men's' bad reputation was well-known in Ginza. Nobody ever argued with them, but, just now, a frail Gaijin female was. Angela wanted to stand her ground. She wasn't going to let a group of thus come along off the street and ask for two thousand dollars cash, just like that.

"Who do you think you are?" Angela asked as she turned around.

They were murmuring in Japanese, surprised at Angela's tenacity. They couldn't believe how strong this Gaijin was. "She's not like a Japanese girl," one man said in Japanese. Angela could understand a little of what they'd said. Her Japanese language had considerably improved since arriving in Shinjuku, so many months ago. Angela had learnt a lot, particularly from her clients. She knew enough street language to understand what they were talking about.

"Yes," the man said. "She's going to be a problem, she's too strong." Then, he walked up to Angela and uttered, "We want from you, ich-ju-man en (one hundred thousand yen) per week, every week, payment to Ginza Yakuza. The name of this Yakuza is 'Kozan.' Kozan Yakuza Abunai (Kozan Mafia is very dangerous). We are Japan's number one Yakuza and what we say goes. We will come back in ten minutes, and then we'll want your answer. If you don't co-operate, you should leave Ginza, Tokyo and Japan, right now."

The Voice said, "Be strong but don't take any risks. Don't give in easily, but don't do anything dangerous. Seek the way of peace, find a peaceful solution."

Angela believed if she began to pay Yakuza, they would want more as time went by and, eventually, would own her. It didn't take much intelligence to realise that merely handing over money was more involved than what appeared at first sight. Angela remembered experiences with the Kings Cross Mafia, realising that she would be working for them once she started paying some Mafia organisation. Consequently, they would do with her whatever they liked. Angela didn't want to be involved in anything like that. She wanted to try and scare them away. If she couldn't scare them away, perhaps it would be best if she left Ginza.

Ten minutes later, the men came back. Angela's palms were sweating intensely, but she smiled casually and merely glanced at them, focusing her attention at passing customers, continuing to do her business.

"Komban wa, komban wa," Angela uttered to passing men.

The Yakuza were perturbed at Angela's casualness, so began to poke her in the chest with their fingers. "Okay, what's your reply, Gaijin?" the English-speaking man asked.

Angela pushed the man's finger aside and walked away, replying, "This is my spot, and this is my city, too. I am going to stay here."

The men laughed amongst themselves. They couldn't believe the guts this girl possessed. They had never encountered someone so single-minded or so stupid, it was hard to tell which. Then, after forgetting themselves for a minute, their personalities changed.

"There's no use in fighting us because you will surely die. You must do as we say, we are dangerous," the man said. "If you don't pay us, I will pull out a knife and stab you in the heart." Then, he lifted his coat pocket, to reveal a shiny Tanto (dagger), placed neatly in his belt.

Angela reacted unconsciously with a laugh. "And what have I got in this bag of mine, then? Perhaps I've got a gun. You pull out a knife, and maybe I'll shoot you through the head," Angela uttered, thinking it was only a game.

The people gazing from across the street were shocked at Angela's reaction. It appeared as if she wasn't afraid of them in the slightest.

"But then, we will only send someone else to shoot you. There are many of us and one of you. Eventually, we will kill you, even if you kill one of us," the man said with unshakeable confidence.

"Alright, then. I don't like violence, and I would never kill anyone. I don't have a gun, but I'm a Gaijin, you can't push me around. I'm not Japanese, and I don't fit into the same rules. The police know I'm here. If you cause me any trouble, I'll go to them."

"The police are nothing to us, they are frightened of us. Go to the police and see what happens."

The man who watched the street turned around and picked up a garbage bin and raised it above his head.

"Abunai, Abunai! Gaijin Ginza get out! Get out!" the man shouted and threw the bin at Angela. It hit a parked car on the street, in front of her.

Pieces of glass and garbage went everywhere. Everybody standing in the street, in front of the clubs and shops, hurriedly ran inside. Angela stood her ground and didn't move.

"Alright, then, it's the police for you," Angela uttered, as she walked off, very determined, and proud, to the police station.

The Yakuza followed her, thinking she was leaving Ginza. It

would take much more than that to move Angela Krukowski. She was a very determined girl. Significantly when she had sacrificed so much and come so far, simply to follow her dream. Angela turned the corner, and as she did, she noticed the Yakuza were still following. They weren't laughing now, but were in fact, very serious. One of the men had his hands in his pockets, and the other waved his hands wildly, as he walked. They talked to each other as if they had to do something they'd rather not. It was apparent they weren't acting on their own. They were, merely, street people controlled by a much higher power, by somebody at a high level. Angela would never have guessed who. However, she would eventually find out. In the meantime, Angela couldn't do anything about these men, who were simply messengers. They weren't in power and in no position to make decisions. They were merely messengers and procreators of violence.

Angela reached the police station. The men stopped at the next corner and watched. She went into the police station, to the surprise of the officers inside.

Angela began to speak as her hands started to tremble.

"Monroe Chan, what is it? What is the problem? Are you alright?" the policeman asked.

It seems, after all this time, the police had developed an affection and respect for her. Undoubtedly, because of her honesty and also, perhaps, her beauty. Angela told them the story of how the Yakuza had come to her in the street, demanded a large sum of money, and then threatened to kill her. The sergeant became seriously disturbed and told Angela to quickly return to Australia.

"It sounds like a very violent situation," the policeman said. "These Yakuza are the most violent in all of Japan. If they make a threat, they usually carry it out."

Angela was distraught and began to cry. One of the younger policemen then put his arm around her. "I'm sorry, but we can't do anything about it until they've committed a crime. It would be terrible to have to arrest them, only after they've hurt you. You should leave now than take any risk," the younger policeman said, caringly.

After thanking the police, Angela ran out of the police station. She grabbed a taxi to return to her little apartment in Hirai, Edogawa-ku. It was not so far away, but hopefully far enough for the Yakuza not to follow.

As the taxi sped along the main road of Ginza, heading towards Edogawa-ku, Angela looked out the back window, to check that she wasn't being followed. Then, Angela noticed headlights, not so far away, that seemed to turn every corner. A prudent Angela asked the taxi driver to stop for a moment. As the taxi driver stopped, the car following sped past. It was merely another taxi. Angela's nerves were really on edge now. She knew that it was simple for the Yakuza to follow her. Not only would they have cars, but also a network of people and vehicles. The Yakuza would consist of many hundreds of organised criminals. Angela could never be sure if she were being followed or watched at any particular time of the day or night. She was now living a dangerous life. It was transparent that all the stories and legends Angela had disbelieved were now becoming the most essential reality of her life. Danger and fear were the most predominant emotions Angela was feeling at this particular point in time.

The taxi driver continued and was a little annoyed with the seemingly inconsequential, brief stopping from time to time, but, nonetheless, continued to do what Angela requested.

After about half an hour, Angela became worried, thinking, "Any of these cars could be turning around and coming back. I shouldn't go straight home."

Angela redirected the taxi driver to Tokyo station, then caught a train and disembarked one station before her stop. Angela was now sitting in a coffee shop at Kameido station, watching the road to make sure nobody was watching. After some time, she went to the lavatory and out the back exit, to the station platform. Very cautiously, she boarded another train, only to disembark at one station past her destination, Shin Koiwa. Angela then swapped train carriages, watching her back to be sure nobody else did the same thing. She jumped on the train that was going in the opposite direction, back to Hirai. Angela was now safe. No one had followed her, as no one had swapped trains, so, no one would know where she lived.

A feeling of relief came over her as the Voice came to her. "You have done well, Angela, very well. Remember to always be careful. Remember, now your life has changed, things will never be the same. Always follow the peaceful path. Don't react with anger."

Angela knew she would remember that as a peaceful and serene feeling encompassed her. Arriving at Hirai station, Angela quickly scrambled down the stairs and into another taxi to return home. Angela entered her room, lay down and began to cry. It seemed she had struggled so hard, persevered so long and built up a profitable business, only to have the Yakuza come along and destroy it, all in one night.

It was very upsetting. Angela didn't know what the next step would be. All she knew was that now, Ginza was the most dangerous place in the world for her.

The next day, Angela stayed at home all day, as she didn't know what to do. "Perhaps if I leave for a little while they'll forget me, and they'll leave me alone," Angela thought.

Angela stayed at home for four days, which was very difficult. All she did was sing and dance. It was a welcome retreat, but in the back of her mind, the worry continued. Perhaps it may be time to leave Japan, and if she didn't, what would be the consequences? Where could she go? Ginza was the only place Angela believed she could work. There was no other place in Tokyo like Ginza.

"Ginza's my home," Angela said, as she stared in the mirror to put on her makeup the next morning. "There couldn't be another place in Tokyo like Ginza." Indeed, there wasn't, but that didn't mean that she wouldn't change location. Eventually, she would have to change territory; otherwise, she would be risking her life.

Five days had passed, and Angela decided to give it another try. "Sure, I'm a Gaijin. They're not going to hurt me; they're just going to try to scare me."

That night, Angela went to Ginza, to her spot, the very same place where she always stood. The people in the area couldn't believe their eyes.

Some said, "Monroe, please go, it's too dangerous. They want you. They will hurt you, or they'll catch you and put some drug into you, then they will take you away."

People who worked in the area were seriously concerned about her wellbeing. Angela had become a part of their adopted family of friends, so they didn't want to see any harm come to her. However, Angela believed if she stayed in Ginza and stood up to the Yakuza because she was a foreigner, a Gaijin, then maybe the reaction would be different. It didn't take all that long, about two hours before the Yakuza came back. This time, they didn't appear to be annoyed, but respected Angela in an odd way. They seemed to admire her strength. She was braver than most Japanese people, as a Japanese person never would've returned.

"Good evening," the men said.

"Good evening, Komban wa," Angela replied, respectfully.

"Your business is your business, right?"

"Yes," Angela replied.

"Violence is our business. Do you understand?"

"Yes, I understand," Angela said. "I am prepared to pay money."

"Our boss, my boss, has decided that he doesn't want you here unless he owns you completely. If you work exclusively for him, he will pay you a salary. If you don't, you must leave. If you don't do either, then we must kill you tonight."

Angela was very aware of the meaning. The word, 'kill' echoed in her mind. It wasn't a word that people used frequently, and it certainly wasn't a word a stranger used lightly in public. The term held a tremendous amount of power and fear. The man lifted the side of his jacket, this time to reveal a gun.

"I will not work for you. I do, however, want to meet your boss. I'm sure he's a reasonable man. Perhaps, we can come to some type of agreement," Angela said firmly.

The man spat out of the side of his mouth and shook his head back and forth. "No, you are not allowed to know who he is. No one is allowed to meet him. You must do as you are told, or you will suffer the consequences."

The man's English had obviously improved, so much so, he'd

made his point understood, too well, in fact. Angela sighed wearily and looked down at the ground. She inspected the men standing before her, then glanced to the side to see the people on the other side of the street fearfully watching.

Then Angela heard the Voice say, "Follow the peaceful path."

Angela then knew what she must do. The Voice said, one more time, "Do what you must do."

"Alright then, I'm leaving. I'm going. I give up. You people are just too cruel and too strong to stand up against, and I am just a Gaijin, right? A worthless Gaijin, something to be exploited for money, or to be destroyed, if you can't own me. You have nothing inside you that I need, but I have something in me that you need and that you'll never get. I forgive you, but I dislike you," Angela uttered, as she turned and walked away.

Slowly, the men, proud of what they had done, looked at one another with a grin of success. Then, Angela turned around and added, "I know one day you will get what you deserve. Until that time comes, you just feel like big men. Uh!"

Then, their success turned into shame. The men felt momentarily disgusted with themselves. Angela had made her point, exceptionally well. The men dropped their heads, then looked across the street, at the people who were watching.

"What a big Yakuza they are," Angela thought, "But what small men live in it!" Indeed, she was right. She returned home and refused to cry as she was not going to give up.

"Ginza cannot be the only place in Tokyo. I must find another place like it," Angela said to some friends she knew reasonably well.

"The next best place in Tokyo, for night clubs and entertainment, is Akasaka, but Akasaka is a dangerous place, Angela. You shouldn't go there alone. It's called 'Yakuza Island.' It's extremely dangerous. Every second man is a Yakuza, but you won't know it, because they dress like businessmen. They control the rest of Japan's Mafia, and that's their headquarters. As for a Gaijin in Tokyo, they may want to catch you and take you away, somewhere," one hostess said.

She knew they were trying to scare her away from Akasaka. They added, "Why don't you go to Shibuya? Shibuya's a nice place, but it's not as expensive as Ginza and Akasaka. Ginza and Akasaka are almost identical."

Angela's business ethic always aimed for the highest level and not settle for second best unless it could be absolutely avoided. Angela knew that the next place she would go to was Akasaka or, as some called it, 'Yakuza Island.'

Angela caught a train on the Marunouchi Line to Akasaka Mitsuke. It was a strange, little place, kind of like an island, a city surrounded by parks. The sub-city centre was hundreds of night clubs like Ginza, only smaller, yet the same standard. It wasn't quite as pretty. There were lots of Mercedes cars driving around, which were almost always Yakuza. Angela knew that much. She was quickly learning that the imported Mercedes cars with the dark windows and two-way radio aerials, were Yakuza. There were as many of those Mercedes cars around Akasaka, as there were night clubs. It was frightening. Angela then knew that this was a scary place. Ginza didn't look dangerous. Akasaka had a very fearful atmosphere about it.

The people who walked around didn't seem to be enjoying themselves as much as in Ginza. There were many men and women in Ginza at night, they seemed happy and carefree. In contrast, the people of Akasaka were mostly men. The women who were walking around were hostesses or working in a bar or nightclub. They weren't just female visitors but were working girls. It was clear that there were working girls, like Angela, there, also, but not in the street. Nobody worked on the footpath in Akasaka. Apparently, it was too dangerous. The Yakuza didn't allow it. They controlled all the sex parlours, and anybody who worked there worked for them. Angela spoke to some Japanese girls who were standing near the subway who spoke excellent English. They were hostesses and told her that there were more brothels in Akasaka than there were in the rest of Tokyo, except for one other place, Shinjuku. However, Akasaka was high class, so all of them were controlled by Yakuza. It wasn't a safe place to work because they were extremely dangerous. It was easy to get involved in drugs in these places because the Yakuza would push pills to the girls to control them. They would pay them a small salary for having sex with many men. Angela became very frightened and realised that she must not ever work in a place like that. She believed that the street was the safest place, even if the Japanese disagreed. It was the best way for her.

Angela knew that the Voice would guide her, and all she had to do was believe and trust the Voice completely, without hesitation.

As Angela walked down the street, the Voice said, "Don't worry, you are safe now. Ginza is the danger area. Akasaka is your new territory, it will take a while before it becomes dangerous. Just continue the same way, and everything will be alright."

CHAPTER TWELVE
'Tokyo's Landlords'

A KASAKA BY NIGHT was somewhat similar to Ginza, except, it lacked something, at least, for Angela. Ginza was an exciting place, yet Akasaka wasn't. It was very conventional, perhaps traditional and only about a quarter the size of Ginza. Nonetheless, there were many night clubs and places where businessmen could gather at night. Therefore, it was the perfect place for Angela to do business. She'd been told that there was many Yakuza in this place, but only time would tell. Angela noticed many men who looked like Yakuza. However, they did not hold the same fear as the Ginza Yakuza. Probably, because the experience in Ginza had been so shocking. Angela didn't know who the Yakuza were any more and was going through some kind of mental block.

Angela found an appropriate, little spot outside an English school, ironically enough. She stood there and continued to work the same way she had at Ginza. Most people were thoroughly shocked, while some men were excited. Everybody reacted individually and differently. Evidently, Angela was a kind of catalyst for Japanese people to release their built-up emotions. Feelings they couldn't usually express, whether it be joy, laughter, anger, excitement or even arousal.

One gentleman walked up and said, "I am so pretty to meet you," while being proud of his English skills.

Angela began to laugh. "Don't you mean you are happy to meet me?"

"Oh, yes, of course. That's what I mean." He was obviously a little confused.

Another man asked, "Why are you here? Why aren't you on television, in movies or something just as glamorous?"

"I guess because, perhaps, I'm not as pretty as you imagine," Angela replied with a smile.

The man couldn't understand the answer and walked off, shaking his head to himself. To him, Angela was stunning, and it seemed like a terrible waste for a gorgeous Gaijin to stand in the street.

As time passed, Angela noticed that there were fewer businessmen in this area than in Ginza. Despite that, Angela had to get Ginza out of her head. She couldn't go back there; it was just too dangerous.

"After all, it's only money," Angela thought. "Money is nothing without life."

A little more time went by, and Angela had managed to make many lucrative contacts, funny enough, through the subway. Then Angela noticed a new type of man in the street, who didn't look like Yakuza. They drove foreign cars, yet, their hair wasn't noticeably permed, and they wore dark coloured suits. They seemed a little scary. However, their reaction to Angela was positively overwhelming. They liked her very much, probably too much. One night, two men in dark suits walked past her. One was relatively large and wore a double-breasted suit that flapped open as he walked.

In contrast, the other smaller man wore a black suit and dark sunglasses, who, most definitely, looked like Yakuza. As they noticed Angela standing there, they burst out laughing. They couldn't believe it, as it was such a crazy thing for anyone to see in Tokyo. Then the two men stood watching her for a little while and quietly walked away.

Angela said to herself, "Just as well they went away. I didn't like the look of those two. I hope I never see them again."

A little while later, another older man walked over.

"Are you Yakuza?" he asked.

Angela shook her head back and forth, then began to laugh. "Me? I'm a Gaijin. No, I'm not Yakuza. I am alone."

The man sighed heavily, looked at the ground, looked up at Angela and said, "Then, you will be killed, as this place is known as Yakuza Island, and you should leave now. Here is very dangerous."

Angela cringed into the corner of the building while looking around. "How do you know that?"

The old man tilted his head and uttered, "Because it has always been that way. Either you work for them, or they will destroy you. This is Japan, and that is Japanese tradition."

The man, sadly walked away, thinking that he had given Angela excellent advice. He quite liked her and didn't want to see the foreign girl hurt and tried to scare her as much as possible. It worked. Angela believed it was better not to stay in one place too long. Moving around would make it difficult for the Mafia to know what she was up to. Angela walked around and acted casual to not attract any undue attention from some group of Mafia. In any case, it had taken about six months before Ginza Yakuza had caught up with her. It may take that much time in Akasaka, or so Angela believed.

"I have plenty of time before they give me the warning to get out. It will be the same kind of situation, I can make a lot of money before I'm told to leave, and then, I'll just quietly leave. There'll be no violence," Angela thought, trying to comfort herself.

"Don't worry. I'll guide you. Trust Me," the Voice reassured.

Angela walked among the people. It was beginning to rain, so Angela held up her French, yellow umbrella. With Angela's blonde hair and the yellow 'Kasa' amongst the sea of black hair and dark umbrellas, she could easily be seen from at least a mile away. Angela was, undoubtedly, a woman of the evening and, to the Japanese, the woman of the evening. The reaction to Angela as she walked through the crowd in Akasaka was overwhelming. Most men in the street stood and stared as she walked past.

Men uttered, unconsciously, in English, "How much? How much?"

Angela knew that was merely for show. Angela would not engage in any conversations about business with such a casual encounter. She understood that real opportunities would seek her out and not just casually drift by. Such options would follow her and impress themselves upon her, then in confidence, ask, "How much?"

The night drew on and eventually, a man came to her.

"How much?" Angela gave the usual response.

"Oh, it's so very cheap! I can't believe it," the man said.

The man couldn't believe it was so cheap! Angela went with him and spent the night in Akasaka Love hotel. It was very elaborate, more than she'd ever seen and was in a castle. Each room had a different theme, such as 'The King's Room,' 'The Supper Room,' 'The Play Room' and, funny enough, even 'The Dungeon.' It was quite humorous. They would stay at 'The Royal Room,' pitifully enough.

Angela thought, "Better that than the dungeon. My past experience with dungeon-like sex has scared me off it. I hope I don't reencounter that sort of thing. I would like a nice, easy business with normal people. It would be the best and safest way."

Angela had been allowing penetration to particular clients in the last month or so, only, to avoid the freaks. Such clients became satisfied with things other than regular sex. As long as Angela engaged in safe sex, she believed it was relatively safe, especially from AIDS. Angela felt that there was some kind of power protecting her. A voice was, merely, a voice, but it came from something more significant than that. It came from 'the power,' a force that protected Angela, no matter where she went, even in the centre of Yakuza Island.

During the following week, Angela went to the same area. There hadn't been any trouble with the Yakuza. However, it was quite apparent that there were thousands of Mafia men. Many were all interested in sex with Angela, rather than exploiting her for money. Most of them would ask, "How much?"

Angela would shy away and reply, "Yakuza Abunai desu (Mafia

is dangerous)." She refused on many instances, just in case, it was a trap or a violent situation she couldn't escape.

She decided that average businessmen who wanted regular sex would be her best target. It seemed like a pretty simple plan. All she had to do was stay away from Yakuza, but, as she would soon learn, it wasn't easy to tell who was Yakuza. Sometimes, Angela thought certain people were businessmen but were, in fact, the ones who she feared the very most.

In Angela's area was 'Soapland.' 'Soapland' was the new title given to massage parlours and brothels. Initially, they were called 'Turkish Baths.' However, the Turkish community in Tokyo kicked up a fuss about it. So, all the names were changed to 'Soapland.' Soapland was very popular with the Japanese businessmen. They could go there and have 'playtime,' as it was called, for up to two hours, from twenty thousand yen. That was really cheap, compared to the prices Angela charged.

However, Soapland's services were only for short periods. The people who pimped in the street for Soapland would approach businessmen and offer their card, suggesting they go to Soapland to meet some nice girl for play. There were at least twenty or thirty of these men in the street. They were spruiking to businessmen the pleasure houses nearby. They had noticed Angela, as they were also a type of Yakuza, a sex Yakuza.

They seemed to really like Angela. One of the bosses came to her and offered her a job. It was in the most prestigious Soapland in all Akasaka.

"I will give you one million yen to start," the boss said.

That was about ten thousand dollars just to start, and Angela would receive the same amount of money every month.

"No, thank you. Thank you for the offer, but no, thank you," Angela replied and walked away, very quietly.

Angela didn't want to be involved in any organised crime group. Moreover, she didn't want to go anywhere where she could be trapped or where there were drugs, for, she knew that was a formula for disaster. In that case, her dreams of dance and stardom would never be realised. In fact, merely surviving seemed to be a big ordeal. Even though the money was good, the risks outweighed the price. Angela was bringing in about that much every month, and she didn't want to risk being involved with Yakuza.

One evening, a group of men walked past and said, "It's Monroe Chan, it's Monroe Chan!"

They all stood there giggling like schoolboys, shaking her hand and asking her why she'd left Ginza. At least, in Ginza, Angela was a famous personality, and many people were sad to see the back of her. When she explained, the men couldn't believe Angela's story. They thought it was a fantasy. They really weren't in touch. The average Japanese knew nothing of the real Ginza or the real Tokyo nor the legends they talked about. None of them really believed the stories, for, ordinary people never encountered such situations. Anyway, they were glad to see her, and some said that they would tell their friends about her new territory. She was so popular in Ginza. Perhaps, now, she would attract a new kind of attention in Akasaka.

'Akasaka's Geisha,' that's what the men from Ginza would now call Angela.

Angela's Monroe image stayed with her but slightly altered, yet she kept the style the Japanese liked most. Akasaka was a difficult place to operate in. On some nights, she would not get any business at all.

If Angela didn't get a client, it wasn't because they didn't find her beautiful. Instead, it was because rich men only went to Akasaka on Wednesday and Friday nights. Monday nights, which had been profitable in Ginza, were quite here. It was a seasonal thing, but, unlike Ginza, Angela would spend only one hour with a man and take him to France for fifty thousand. She wouldn't have to do 'all-nighters,' for, there was a different kind of client in Akasaka.

So, on some nights, Angela would stand all night and not meet anybody. Then, on the next night, she would go with someone for one hour and receive the money she would've received for a whole evening at Ginza. Akasaka was a strange place.

One night, Angela noticed a group of Yakuza standing near her spot. They were all young and seemed harmless enough. They stood across the road, watching Angela, as they made calls on the public telephones. Angela ignored them. The leader of the group was the same man who had previously laughed at Angela. A short while later, they came over to her and said that Akasaka was Yakuza Island and that they must receive money from her. After payment, Angela would be allowed to freely operate here. The leader decided that each time they approached her; she must pay them twenty thousand yen.

"It's cheap, it's okay. I can pay that, no problem," Angela said, "But just now, I don't have any money. I'll have to be next time."

They agreed and walked away. Angela would have said anything to get out of a confrontation with a Yakuza group. They didn't seem as professional as the Ginza gang but were obviously capable of causing harm if they wanted to. Violence scared Angela, not their professionalism, but their ability to hurt her. Angela believed that she could avoid them, and only in certain situations would she pay them the money they asked for. The plan was to keep twenty thousand at all times, in case they ever caught her again.

A few days went by, and Angela noticed a strange thing beginning to happen. The Soapland people had started to realise that Angela was in direct competition for their business. She'd been taking away affluent clientele because she was operating in the street. The Soapland boss designated one of his men to stand near Angela at all times. Then when a businessman would go up to Angela, he would drive him away, in the direction of Soapland, by speaking to the businessman in Japanese. This annoyed Angela immensely, for, wherever she walked, there were always one or two of the men shooing away her business.

The men would say, "O-kama desu (it's a man, implying it's dangerous, and this person will probably steal your money)."

They would tell outrageous lies to drive Angela's customers away and nine out of ten times, it would work. These were a different kind of Yakuza she'd never encountered before. They didn't want to harm her but just destroy her business, hoping she would leave, leaving Soapland with all the clients in Akasaka.

It didn't take long before Angela realised the Yakuza was all one, huge Mafia. At first, Akasaka looked like it was of a mixture of small

Yakuzas. Soon, it became apparent that they were all part of one big organisation. The Soapland and street Mafia were all a part of the same group. Angela couldn't understand why they had agreed to let her operate there for a fee. In contrast, another group of the same organisation had sent men to drive away all the prospective clients. She was determined not to pay the twenty thousand yen until Soapland stopped ruining her business.

"If they leave me alone, I'll pay whatever they ask," Angela told one of her clients.

The client still didn't believe Angela and couldn't believe that they were determined to drive her out. Needless to say, they were very committed and more determined than Angela would ever realise. Yes, Akasaka was, indeed, a strange place. Sometimes, Angela would get a twenty or thirty-thousand-yen tip from a client, without having sex, merely for a quick coffee. The money was considered a present.

On the other hand, two or three days would go by, and Angela would get nothing. Then, occasionally, she'd make two thousand dollars in one day. This new place was very inconsistent and unpredictable, so were the people there, especially the Yakuza. It was driving Angela crazy.

It was the same thing every night. "Okama desu. Abunai (it's a man, dangerous, stay away)." Then, they'd grab the client and lead him up the hill to Soapland.

It was a mean trick that often worked. It got rid of most of the men who seemed interested in Angela. She was very furious.

One evening, the Yakuza men, who had asked for the twenty thousand yen, came to Angela in her spot and said, "Now, please pay us."

"No, I refuse to."

The men were shocked. "You must pay us."

"I will pay you when you stop Soapland from ruining my business. I will pay you then, no problem, but you must stop that nonsense first."

The gang leader acted as if he didn't understand, but it was clear that he didn't care about Angela's business. All he cared about was the money.

"Pay me now or else," the leader uttered with the help of someone who spoke English.

The man was tough, big and muscular, but not so intelligent.

"You must pay him now or else, he will hurt you," the translator said.

"Tell him I refuse to pay any money until he stops these people from driving my business away."

The man translated it back to the Yakuza leader, who then became furious. He squinted his eyes and started breathing heavily as his nostrils flared, then clenched his fist as he stared at Angela.

"Ima, ima (now, now)!" the Yakuza shouted, loudly.

Everybody in the street could hear him. However, Angela refused to give in, merely on principle. It wasn't just twenty thousand yen. That meant nothing to Angela, it was the idea that they were trying to destroy her business and take protection money from her at the same time. Everyone stood to watch what the outcome would be. Angela shook her head, one more time.

"No way," Angela said. "You're not going to manipulate and destroy me."

The man pushed the interpreter to one side, took a step back, then brought his back leg forward and kicked Angela, as hard as he could, in her shin. Angela didn't move, but just stood there, stood her ground.

"Is that the best you can do?" Angela muttered, sarcastically, rolling her eyes at him.

Angela was determined to prove her point of not being scared away easily. Angela had sacrificed so much and had been pushed around by so many people. She believed this was the last straw.

The Voice inside, said, "Now it's time to leave. Take a peaceful solution. Don't engage in violence. Choose a peaceful path."

Angela, being proud, ignored the Voice.

"Is that the best you can do?" Angela repeated as if she really wanted him to do something else. Perhaps, the man was not as strong as Angela had initially thought. Angela should have listened to the Voice and left, peacefully, but, to her regret, she didn't. Her pride had taken the better of her.

The man took a giant step back. This time, he did it so quickly that Angela couldn't react. Then, he kicked her, far harder than before. Angela stumbled. Her leg was cut open, and blood gushed out onto the ground. Angela was stumbling and leaning on her left leg.

The Yakuza man then yelled at her, in Japanese, "Fall down, you whore! Fall down!" All the businessmen in the street stood, helplessly, watching on with sad expressions.

They wanted to help but knew they couldn't. This was a very violent gang, and if any member of the public were to intervene, they'd become victims also.

The Voice said, once again, "Leave! Leave now!"

Angela turned and limped away. Then gazed back at the thug. He was furious, for he wasn't finished with her. When they were about ten feet apart, she turned around and uttered her last words.

"What a big man you are! What a big, little man!"

Then she turned back and continued to limp away, sadly. She began to cry as the pain was so intense. It felt as if her leg was broken. Her spirit was broken, and her leg was partially intact. Like a wounded soldier, she retreated from battle, stumbled down the slope, towards the main road, away from the danger zone. Looking back, she noticed the Yakuza were now grouping together, where Angela had been standing. It was evident they were making further plans. They weren't finished with her, yet. Angela didn't know what the outcome would be. She realised that they may follow her and try again, but they didn't. They just watched her limp away.

Then, a businessman ran up to Angela and said, "Look, Miss. You must get out of here, now. It's too dangerous. Please go."

He helped Angela around the corner, away from the field of vision of the danger zone. She walked a little further down the road and began crying again. Angela reached into her bag for a handkerchief and tied it around her leg, into a tourniquet.

The Voice said, "The peaceful solution is always best, Angela.

Always trust Me. Don't doubt Me and if I tell you to leave, leave as quickly as you can. If I ask you to stay, then stay."

Angela apologised to the Voice and said, "I'm foolish. Forgive me. It's just so horrible that they can do what they do and get away with it. It makes me sick."

Angela had a very ill feeling in the pit of her stomach, a nauseous feeling combined with pain. It made her hands tremble.

Just then, a taxi pulled up beside Angela, and a young man got out, ran up to her quickly and asked, "Hello. How are you?"

Angela sat down on the chair near the bus stop and replied, "I'm not very well. I've been injured."

Angela told the young man the story of how she was doing sex business in the street. A member of the Yakuza had attacked her because she refused to pay them money.

"I'm looking for somebody just like you. Isn't that strange that I should find you just now?" the young man said.

Angela was now a long way from the danger zone, somewhere she'd never thought there would be business, but yet, here was a man who wanted her.

"How much is it?" the young man asked.

"Fifty thousand."

"Come with me. I'll give you eighty thousand because you are so beautiful. I could give you anything."

Angela got into the taxi, and they drove off. It was a somewhat ironical ending to the evening. Angela knew to go back to Akasaka would be more dangerous than to return to Ginza. Ginza and Akasaka were areas where Angela may not be able to return to, ever again.

A few days passed, and Angela became worried. She knew that Akasaka and Ginza were the only places where high-class businessmen went and could pay the kind of money she wanted. Everywhere else was rather low-class. If she worked there, her salary would be lower.

She may even have to lower her price, either that or not get anyone at all. To reduce her fee would be to diminish her spirit.

"I must go back to Ginza, one more time, just to try it. Maybe, by now, they've forgotten about me," Angela thought to herself.

The Voice said, "If you go, be very careful. I'd rather you didn't, but in any case, if I tell you to go this time, you must leave."

Angela went back to Ginza. She'd been there three days and had met three very wealthy clients and had excellent business dealings. By now, it seemed Ginza Yakuza had been forgotten. It was as if things had changed back to the way they had been before she'd ever met them. She stood in a different area, Hachi-chome (area eight). It was a little distance from the other place. Angela had changed from her Monroe image into an entirely different look. Angela's hair was straight, her make-up was different, and there was no mole. She'd chose to dress in an altogether different fashion, with a mini skirt and black leather jacket. She almost looked like someone else.

"If I don't look like Monroe, but say, like Bardot, then, they won't know who I am. They'll think I'm someone else," Angela reassured herself.

However, Angela was so outstanding that it didn't take anybody all that long to realise that it was Monroe Chan beneath the new image.

People walking past would ask, "Isn't that Monroe? Isn't that her?"

Angela deluded herself to think she tricked them and felt that they didn't know who she was, but, indeed, everybody knew.

On the fourth night, a group of men walked past in business suits. Then, one man from the group returned alone.

"Monroe, it's you?" the man asked. It was the inevitable event that Angela had dreaded most. Before her very eyes stood the same man from the Ginza Yakuza.

"You are so crazy. Don't you understand how crazy this is? The others don't know you're here, yet the only reason I'm here, by myself, is because I like you, but I'll explain it to you, one more time. After that, if the others find out, I can't help you. Business is business in our group. My boss is responsible for foreigners in Ginza. If there are any foreigners here, who are not supposed to be here, then, he has his little finger cut off. He doesn't want to lose his little finger;

he'd rather lose you. So, please, Monroe, leave and don't ever come back. Go to Roppongi," the man stated. "Everything will be alright there. Go to Roppongi, no problem."

Angela had never thought of Roppongi. After all, that is Gaijin City.

The Yakuza man had two personalities. He had been ruthless to her before, but now, was being extremely pleasant. He held Angela's hand and spoke softly.

"You are beautiful. I'd hate to see anything bad happen to you, but we will have to kill you. It's nothing personal, you're lovely. It's just business, you must understand this."

That was something Angela could understand, the separation of emotion and intellect in business. In her line of work, she often had to do the same thing. So, even though she didn't like what this man said, he'd made it clear that killing her wasn't a personal gesture of dislike. He could fancy her and still kill her. It was merely his work.

Then, at the corner of the road, a black limousine pulled up. The man pushed Angela to one side and added, "They're here now. If he sees you, it's all over."

Angela looked to see the same old man who had come up to her one night, so long ago, with the group of bodyguards. She remembered how he had said she was beautiful. It was the same man.

"That's him," the man said. "That's the boss. He's the one who makes the decisions, and you can't change his mind because he's old. His thinking is old, so he will never change. The only time things will change is when he dies."

The old man strolled into one of the high-class night clubs with his entourage.

Then, the man talking to Angela, added, "Now, get out!"

The Voice also said, "Yes, leave, peacefully."

Angela did precisely that. As she did, the Yakuza man seemed to become somewhat emotional. You could almost see tears in his eyes.

"How ironic," Angela thought to herself as she hurried away. "Here's a man who's just threatened to kill me yet seems to care for me. How strange this place is and how strange these people really are! It is not the kind of system I know. It is a corrupt system.

One who goes against human emotion has to be evil." Angela left Ginza that night, for the last time. To return, would inevitably mean certain death. She had no other option but to go to 'Gaijin City,' Roppongi. The name was Japanese for 'six trees,' but there weren't any trees there, just many night clubs, coffee shops, restaurants and live houses. Angela would work on the street but didn't know where. Roppongi was the most challenging place she had been to, so far. Probably, because there were some foreign people, like her, well, not precisely like her. She was different from everyone else, but some non-Japanese people there, and Angela felt very uncomfortable about that.

The first day Angela went to Roppongi, she just walked around, looking for the right spot. There wasn't any business, at all. Perhaps, she had a psychological block. Roppongi didn't feel like a real Japanese city. Sure, there were lots of Japanese, but Angela didn't feel the same. It was tough to psyche herself into a position where she could work among Gaijins, without a feeling of inadequacy. Angela did feel inadequate, mainly, because, in Western countries, the attitude toward street prostitution was far more derogatory. In Japan, prostitution was considered as merely another profession as simple as office work. Anybody who made a significant amount of money, being a prostitute, held respect, for, the Japanese are amoralistic. They didn't believe in good nor evil, or so they thought. So, it was easier for Angela not to be judged by them. Still, among the Gaijins, it would mean discrimination, defamation and, perhaps, even verbal abuse. These were the things Angela dreaded, especially violence. Angela could handle being kicked out of Ginza and Akasaka by the Yakuza, being threatened with a knife and at gunpoint and risking her life daily with the killer disease, AIDS. However, what she couldn't handle was humiliation. Roppongi seemed to represent a place of shame, a city where Western society's ethics and morals had rooted themselves in a subculture of the Japanese community in Tokyo.

Nonetheless, Angela went back the next night and continued to return every night. A week had passed, and Angela hadn't met anyone, nor did she stand in a particular spot, but just walked around. The Voice always told Angela to be patient, and that things would all work out fine. Angela knew Roppongi like the back of her hand, having gone over every inch of it several times over. She realised that the best thing to do was to go to Ni-chome (area two). There were possibly no Gaijins at all there. It was a Japanese part of Roppongi, a place where there weren't any nightclubs, simply, Japanese drinking clubs, like a small Akasaka or very tiny Ginza. In that area, Angela believed she would find work.

Angela stood in area two, near a flower stall, where beautiful flowers were sold. Her taste in places was always excellent. She found spots that highlighted and adorned her appearance. It made a lovely image being next to the roses and daffodils. She stood beneath a light that shone down from the roof. It was just like a stage setting or photographic studio set. She stood out so beautifully. People walked by, and their reaction was always overwhelming, only as it had ever been.

"Roppongi is not so different," Angela thought. "It just took a little while to know where to go. It's funny, but I don't feel threatened now."

Occasionally, a Gaijin would walk past and, in horror, exclaim in English, usually something distasteful. However, such incidents were few and far between, so Angela's personality was always carefree.

Almost one week had expired, and Angela was standing in her new spot, on a Saturday evening. She met a client quite early, after being there for only ten minutes. It was the same situation as it had always been in Ginza.

"All night?" the man asked.

"Fifty thousand," Angela replied.

The man wanted Angela to go drinking with him first. Angela went to the club and served his drinks and sat like a good, little hostess with the other hostesses. As he absorbed the feminine custom, he talked to Angela about how Roppongi was also Yakuza territory and take care.

"This man doesn't know what he's talking about, but, anyway, I shall just go along with him, nonetheless," Angela thought, cynically.

After the drinking session, the man insisted that they go to a love hotel in Akasaka. Angela didn't want to go to Akasaka, but the man demanded. They went to the familiar place she knew, 'The New Akasaka Love hotel.' It was quite expensive, but charming, although, outside represented a danger to this blonde Gaijin.

"The best thing to do in the morning is quickly run down to the subway," Angela muttered to herself under her breath.

After all, Angela would be inside the hotel all night with her client and believed she would be relatively safe from harm. The client was easily satisfied. He didn't actually require much sex, just enough to absorb fifteen minutes.

Then the man said, "It's alright now. You're free to go. Thank you very much. I had a pleasant time."

Angela was happy to have earned so much money in such a short period, especially after having such a tiring and uneventful week.

The man left, and so did Angela. It was late, 2:00 a.m. It was precisely the 'dangerous time', and Angela was in the most dangerous place, where she had previously been attacked. If they saw her again, they would most probably kill her.

Angela thought, "I shall just grab a taxi, quickly get out of this place and go back to Roppongi."

Angela stood in the corner of the main road that leads to Roppongi, waiting for a taxi. Meanwhile, two men walked up, started looking at Angela and talking about her. They didn't seem harmful or dangerous, although one did look like a Yakuza. Although different somehow to the other Yakuza, who had caused Angela so much pain, he was, perhaps, another kind of Yakuza. The other looked like a businessman, seemed pretty harmless, and even quite handsome. He took a liking to Angela and started talking to her while she waited for a taxi. He was very polite and well dressed, in fact, a little too well dressed, one might say. He had many diamond rings on his fingers and a belt buckle by Christian Dior. It must have cost quite a lot, for, it was real, not imitation.

"So many little stones in that belt! You must be very rich," Angela said.

The man nodded his head and said, "Not really, just a little, but how about you? Looking like that in Tokyo, I think you must be pretty rich, too."

"Spiritually, very rich, but materialistically, always poor," Angela replied.

The man didn't understand Angela's response but insisted on talking further. The other Yakuza man soon left.

The nice man said, "I want to be with you, all night."

"But I am very expensive."

"How much?"

The price was then negotiated, slightly higher than the usual rate, seeing the man was so well attired with diamonds. He was prepared to pay ju-man-en (¥100,000, A$1,000).

They walked to the very same love hotel where Angela had been previously, in fact, the very same room. Angela and the man entered. He seemed like a businessman of some sort, although dressed more colourfully. She liked him.

"Perhaps, he is bisexual. He does seem to have some kind of bisexual tendency about him, yet, he is masculine, but then again, he does wear Christian Dior. It's most strange for Japanese. Nearly all Japanese men are straight, up and down, so conventional," Angela thought to herself.

The man was sensitive, and they talked at great length.

Then, the man said, "Now, we shall bathe together."

"I don't take baths, only showers."

"Why is that?"

"Because of AIDS," Angela replied. "Hot baths can transmit diseases, showers can't."

The man understood and agreed to shower. They took off their clothes and entered the bathroom. Angela stood in the warm water, then, surprisingly, caught the reflection of the man's back. She hadn't paid much attention to his body, until now. Then, she saw a large tattoo. It started at the top of his neck, spiralled down his back, onto his right leg and to the heel. It was of a dragon with wings, such a beautiful tattoo. It didn't scare Angela as the other ones had. Angela wasn't that surprised that he was Yakuza, but, found herself somewhat enchanted. He didn't have the personality that fitted the

Yakuza profile, like the ones she had met. This man's nature was unrelated to his profession. That fascinated Angela, and she wanted to know more.

They went to bed, and Angela said, "Kowai (frightening). You are Yakuza."

"But you are so beautiful. You have nothing to fear from me. I will not harm you, for I love you." He caressed her with a sensitivity she had rarely felt before.

Angela couldn't understand this absurdity. Such sensitivity was coming from a man who was part of the organisation that detested her. She also despised a group that she was at odds with, in fact, at war with. Her feelings had been thrown into a whirlwind of emotion. A tear formed in Angela's eyes as she thought how sad the world had become in Japan. The sensitive individuals, like this man, had been drawn into such a treacherous, Mafia group. He made love to Angela, very gently. His fingertips stroked her leg, as if he was, perhaps, the most sensitive man she'd ever met, strangely enough. As they lay on the bed and engaged in intercourse, Angela could see the tattoo in the reflection of the mirror. It enchanted her. Then, she remembered what it represented. That is when Angela switched off her emotions. She couldn't let this man touch her soul, the way he was trying so desperately to do. He was reaching out to Angela, for being part of a Yakuza group meant great loneliness. It is not as if a Yakuza member can be married and have children, as that would be, virtually impossible.

They had to dedicate their whole lives to the group, wholly. In most cases, they'd even live together to protect one another. In any case, it was a lonely life to live, and so, most of their private lives were spent with prostitutes when they required sexual companionship. However, this man wasn't so interested in sex, in fact, he didn't even expect an orgasm. What he wanted from her was simply sensitivity and intimacy.

Then another half an hour of cuddling passed, without intercourse. The man lay on his stomach, so his tattoo could clearly be seen. Then, he dimmed the lights and held Angela's hand as he drifted to sleep. Angela had agreed to stay until the subway opened at 5:00 a.m. It wasn't long, only another two hours, but it was long enough. Angela felt nervous. Even though the man was kind, he represented the very evil that was threatening her life. Angela lay there, in the darkened room and could barely see the tattoo in the darkness. She could see some lights on the wall across the room, which had something to do with the computer. All the rooms in this expensive love hotel were computer-controlled. The doors were locked automatically by a computer. No one could leave, until the man who rented the room picked up the telephone and authorised it to happen. So, Angela couldn't get out, even if she wanted to. The doors and windows were locked, automatically from the inside, by a machine on the wall. The device was glowing in the dark with its two, tiny, red lights.

Angela lay there, saw the tattoo and then the two red lights shining in the darkness. It was as if those two, red lights represented an evil face of capture, by Yakuza, an evil look of the Devil, himself. She lay there, and just when she was beginning to feel a tremendous sense of anxiety, the Voice came.

"Fear not. All is well. Just be patient, everything is alright. He shall not hurt you, for he is not like the others."

Then, Angela, trusting the Voice, fell sound asleep.

At 5:00 a.m., Angela woke. She possessed a mental alarm clock. If she wanted to wake at 5:00 a.m., 4:00 a.m. or 3:00 a.m., she could, by merely programming herself to the time she wished to wake up. Windows were always covered in love hotels, but in this instance, there was some stained glass in one particular area of the bathroom, and a tiny beam of light came through. There was just enough light to make those two, red lights disappear. By now, the man, during his sleep, had rolled onto his back and so, the tattoo had become invisible. The man was still clutching Angela's hand and wouldn't let go. Angela, slowly, tried to pull her hand away, but his hand was stuck to hers. Then, she pulled a little more forcefully, and the man woke.

"No, don't go. I am lonely. Please stay with me," the man whimpered.

"I'm sorry, but it's 5:00 a.m., and it's time for me to leave. I must go."

The man, pulling Angela closer to his body with his eyes still closed, pleaded for Angela to stay a little longer.

Angela held the man, sympathetically and said, "You are a delightful person. It's a shame you are Yakuza, it's a pity really."

The man shrugged away from Angela and sneered at that remark as if he was proud of who he was.

Then Angela added, "I'm sorry. I must go."

He gently stroked her arm as she began to slide off the bed. Then, he turned onto his side and returned to a morning's sleep. Angela got dressed, quickly left and found the subway. She didn't want to wait in the street if she saw the other group members, the dangerous ones.

The man had clearly been an echelon Yakuza, someone high in the organisation, someone who didn't engage in street violence, someone who did one of the two things. He could be a hitman, a professional killer or one who, perhaps, pressed buttons on people. In any case, he was, obviously, somewhat high up, and that was something Angela was beginning to understand. There were street Yakuza and controllers or bosses. The latter were the ones who Angela need not fear for now.

The ones in the street were the dangerous ones. Perhaps, this man was a single exception and, maybe, the others weren't so exceptional. Only time would tell.

The following Monday, Angela returned to Roppongi. Gaijin City was still a challenge, something of unmapped territory. There was a distinct Western feeling there, even in the Japanese city. Angela didn't like it because it wasn't like the rest of Tokyo. Ginza was always in Angela's heart. She remembered all the good fun and all the people she knew there, not so much the business. She didn't care that much about the money, for what use is money if you're not around to enjoy it? No, it wasn't money, it was the enchantment.

Soon, Angela met another man, then another and so on. In Roppongi, sex business was less frequent, as there were fewer businessmen. Therefore, she only met the occasional client, so her salary had decreased. Angela didn't mind, as long as she had enough to survive and plan her dream.

Angela practised her dancing in the daytime. After a long, hard night, she would get up early and dance wildly. The living room had no furniture, just an empty room with wooden floors, her own personal dance studio. The bedroom was right next to it. Each day, she danced with passion and determination. It seemed the more Angela sacrificed, the more passionate and more exciting her dancing became. It was as if, through sacrifice, her spirit was made more robust. It seemed strange because she always thought it would be the opposite. She believed that, if compromised and did what people wanted, she would die. Ironically, Angela had become more determined and much more ambitious. Now, when she dreamt of dance, she dreamt of dancing on a stage while she sang. The vision had grown to include singing. Then, it increased even more, as she dreamt of also acting on film.

The next night, Angela went to Roppongi and stood in the street for about half an hour, next to the flower vendor. Then, suddenly, in the background, Angela saw two Japanese men she recognised, in suits, walking toward her. Angela looked in the other direction, to see if anyone else was coming, then, before she knew it, the two men were standing right next to her. They cornered Angela into the side of a building. They were the Akasaka Street Yakuza, one being the same person who had hurt Angela so severely.

The man kicked her, once again, quickly and in the same place. Angela pushed her way through the two men and ran onto the road and into the traffic. The men ran after her, yelling abuse after her.

Then, Angela hid behind a car. "This is Roppongi! This is not your territory! This is Roppongi! Leave me alone!" Angela cried loudly.

The man laughed and spat on the ground. He then peered at Angela with evil delight as if it were merely a game.

"Ha!" the man said. "Roppongi and Akasaka are my territories, and you are mine!"

Apparently, the man had planned the whole thing. He'd heard about Angela's new location and came for her. The other man was standing on the street, looking out for the police. They had a system they operated by. Suddenly, the harsh reality of Yakuza had been brought home to Angela. The Yakuza man who she'd met a little while ago was nothing like this man. Then, the man walked around the car and went up to try to kick her again. Dangerously, Angela ran away into heavy traffic, once again. He wasn't going to kick. This man was dangerous and wanted to really hurt her. Then, Angela ran into the middle of Roppongi Square. It was extremely dangerous. Then, a car drove past and slightly hit Angela on the hip, knocking her to one side, to which, she began to cry.

The Voice said, "It's alright. Now you are safe. Don't worry."

Angela realised she had made it across the other side of the road, as the man stood there, watching for some time. It was almost as if Angela could read his mind. He was like a primitive animal. Planning how to get across the road to harm her. This would persist until Angela gave into the man, until she gave him all her money or, even worse still, gave herself. It's hard to say what he really wanted. Perhaps, in the beginning, he only wanted the money, but now, he wanted Angela. In any case, Angela knew the only way to get rid of this guy was to go to the police. The best thing a person could do was go directly to the police, for, even Yakuza were frightened of the law. Angela quickly walked to the police station.

The Voice said, "You are safe now. Don't worry."

Angela stood near the police station, as the man watched from a distance. Then, he gave in, started kicking the ground and hitting the side of a wall with his fist. He was crazy, very violent and madly determined. That determination only matched Angela's. She didn't respect him, but instead had contempt, yet understood his commitment. Angela knew that Roppongi was no longer safe. In fact, nowhere was safe.

For the next couple of days, Angela stayed at home and spent most of her time worrying about her next action plan. She thought she may have to return to Australia with the little money she had saved. It wasn't an enormous amount when one deducted all the clothes, the apartment and the cost of living in Tokyo. Angela would probably go home with only a few thousand. That wouldn't help her dreams very much and meant she wouldn't be able to travel to the places and do the things she planned to. If she was to leave now, it would mean failure.

The Voice said, "It's alright. You can go back to Roppongi, as long as you are extremely careful. It might be wise to stay close to the police station, but, if you do as I say and trust Me, you will be safe."

Angela wanted to go back to Gaijin City. She hated not knowing if she could survive financially. A little doubt clouded her mind. She refused to go back until she had recovered from the fear that man had instilled in her. He'd haunted her dreams. Angela would be dancing, then he would emerge in a black cape, grab her and start to carry her away into the darkness. Angela would wake in terror, screaming at the top of her voice, realising it was only a dream. She would realise that the fear was part of the Yakuza way. They embed fear into the victim, so they'd eventually co-operate and do anything they wanted. Yet, Angela was tenacious.

The Voice said, "They will not catch you. I will protect you. Trust only Me."

For the first time in a few days, Angela fell asleep and had a very peaceful, dreamless sleep.

CHAPTER THIRTEEN
'The Star Breaker.'

ANGELA HAD BEEN very concerned about the future, desperately planning a chance at stardom. It was strange how she was always having premonitions. She sometimes gave people readings by holding a piece of their jewellery and picking up vibrations. Many of her friends had asked her to provide them with psychic readings, and Angela foretold their futures with uncanny accuracy.

"It's a gift from God. I should never make money out of that. It's a spiritual gift, and so, I should only use it as such, a gift. So, when I give a reading, it's a piece of me that I give to you," Angela would always say.

The only unfortunate thing about Angela's readings was that she could never use clairvoyance for herself when she was probably the one who needed it most. However, since the sex business compromise, she had come closer to the Voice inside her. The Voice was her only reality, her closest friend, protector and adviser. Next to the Voice was Barb, who lived a great distance away and even further away was Lyn.

Some years ago, Angela had given Barb a reading and foretold just what would happen in her life. It happened as Angela said it would. Angela now needed that kind of certainty in her future. The Voice suggested that Angela write the words it gave her, in a little book and call it 'Conversations with the Voice.' Angela was, by now, anxious about her future and her sex business. She would sit over coffee with a little, pink diary and write from her heart: The material that came to Angela was a bit frightening. Words detailed why she was in Japan. Including the real motivation for sex business. Yet, she was cleansed of all the things, especially the things that happened with the Yakuza. In fact, everything, up to this point. Everything had been so clearly explained in the little diary. Then, one day, a new entry came.

It was late in the afternoon. The sunlight was beginning to fade, and the shadows of the curtains flickered over the little book, as Angela wrote.

The Voice spoke through the pen. "Now you will meet a bad man, but fear not, for I am with you."

Angela cherished the journal. It was the most important thing to her. However, the last entry was a rather unusual statement and opposite to everything else in the diary. This was, most definitely, from the one who mattered most, the Voice.

It read, "The wicked man will come sooner than you realise. Don't worry. I will protect you. Trust Me."

The next day, Angela went to the bank and found her account was dwindling. She hadn't been working for some time because of the incidences in Ginza, Akasaka and Roppongi. She didn't know what to do. It was clearly time to enter a new phase in the sex profession. It wasn't a chosen option, but one selected by the violence of the Yakuza. Angela decided that the best solution was to lower her price and go to Shinjuku. This would mean that, instead of fifty thousand, it would be more like twenty to thirty thousand yen for short times. That suggested, she would have to do more than one, in fact, would have to do as many as possible.

The Voice said, "It's not the price that determines the standard, it's the men you select. Don't go with those you have bad feelings about. Always follow your instincts."

Angela believed that she wouldn't have any trouble, with the tremendous amount of guidance she possessed, and so went to Shinjuku.

Shinjuku was called 'Play City.' There were many 'Soaplands,' strip clubs and 'Pachinko' (Japanese gambling parlours), pretty much everything, except for one thing, a beautiful, blonde prostitute. There were many Japanese hookers on the streets. One could see Japanese girls leaning against buildings, obviously, employed in the sex business. Still, there were no Gaijins and no one like Angela. When she walked down Shinjuku streets, all the men couldn't take their eyes off her. Angela felt as if she were on stage or a model in a fashion parade, attracting everybody's attention. It was bizarre because Angela never thought of herself as beautiful, nor even pretty. Yet the Japanese's reaction was a powerful one. She could never understand why.

There is a place in Shinjuku, called the 'Koma Theatre,' near all the picture theatres. It's the favourite area for girls engaged in the sex business to operate. Although Angela had been there before, she didn't like to work there, for it seemed low class and sleazy, indeed.

"Perhaps, I should give Roppongi one more try," Angela said to herself.

So, Angela left Shinjuku and left a lot of business behind.

Many men were waiting to talk to her, but she turned and walked the other away. She didn't want to go to that point in her life unless it was essential.

That evening, Angela went back to Roppongi.

The Voice said, "Tonight, you will be surprised, but, remember, stay near the police station and don't be frightened."

It was funny, really. In the street, Angela was standing directly opposite the police station and obviously engaged in the sex business. The police saw her and began laughing, loudly. They couldn't believe their eyes. It was hard enough trying to catch prostitutes when they knew where they were working. Still, they'd never seen a Gaijin, blonde prostitute, so outstanding as Angela. They were so astonished that they just remained seated and watched the brazen Gaijin for hours. The police saw many men come up to Angela, talk for a while, then shake their heads because it was obviously too expensive. They couldn't actually do anything about it, except watch, unless they made a trap, but they didn't.

Then, Angela noticed a man across the street, near the police station. He was big and chubby. The man obviously had a vision problem and unconsciously passed in front of a moving car while walking directly towards Angela, seemingly hypnotised by her beauty. He didn't see anything, except Angela. As he gazed at her, he kept walking, then, almost fell over a fence, then, tripped over a garbage bin and fell on his knees as his hands touched Angela's shoes. He lay on the ground before her and looked up at her, seemingly speechless.

"Oh, what are you doing here?" the man asked.

He was so surprised. Angela began to laugh, as it was such a silly situation.

Angela had never seen anybody humble themselves so much before and replied, "We must stop meeting like this."

The man could speak excellent English. Then, he stood himself up, shook his trousers clean from dirt and began to talk.

"Hello. My name is Ariyoshi. What are you doing here?"

Then, Angela began the same old story. It was almost a repertoire, by now. She had it down pretty pat.

"I'm doing sex business."

"No, no, you are far too beautiful!"

Angela raised her eyes to the sky and began to shake her head up and down, saying, "Yes, I know you think I'm too beautiful to be standing in the street, but I am. Everybody tells me the same thing, but that's life. I can't do much else at this point in time."

"I'm not interested in you for business, I just want to talk to you for a while. Is that okay?" the man asked.

Angela agreed. She didn't pay the guy much attention after he wasn't interested in sex. Angela started looking at other men passing by and unconsciously chatted to the man. She hardly even looked at him, but just talked and, before she knew it, Angela had told Ariyoshi the story of her life.

The police were really watching, as a man was standing right next to Angela, for at least half an hour. However, they weren't doing anything except talking. Then, one of the policemen came closer. He wanted to hear what they were saying, perhaps, so they could catch Angela and arrest her. Ariyoshi didn't notice the policeman, but Angela could see a policeman from a mile away or so she believed.

Ariyoshi presented his card. "I am a promoter. I promote big stars, like Madonna, Ray Charles and so on."

"Oh! Oh, yeah, sure! Yeah, I believe you, you and everybody else. That's the most famous profession in Japan for the guys I meet. They're always star makers, movie directors and this and that. In fact, you're the third one tonight, honey!"

Ariyoshi began to laugh, as he added, "Please, look at my card more closely. My office is here where you are standing. I am very well known. My company is 'Bomb Promotions."

Angela laughed at the name. She thought it was hilarious. "You mean, you're still in business, with a name like that?"

Ariyoshi shook his head and said, "I deal in the best, and I feel something with you. You have a strange personality about you. You talked about the fact that you were a dancer and that you play music. I feel as though you have something special to give. While ever you have the talent, which I believe you do, it's wrong to stand in the street. Come with me and leave the street behind, Angela."

The policeman was still watching but was not close enough to hear what they were saying. The look on his face meant he suspected the worst.

The Voice said, "Go, go with Ariyoshi."

Immediately, Angela grabbed Ariyoshi's arm and said, "Let's go." She didn't want to get arrested and knew that she always followed the Voice no matter how absurd it seemed.

As they walked, Ariyoshi said, "We shall go to dinner. I want to talk to you and introduce you to a friend of mine. He's a movie director."

Angela laughed at this, only half believing what she heard from this man, began to talk seriously of her dream of dance and stardom. Ariyoshi listened intently and, as he did, he inspected Angela, as if examining an elegant, porcelain vase.

"We'll have to change many things about you. We'll have to

change the way you look, the way you talk, even the way you walk. We have to take you from the bottom to the top," Ariyoshi stated.

Angela laughed and said, "What do you mean? I'm just going with you, only to talk, nothing else."

"I already know your mind. You must do as I say and I will put you where you belong, but only if you do as I say."

Angela really couldn't believe what she was hearing. She'd been working in Tokyo for about ten months. During that time, this Australian dancer had experienced every trick in the book, well, almost all. Angela thought she knew men and did, well, most men. This was something new. This was a guy who said he just wanted to make her a star. Ariyoshi thought of himself as a star-maker and saw Angela as his new starlet.

"If I take you home, to meet my wife, will you then believe that my intentions are honourable?"

Angela sighed and said, "I don't know what to believe anymore. Men always lie about sex and money. I can never trust them. They tell me something, and it always turns out to be untrue. Most people consider prostitutes to be worthless garbage, and it's only real friends who count. Anyone else who's passed in and out of my life was like passing cars in the night."

Ariyoshi seemed sympathetic and sensitive. He said, "Angela, leave the street behind. Take my hand, and I will make your dream come true. I love you."

Angela laughed once again. "You know, every man who wants sex from me thinks he makes love to me and says he loves me, that's until they reach orgasm. Then, they all change their personality, and the next thing they ask is, what's your name, again?"

"Angela, you are special, and I will treat you preciously," Ariyoshi said, softly.

They sat, eating a rather exquisite seafood dinner, when another man came in, a very young, handsome man. His name was 'Mike'. Apparently, he was Japanese with a Gaijin name. It was very fashionable for many of the 'in vogue' people to adopt Gaijin names. He sat down and started talking about how he'd met Steven Spielberg and all the big names, obviously trying to impress Angela.

Then, he presented his card and said he would like to shoot her when she had free time. Angela laughed in disbelief. Was this opportunity for real?

As all men want, Angela knew what they wanted, which was sex. She also knew that her business was changing direction. She was going to treat Ariyoshi and Mike, as well as any others who came along, as merely business. Angela would never love any of them. They were looking at her body, like all others. Angela's instinct told her that nothing had really changed. It was just how remuneration was modified. These were favours for sex instead of money.

Then, Ariyoshi took Angela to a rather expensive cocktail lounge. It was tucked away, right down the bottom of Roppongi, where no one could see them. After they sat drinking, Ariyoshi went to talk to some people he knew. Anglea remembered the 'Conversations with the Voice' and how the Voice had told her that a surprise was coming. It had also told her many other things, so many things that, with the alcohol clouding her mind, were difficult to remember. She wanted to read that journal now, but it was a highly inappropriate time. In the meantime, everything the Voice had said, had happened. Angela became nervous, and the hairs on her arms stood up with goosebumps, as she thought of how the Voice had predicted the meeting of a bad man.

Angela didn't know who the identity was and asked her heart, "Who is it? Please tell me, please tell me who it is."

The Voice said, "Don't worry. I will tell you when it's time to know. Now, be happy that you're not on the street and free from danger. Trust me and go with this man."

Angela was amazed. This was the first time she'd ever gone off with a man without some kind of deposit or financial negotiation. Was this business or personal, or was it both at the same time? The only thing to do was follow her instinct, play along and see just where this lead. One thing was for sure. The guy seemed pretty legitimate in his business. The question was: what was his real motivation? Only time would reveal that fact.

Ariyoshi came back to the table. They chatted for a while, about what Angela liked, what she did, what she wanted and every aspect of Angela's dream. Now, Ariyoshi knew Angela very well, in such a short time. He was the only man she'd ever met who had managed to draw out her wishes, hopes and desires so quickly. Angela was surprised and couldn't believe the things she'd told Ariyoshi.

"That does it. Now, we'll go to my home, and I'll introduce you to my wife. Then, you'll believe me."

Angela went, for the Voice told her to. Ariyoshi lived outside Tokyo, very far away, about two hours by taxi, which cost over two hundred dollars. As they sat in the cab, driving along, Ariyoshi's intoxication became obvious. First, he put his arm around Angela, then, held her close and, after a while, began to kiss her on the cheek. What had started off as being a non-sexual encounter, was turning into a special meeting. In fact, soon, it would become a powerful sexual encounter that Angela hadn't experienced before, full of a man's lustful passion. Previous encounters were rather casual intercourses or, merely, fantasies. However, this relationship would quickly become passionate and powerful. This man would impress himself upon Angela, in such a way, she had never known to be possible before. Angela didn't know how to respond to Ariyoshi. The rules must be adhered to at all costs. The nature of the transaction was different. However, there must be no deep kissing and only safe sex, regardless of the payment method.

As the taxi sped along the expressway, leading out of Tokyo, Angela could see the stars.

"Perhaps, this is really the start of my dreams," Angela said softly to herself.

The Voice said, "Yes, it is."

Then, the man grabbed her, pushed her down, onto the taxi's back seat and mounted Angela, as if she were a horse.

"I will give you everything. I will give you the world, but you must be mine and only mine. Promise me."

Angela said nothing but merely giggled, as she couldn't believe the things she'd heard. The man didn't even know Angela, yet suddenly he was claiming her as his own.

"Please don't do anything here. This is not right, in a taxi. The taxi driver's watching, and I feel cheap," Angela uttered.

Slowly, Angela pushed Ariyoshi off her body. They sat together, and embraced tightly, as he kissed her hand, arm, then her shoulder and neck. Every time Ariyoshi got close to Angela's mouth, she would think of an excuse to stop him, remembering that deep kissing was taboo. Ariyoshi was a lustful and passionate man. At the first meeting, he seemed so genuine in his attempt to seduce Angela. 'Seduction' was the name of this particular game.

On the other hand, when Ariyoshi spoke about stardom, he became a different person, a businessman. He had multiple-personalities, one moment, emotional, tender, passionate, and lustful. Then, the next moment, this man was a non-feeling, insensitive, businessman, who only cared about profit and success. It was hard to distinguish who the real Ariyoshi was. He moved from one personality to the next, from moment to moment. Angela had been with many men, hundreds of men, perhaps by now. In many different ways, Angela had known many men but never had any of them held her in this way. This man was doing more than merely touching Angela. He pressed buttons inside her that had never been pushed before. He played with her dreams and enticed her with a desirable future. Indeed, it was a very passionate seduction, and what ended in the taxi would soon begin elsewhere.

The cab promptly arrived at its destination, Ariyoshi's house. It was dark in a small suburb, very far from where Angela lived.

The Voice said, "Don't worry, everything's alright."

Angela sighed with relief and knew that everything would be alright, regardless of where she was or who she was with. The Voice was there, always, to protect her and guide her. While driving in the taxi, Angela had thought a lot about the Voice. As Ariyoshi paid the taxi driver, Angela remembered the words of the Voice.

"You will find great stardom, Angela. Patience and faith in Me is the key, for you deserve it. You have paid the price, and you have the talent. Just believe in yourself and in Me, only."

Then, Ariyoshi all but dragged Angela out of the taxi and across the street, to a large, three-storey, brick house. It must have been expensive because it was gigantic. In Tokyo, even the smallest, humblest dwelling costs the earth. This place was a mansion.

"This is my home," Ariyoshi exclaimed. "Please wait here. I must go and tell my wife that you're coming."

After ten minutes, all the lights in the house came on. It was 3:00 a.m. Obviously, Ariyoshi's wife had been asleep. A few minutes afterwards, the door opened. Ariyoshi came out and ushered Angela inside and into the lounge room, where his wife was waiting. They all sat down together at a table. His wife was younger than he was, lovely, intelligent and utterly the opposite to Ariyoshi, more like Angela. Angela was surprised and liked the woman straight away. There was something sweet and honest about her. Ariyoshi's wife liked Angela too. It was as if they were old-time friends, who had been reunited. They talked for hours and hours until the sun came up.

Meanwhile, Ariyoshi just sat there and poured whisky into his glass, then straight into his mouth. Perhaps, Ariyoshi listened to their conversation because his English wasn't as good as his wife's and certainly no match for Angela's.

Then, when the sunlight started shining through the window, onto the floor and silhouetting the bodies that sat around the table, Angela began to yawn. She was tired, and Ariyoshi sensed it.

"Would you like to go to sleep in the guest room? You have all day. We won't even talk about business until tomorrow. I want you to have a good rest," Ariyoshi said, caringly.

Ariyoshi lied to his wife about why Angela was here. He'd said Angela was the wife of one of the musicians, who he had noticed singing in the studio and wanted to record her. It was apparent that Ariyoshi's wife didn't believe him. They winked at each other, knowingly. However, Angela didn't feel bad because Ariyoshi's wife didn't seem to care. This hadn't been the first time and certainly wouldn't be the last. The fact that Ariyoshi's wife liked Angela, seemed to make it a worthwhile encounter, at least, for the two women. Angela's life had been transformed so significantly in such a short time. One moment, a prostitute and the next, she was a budding starlet or, shall we say, aspiring starlet, part-time mistress.

Ariyoshi's wife excused herself and said, "Now, I must get ready for work."

Her name was 'Mieko' and was the principle of an English school and so, had to be at work very early in the morning. Mieko also had a son to take to school, who looked a lot like Ariyoshi. While they got ready to leave, Angela went to bed in the guest room. Then, Mieko and her son left for the day's activities.

Angela began to doze off to sleep when she noticed the door of the guest room slowly opening. The guest room was very dark. The sunlight through the doorway shone in. A silhouette of a naked Ariyoshi could be seen clearly.

Angela said, under her breath, "Oh, so it's just business, as usual."

Then, Ariyoshi moved closer to the bed. He was different from the others, like an animal, rather than a person, calculating things by scent and instinct. He was a beast, hard to contain and a little fearful. All the while, the Voice reassured her. "Don't worry. It's all part of the plan."

Angela believed there was a purpose of standing on the street. Although, standing on the footpath to make money, wasn't going to help her achieve stardom. Angela didn't know what form this would take. Still, her instinct and the Voice have said that it would eventually happen. The plan was to work hard, continue to believe and never lose sight of her dreams. Angela did that, even while she stood face to face with the beast, Ariyoshi. He slowly sat down, with very lust-filled motives. His eyes revealed years of frustration and sexual desire. Then, he suddenly pounced on Angela, like a panther and grabbed her with his claws, capturing her body, so she couldn't move.

Then, Ariyoshi pulled Angela out of bed, dragged her onto the floor, and rested on her. The panther-like body leaned over Angela and uttered, one more time, "You are mine and mine, only. I will give you the world, but, in return, you must give me yourself."

Angela couldn't believe what she was hearing.

"And how am I supposed to survive?"

"Be quiet. I will provide everything for you, and you will be there whenever I need you. I will put you on tour when you are ready. You will be a huge star, but I will never, ever let you go with anyone else. If I hear that you have been with another man, I will have you killed," Ariyoshi stated, boldly.

Angela began to cry. She had mixed emotions about this, and Ariyoshi was manipulating them. He knew what buttons to press and smiled with delight as a smug look overcame his face. Angela's weeping turned to a sob, as she looked at Ariyoshi.

"You are just going to use me. You are trying to trick me. You only want sex, you're like the rest. Why did I come? I'll never know," Angela said, empathically.

"No, Angela. I'm not like the rest. I'm not like anyone you've met, and you're not like anyone I've ever met. We are different, and we belong together. You want to be something, so badly, that I know you already possess. I'm the one who has the power to make it real, and you have the beauty that I've long dreamt of."

Then, the man held Angela, as he began to entice her a little more, physically. Ariyoshi would touch Angela's body, then squeeze her, as a bear would, then bite her neck and say passionate, lustful things. Angela wouldn't allow Ariyoshi to penetrate her body, so it just became a form of seduction.

Ariyoshi spoke as he kissed the blonde Gaijin's body, endlessly. "You will be my Marilyn Monroe. You will be my Angela. Don't worry about money or anything, anymore. I'll provide everything for you. Just do as I say."

Ariyoshi repeated these words again and again as he kissed every part of her.

"I won't have intercourse with you until I know you are clean. You'll have to go to a hospital and be checked first. I must be sure you're clean and that you'll be mine and no one else's, then, I'll take you. Until that time, I'll want you," Ariyoshi said fiercely.

Ariyoshi did everything, except intercourse, then he masturbated. As he orgasmed, he admired Angela's body. Afterwards, there was a feeling of serenity, strangely enough, between the two of them. Angela wondered, now that he'd orgasmed, whether he would change personality or say different things, as all the others had, but he didn't, oddly. However, Ariyoshi kept saying the same things, talking more in a business tone than a sexual one. He started planning when Angela would have her first singing lesson, when the first rehearsal with the band would be, and when Angela would go on tour. Ariyoshi's first plan was to take her with him next month around Japan for ten days. They could be together then. In the meantime, while they were in Tokyo, Angela would have to work very hard with the musicians. Ariyoshi believed that Angela's stardom would come through music.

"Dancing is good. It could be a part of your act. Still, I'm sorry, in this day and age, no solo dancer becomes a big star unless they are versatile and can do many things," Ariyoshi said, knowingly.

Angela agreed and said that she'd known it was limiting. Some time ago, Angela had realised that she must do many things to find stardom.

Ariyoshi began to write things down. He was solemn. He had his briefcase at hand and date planner and started to plan Angela's schedule. Angela's eye, for a moment, twinkled, as she looked out and saw a beam of sunlight shine through the window.

The Voice said, "Trust me, Angela?"

Angela blinked and then, a tear fell from her eye, onto her arm.

Ariyoshi noticed it and asked, "Why are you sad?"

"I'm not sad now. I'm happy, because, perhaps, you really will love me. Perhaps, you like me enough to take me off the street and make the world see the person I truly am inside."

Ariyoshi closed his briefcase and embraced Angela, tenderly. It's strange because what had begun as a lustful, passionate, sexual encounter, was becoming an affectionate embrace. She never thought a situation like this would ever happen. Angela hadn't faced any real emotions, not since her boyfriend, Theo, almost a year ago. She had nearly forgotten how to feel, forgotten how to love.

Then, Ariyoshi said, "There are many things we must do today. I think it's best we get dressed, and I'll take you to my office. We have many things to do and must not waste time."

As they showered and dressed, Ariyoshi became sexual again. They ate breakfast; then, Ariyoshi began to forget about business and thought only of sex with Angela.

"I must have you again, Angela."

Angela, confused, replied, "What about going to the office?"

"We can do that tomorrow!" Ariyoshi exclaimed. "Today, I want to be with you. I want to make love with you, all night. Tomorrow, we can begin the business. Today is for us."

Angela now trusted the man because the Voice had told her it was her destiny to meet him. She agreed, although, wanted to go home first, as there were many chores for her to do, but said she could return later.

They sat together in a coffee shop. Ariyoshi talked about many plans, long term plans concerning Angela's tour when she could sing properly. After which she could choreograph material to go with the songs. Firstly, Angela would have to sing jazz standards and Ariyoshi would choose every number. Ariyoshi planned to tell Angela how, when and why to sing those numbers. He demanded to oversee everything. Angela had always been an independent person and was now finding it difficult to come to terms with this new kind of manipulation and management.

Angela went home and did the things she had to do. Then, Angela began to doubt, "There was lust in his eyes. I can't trust a man with lust in his eyes. They all want the same thing, and afterwards, things change."

It was strange. Listening to Marilyn Monroe, it seemed the words were about the same experiences Angela had. She'd realised the same things about men that Marilyn had. However, Monroe had succeeded, and Angela certainly hadn't. Monroe was dead, and Angela was alive. There wasn't a lot of difference in the sentiment, just the physical situations. Angela felt some kind of spiritual link with Monroe, as the words to her songs seemed to echo doubt across Ariyoshi's proposal. That echo turned into distrust. Suddenly, seemingly without reason, Monroe's postcard fell from the shelf and landed at Angela's feet. Angela froze with uncertainty. She believed it meant something but didn't know exactly what.

The Voice said, "Don't fear. I'll guide you."

Then, Angela remembered that Ariyoshi was waiting in a hotel room in Shibuya for her. It was challenging to know what to do. Perhaps, it was best to go back to work and forget about his proposal.

The Voice said, "But, then, you'll never know. You must explore every possibility, Angela, every possibility and one time when you least expect it, the possibility will be realised."

After sitting for a couple of hours in doubt, Angela jumped out of bed and realised that she must explore this new path. Even if Ariyoshi wanted to just use her for sex, she must find the truth.

Angela quickly ran to a telephone and rang the hotel where Ariyoshi was staying, telling him not to leave. She told him she had some doubts, but that she was now coming, directly. Ariyoshi was very relieved to hear that and said he would wait and that he understood.

Angela packed an overnight bag and quickly grabbed a taxi, which, Ariyoshi would pay for. She soon arrived at Shibuya. Angela got to the hotel, ran to the room and knocked on the door, as Ariyoshi opened it. He embraced her, wildly, took her inside and immediately began to make love to Angela. It was compelling, intense and passionate.

"There are many things I must talk to you about, first. Before we do anything more, there are some things I must tell you, some things we must get straight. I want to do that now. I want to talk about those things now. Then afterwards, you can have me. Just now there are so many things I must say, so many things I must hear you say before I can truly make love with you," Angela uttered, sincerely.

Ariyoshi agreed, and they went downstairs to a restaurant to have dinner and talk. Ariyoshi ordered a relatively expensive, traditional, Japanese Tempura dish for them. He chose everything and never gave Angela any free choice. This domineering personality would become more evident as time passed.

Ariyoshi didn't want Angela to make any choices of her own. He tried to dominate her completely, in the bedroom and in the outside world. She didn't know how she felt about that but only wanted her dream to be fulfilled. If she had to continue in the sex business, she felt perhaps, she would surely die. Although Angela had become strong, that strength was suddenly lessening and had been ever since leaving Ginza. While ever she was in Ginza, Angela was tough. Now, she was beginning to weaken, due to the violence and persecution of Akasaka and Roppongi. It was all too much; so, this seemed like Paradise. Even though she didn't love Ariyoshi, she could be honest about that, so she told him the truth.

"Alright, you want me to be yours and only yours. I want to be the star that you've talked about. I will be yours. I will give myself to you and only you, but you must do what you promise," Angela uttered.

Ariyoshi agreed. Then, Angela talked about her doubts and how, if she really believed in something, maybe it would happen. Perhaps, after all, it would be with Ariyoshi, and now she was beginning to feel anew. Angela didn't feel like a hooker anymore and didn't feel like someone who had failed. She felt like she'd taken a chance with someone and Ariyoshi was that someone.

"It's a contract, Angela. We have an agreement signed in the bedroom. I must fulfil your part, but you must fulfil mine, also," Ariyoshi stated.

They finished the meal and went to the bedroom. Ariyoshi was now very excited. Upon entering the room, he threw his clothes off. He began to peel Angela's clothes off, delicately as if they were made of precious gold. Ariyoshi smelled each item of clothing and became more aroused. He then gently threw her panties in the corner, as if it was as delicate as Angela's body or as if it were a part of Angela. Then, suddenly, lifting Angela into the air to hold her tightly. Then he began to kiss her breasts. After a moment, he placed her on the bed and pulled the curtains back, to reveal a bright starry night.

"Ah... an Angel in the starlight," Ariyoshi said, "How wonderful!"

Angela felt like a helpless child. She knew that this time, she'd have to do more than she'd ever done before with a client. The man took Angela and had complete intimacy with her, except for deep kissing. He enjoyed her flesh as if it were a whole, hearty meal. Angela lay there, helplessly, thinking only of one thing, the promise that Ariyoshi had made. The man had sex with Angela in so many different ways. Apparently, his imagination had been planning this moment for many years. No matter how lustful, Ariyoshi's fantasy and desires were being fulfilled, voluntarily, by Angela. She didn't enjoy the encounter but kept the contract in her mind.

As Ariyoshi kissed and caressed Angela's body, he uttered, repeatedly, "You are mine, mine only, absolutely mine."

Strangely, that seemed to make Angela feel safe, secure, and happy, even though she didn't love him.

The Voice said, "Forgive Me."

Angela didn't quite understand. Then, she remembered her little diary and the story of the bad man.

Angela thought, "This could not be the bad man, for he is simply an adulterer. Perhaps, that's what it means."

Angela contemplated the words of the Voice as she lay next to Ariyoshi. They had finished the sexual experience and now embraced, endlessly.

Angela remembered the words of the Voice, "Forgive Me for by whom it begins. The world is evil, and people almost always require sinful things in return for good things."

Angela thought about the words of that little diary and tried to make excuses for Ariyoshi. However, she did that only in her mind, for, Ariyoshi was an adulterer. The sin wasn't Angela's, but Ariyoshi's. Despite all that had been said, Angela saw this as a business situation. She never thought, for a moment, to take the relationship seriously. It was merely, sex business but on a different level and with only one person.

Then, they slept the night together. Occasionally, Ariyoshi would wake up and make love to Angela once again, in fact, so many times in one night, that Angela lost count. Indeed, there was a fullness of passion and frustration in Ariyoshi that Angela could relate to, not in a sexual way, but in an emotional sense. Angela felt empathy for his desire, but not his lust.

The next day, Ariyoshi said, "Today I have things to do. I will get you to come to the office another time. Today is difficult. Besides, I want to introduce you at the right moment. You must call me tomorrow morning, early. Then you can come to my office." Ariyoshi then pushed fifty thousand yen into Angela's hand and added, "I will give you all the money you need. Just don't go back to the street. If you go with someone else, our contract will be broken."

Angela remembered very well. She knew what she had to do, first, to go home and practise. It was time to prepare herself, change her image, working harder at her dancing and practice her vocal scales. There were now so many things to be done. But, most of all, what she was not to do was not to return to the street. To do that would break a contract.

When Angela arrived home, she began immediately. Every minute and precious second were utilised totally. Now her ambition and drive were heightened. Ariyoshi had given her new hope. Angela was dancing with more power than she'd ever had and was beginning to sing with a certainty she'd never known before. Before this, Angela never saw herself as a singer, for she believed that her voice wasn't any good. But now, for the first time, Angela was able to hold notes, simply because of her new attitude.

The next day, Angela rang Ariyoshi. He was having problems with his business and so, had to go outside Tokyo. Angela worked hard, all the time. When they met once more, he passionately took her, again. Now, Angela knew only him. This man monopolised Angela's dreams and waking moments. She'd call him at least five times every day. When they'd speak, he'd want to know what Angela was wearing and what she was doing. Ariyoshi would fantasise that Angela was touching herself during their telephone conversations. Ariyoshi couldn't get enough of the blonde Gaijin. He was totally besotted with her sexuality.

"The time for your stardom is not yet, Angela. You must work hard. I want to hear a tape of the work you've done. I want to see your dance routines. You must have everything prepared for me," Ariyoshi said.

Angela worked hard, eighteen hours a day, every day, for weeks on end. Ariyoshi seemed to have really changed Angela's life. From a Gaijin prostitute, standing in the street, to now a girl who could sing at least half a dozen good songs, dance to them and be able to play all music. Angela recorded the whole thing on tape, and it sounded great. She even surprised herself. Angela had lost weight, changed her hairstyle, makeup, and appearance. She was beginning to feel like a new person and indeed, becoming the person she really thought she was.

The first rehearsal with the musicians was arranged. Angela was to meet the band in two weeks. It was all planned on a schedule that Angela looked at with a kind of eager anticipation.

Then, Ariyoshi said, "I have a major problem in my business. We're going to have to delay your schedule. It'll be good, really. You'll need extra time to work."

Angela's money was running extremely low, and so, she said, "I need money, Ariyoshi."

"Next week, I will give you all the money you need. Just bear with me for one week. I have a tour happening right now and many problems with it."

Ariyoshi postponed Angela's schedule for one month. That upset her a little, but she rationalised that it was for the best, needing that extra time to practise. During that one month, Angela worked harder than ever. Ariyoshi gave her a little money from time to time, but not as much as he'd promised her. As time passed, Ariyoshi began to not pay Angela so much attention. However, Angela's work had vastly improved. The singing, dancing and, even composing, was at a good standard. Also, she began to write her own songs. She'd never done that before, until now. Ariyoshi hadn't even heard Angela's work yet.

The Voice came to Angela when she was working and said, "Ariyoshi is the bad man, Angela. This man is the bad man, from which the stardom initially comes." Then, the Voice went away. Angela was confused and didn't understand why the Voice had said that. She believed that Ariyoshi had been kind. After all, he'd taken her off the street. Yet, the Voice had said a totally contradictory thing. Then, Angela began to reflect on the past six weeks, when Ariyoshi had done nothing, except talk and have sex with her. Sure, he gave her some money from time to time, but none of the schedules actually occurred.

Then, as the days followed, the Voice repeated the same thing.

"Don't worry. It's all part of the plan. Don't worry. Sometimes, good things come from bad things."

Angela didn't really understand that statement, but, nevertheless trusted that Voice with a dedication that one could only have for one person, God, Himself.

The days followed, and Angela rang Ariyoshi several times. He became unavailable, suddenly and was too busy to speak to Angela. It was out of character and went on for many days. This was outrageous! Angela went to his office to see Ariyoshi. He wasn't even there, but out on some business luncheon with a new client.

"Another 'new' client," Angela thought. "I know what kind of clients. He likes to spend time with clients, like me." Then, Angela became angry and jealous that, perhaps, the attention was going to be showered on some other 'new starlet.' Sensing his dishonesty, Angela waited outside the office until Ariyoshi returned. He returned alone and then went inside. At 5:30 p.m., the secretaries left the room, so Ariyoshi was alone. Angela went inside and demanded to know what was happening, why he had been so hard to catch and why he wouldn't speak to her or answer her calls. Ariyoshi explained that the contract must be cancelled. He was having problems with his business and maybe in a couple of months or so, when things looked better, they could reunite to reform the contract. Angela suddenly realised Ariyoshi's dishonesty and trickery.

"You lied to me! You've broken your part of our contract," Angela said, sternly.

Ariyoshi looked at the ground as he bit his lip. Evidently, this man was a liar and, in a way, a thief. Angela began to cry as she leaned forward and slapped his face firmly.

"How dare you do that to me!" Angela shouted, then slammed her palm on the table before him. "Who do you think you're dealing with? Do you think I'm some little fifteen-year-old girl who opens her legs to the first guy who comes along and makes promises? Do you know the things I've had to do to get to this point, only to throw it away and believe in your promises?"

"Just give me a couple of months. I just need a little time, Angela.

I know you have talent! I know you do. I know everything about you. I know you have what it takes!"

Angela became furious. "A couple of months! How am I to survive?"

"I will give you some money, but I can't give what I promised before."

Angela threw a tape of her music across the room. "How dare you use me like this! I know it's a lie, it's just another lie. You're trying to trick me, again! You've given me hardly any money. Soon, I'll have to return to the street! If you really love me and really care about me, why don't you do the things you promised? Why is it that men always lie to me? Isn't there one man out there, who can tell the truth?"

Angela cried as she picked up a pile of papers and threw them on the floor. Ariyoshi did nothing, except fall into a chair and look at the ground. Obviously, the man was a lousy liar, thief, and defrauder, who had now met his match.

"Now, I want the truth from you. If you don't give me the truth, I'm going to do something really crazy. You know what I'm going to do? Really crazy stuff. I don't even know what I'm going to do, but it's going to be really wild, so you better tell me the truth, right now!" Angela demanded.

"We have to cancel the contract, right now," Ariyoshi pleaded.

"I refuse to cancel. We have a contract, and you must fulfil it. If you don't fulfil it, I don't know what I'll do."

It was apparent that there was no conclusion to this argument. Then, a silence overcame Angela. She relaxed back into her seat and took a deep breath, looking at Ariyoshi with contempt. He stood up, put his hands in his pockets, walked around the table, then began to speak.

"You know, you don't need me, really. I'm not such a big promoter, and you are already a star. You are very strong, Angela. You really don't need anybody; you can do it all by yourself. Can't you see that now? Can't you see that everything you've done in the last six weeks, was you? Can't you see I did nothing for you, except talk! Maybe, I am a liar, but can't you see that you are all the things I said you were?"

"If you don't do what you promised, I'll tell everyone what you've done. Do you understand?" Angela urged.

Angela was determined to make the man fulfil his agreement; she turned into a tough businesswoman since arriving in Tokyo. She didn't want anyone to ever steal from her again. Regardless of what type of contract it was, this was business.

Angela left the office, went home, thought about the work she'd done and realised that, through all the lies, deceits and even sex, between the two, one thing remained true. Angela had, indeed, done all that work by herself. She phoned Barb, only to cry on the telephone. Barb was always a consoling friend and spoke very little about her own life. Usually, Barb found consolation in thinking about Angela's problems.

In contrast, Barb lived a very comfortable life with children, a country house and husband. So, it was good for Barb to console Angela. They had a rather unique friendship, boarding on sisterhood.

"Yes, Angela. You've done it all yourself. He did nothing for you, except screw you. Can't you see that now?" Barb replied, and she was right. That's basically all Ariyoshi ever did. "If you have no money, Angela, I will give it to you," Barb said. "Just tell me, but you must realise, as time goes by, that you may have to go back to the street, either, that or return to Australia. You must listen to your inner voice for the best advice."

This incident with Ariyoshi had upset Angela, and it wasn't clear what she needed to do next. She believed, if she went back to the street, that would break the contract. Barb convinced Angela that the truth was that Ariyoshi had already broken the agreement. And that it was time for Angela to go back to work, and simply pick up the pieces of her life. However, out of all of this, one thing remained true, one beautiful thing.

The Voice said, "See how far you've come in such a short time? This is how it initially begins. Remember, he is bad. I told you before. Now, understand that it was meant to be. Now you have direction in your dreams. Keep working, day to day in both your dreams and your business. Slowly, it will happen. Don't trust anybody, only Me."

Angela wanted to listen to the Voice and did, but it was challenging to ignore Ariyoshi altogether. She desperately wanted to make the contract stick. She tried to realise the dream, just the way Ariyoshi had said. It seemed the most straightforward path, after all. She probably wouldn't have been able to do it without Ariyoshi in the background, for, Angela lacked confidence in herself.

Determined, still, to make the contract work, Angela kept ringing Ariyoshi, each day. Most rents in Japan are paid monthly, and Angela's was quite late. Ariyoshi had given her a little more money to live off but neglected to pay the two months' rent, which totalled four thousand dollars. Even if Angela did go back to the street, she wouldn't have been able to make that much money in such a short amount of time.

Angela had a strange love-hate relationship with Ariyoshi. On the one hand, she loved the things he'd said, promised and the way he made her feel when they were together. Although she disliked his personality. Their contract conditions took away any personal feelings and most of all the lies. It was these feelings that bound Angela to the relationship with Ariyoshi. It wasn't the money, only the promise of the beautiful dream that could be, that was difficult to ignore. The Voice hadn't precisely said she should leave Ariyoshi, but only said that it had begun, and so it had. All Angela had to do now, was wait and see, but as time went by, money was non-existent.

Angela continued to telephone Ariyoshi, and he soon became annoyed with her persistence. He wasn't the same man whom Angela had known. The promoter was trying, very hard, to get rid of the irritating Gaijin. Once again, Angela went around to his office.

"But you must pay my rent, Ariyoshi. It's very late. Please, I'm desperate," pleaded Angela.

Ariyoshi turned into a different person and replied, "I've broken the contract between us. There's no need to continue this anymore. You have to go back to where I found you. Besides, I'm not sure if you really have enough talent to make it, anyway."

Angela was emotional, still clinging to her dream. "You

promised, remember? We have a contract, and I haven't broken it, so you must keep your word."

Ariyoshi was annoyed and didn't know what to do. Then, a wild, evil side of him reared its ugly head at Angela. "Listen, Angela, you don't know who you're dealing with, here. I'm not who you think I am. I work for someone else. I'm not in charge of my company. I work for someone powerful, in fact, a very powerful Yakuza."

Angela, shocked at the statement, immediately turned back into the businesswoman, which she had now become. "What do you mean, Yakuza?"

"If you persist, I will have to send someone around to shut you up. After all, many girls want to be a star in this city. You're not so special, after all. If you insist too much, I'll have to resort to methods I'd rather not use."

Angela was outraged and began to poke Ariyoshi in the chest. "Who do you think you are, talking to me like that?" Angela was furious and realised that Ariyoshi was, really, a con man. The man she saw now was just another criminal, like so many criminals she'd met since walking the streets of Ginza. Ariyoshi realised just how tough Angela really was.

Then, Ariyoshi said, "I work for... well, you needn't know who I work for."

"Who do you work for? Names don't scare me. I know more names than you'll ever realise. I've had more incidents with Yakuzas than, probably, you have, and you think you're going to scare me?" Angela said.

Ariyoshi became a little apprehensive. He thought perhaps, Angela may be Yakuza. It was a hilarious situation, really. Here was Ariyoshi, a part of some organised crime, threatening to hurt Angela. At the same time, Angela was so firm that Ariyoshi sensed some higher power behind her. However, he believed her strength to be like his, a Yakuza.

Then, out of his insecurity, Ariyoshi asked, "Who do you belong to?"

Angela smiled, thought for a minute, and replied, "I have

someone who guides and protects me, that is the strongest power I know of."

Ariyoshi became very annoyed and slightly concerned. He believed that Angela talked about some powerful crime syndicate when she was actually talking about the Voice. She wasn't prepared to say who it was.

In fact, the Voice had said, "Don't reveal who I am, just how powerful I am."

Ariyoshi evidently was worried. He stepped down and said, politely, "Yes, I will give you the money I promised, Angela. Don't worry. I'm sorry for being upset. I don't know what came over me."

Angela, rather pleased with herself, but still determined to make the contract work, asked who Ariyoshi worked for.

"Ginza Yakuza," Ariyoshi replied.

Angela laughed. It was so ironic. The very people who she'd run away from were the ones she had now run to for help in times of trouble.

Angela detested these people and the Yakuza code but did not reveal her true feelings to Ariyoshi. She smiled and added, "Yes, I know who they are, and I know the Ojiki (father) who controls them."

Ariyoshi picked up his cup of coffee, as his hand trembled with fear. He had underestimated Angela, in intelligence and her business capacity. They departed peacefully, but the personalities had changed. Both had become very businesslike. Angela hadn't threatened Ariyoshi with violence, yet, he had threatened her. Angela simply stated that she possessed a power, one that always protected her. Ariyoshi saw, in Angela's statement, the evil in himself. Ariyoshi then believed that Angela wanted to fix him up. All Angela wanted was to make Ariyoshi an honest man. She didn't want anything else, except what was right, fair and just. Ariyoshi was, as the Voice had said, a wicked man. He would do whatever necessary to get his own way, then, thoroughly wash his hands of the situation, whenever it suited his need. Yes, this man was evil, indeed. However, Angela had a twofold purpose in her insistence: to make the contract stick and make Ariyoshi an honest man. Angela now only felt pity for the man, for he was a weak individual. He apparently had little love or caring for anyone else, except his own lust.

Angela went home to her penthouse. She sat, looked out the window and wondered just how widespread the Yakuza organisation really was. She'd run into it in so many different forms since arriving in Tokyo. It was clear that this Yakuza situation was a significant obstacle to her career. Perhaps, it was this that may stop Angela. She noticed that her feelings were changing. The small piece of fondness she had for Ariyoshi was dying, out of the distrust and hate for the Yakuza. In fact, Ariyoshi would prove to be the last man who Angela would ever feel any love for.

The next day, Ariyoshi deposited one hundred thousand yen into Angela's account. It was enough to pay some back rent. She had not worked on the street for many weeks and so, needed money badly. Angela's lifestyle was expensive and thus, cost thousands of dollars each week to maintain. It wasn't as if Ariyoshi couldn't afford it, he could. The man lived a very glamorous life in a very sophisticated environment, that was quite opulent. It was only right that he should pay her, as had been agreed to do so initially.

The following day, two men came to Angela's door and knocked. She looked out the peephole and noticed the permed hair and colourful casual clothes, they were Yakuza. Angela was streetwise enough to know that they weren't merely salesmen. So, she didn't answer the doorbell, pretending not to be home. As the men walked down the stairwell, Angela overheard their conversation. They muttered about being able to deal with the Gaijin.

Then, looking out over the balcony, she noticed a small, surveillance van watching her apartment. There was a man inside, with binoculars. He sat there for hours on end, staring at the balcony. At first, Angela concealed her movements and pretended not to be home.

The van stayed there night and day. Angela noticed, occasionally, other cars arriving, and operators being replaced. Every few hours or so, men would come knocking on her door. It was, undoubtedly, the Yakuza. Was Ariyoshi desperately trying to silence Angela?

The man wanted to get Angela before Angela got to him or so

Ariyoshi believed, through his evilness. Angela would never hurt anybody and simply desired the promise to be fulfilled.

Soon, it was evening. Angela didn't want to put the lights on, as the surveillance continued. She had to eat, and there was very little food. Angela left the lights off and quickly scrambled down the back elevator, to the nearest shop. As she did, she looked back and saw three men chasing her. Angela ran fast, luckily knowing the area well. She ducked into a side alley, then, down another side street, over a fence and through someone's garden, out the other side of area seven. The men kept running into the first side street. They didn't see where the elusive Gaijin had gone. Soon, she doubled back and went inside the apartment, bolted, and chained the door. This was a frightening situation. Angela's heart was almost beating out of her chest. She didn't know what to do.

Then, the Voice said, "Fear not. I am with you. Don't worry, everything will be alright. Calm down and relax. It's not as bad as it looks."

The Bible was very consoling in peaceful moments. Still, in moments like these, Angela didn't have time to sit down and interpret the words. The Voice, instead, was the power that she needed. The Voice always helped Angela through difficult times. This time, it wasn't the street, this was her home. This time, Angela couldn't run and hide, for, this was where she lived. They had found where Angela lived and could now do with her as they pleased.

"Just another Gaijin, who went back to her country," people would say.

These words crossed Angela's mind, as she lay on the bed in darkness, with the door bolted. Angela kept spying over the balcony to see whether the surveillance van was still there. In fact, now, there was another car there, a dark Mercedes, with tinted windows and many aerials. Apparently, two-way radios. Indeed, it was Ginza Yakuza. They now knew where Angela lived. She was causing a problem for one of the people who were on a high level of this Yakuza, namely Ariyoshi.

The Voice said, "Leave Tokyo, quickly, but quietly. Change your identity. Leave Tokyo as soon as you can."

Angela grabbed a bag and scrambled to the drawer in the darkness, clutching all her underwear, necessary change of clothes and makeup, before throwing them into her overnight bag. Then, she noticed the black wig that she had from her stage act. She quickly placed the fake black hair on her head and dressed in jeans, to look like a typical Japanese girl or, at least, as best she could.

Bravely, Angela left her room and proceeded to the elevator. As she did, she noticed the elevator ascending to the sixth floor, where Angela lived. Frightened, she ducked down the stairwell and waited to see who emerged. They were the same men who had been to her door so many times. They went, once again, to Angela's door.

Meanwhile, she cringed in the corner of the stairwell. Her heartbeat was the only sound Angela could hear. Then, the sound of the men slamming their fists on the door echoed through the empty apartment.

"Moshi Moshi! Gaijin san!!" The men shouted.

The men banged at the door as if they were trying to bash it down. Angela quickly scrambled into the elevator and down to the first floor. Then, she casually walked past the surveillance van, realising that they were looking for a blonde-haired Gaijin, not a girl with black hair. The operator glanced at Angela and back into his binoculars, as if he hadn't really noticed that the girl wasn't Japanese.

Then, a taxi came along. Angela hailed it and quickly jumped inside.

"Ueno-Eki (Ueno station), please," Angela's voice quivered.

The taxi sped away and, as it did, Angela raced away from danger. It was a secure feeling.

The Voice said, "You are safe now. Don't worry."

Angela was indeed safe. So safe, that after fifteen minutes away from her home, she removed the black wig.

Then, Angela caught the 'Shinkansen' (bullet train) to Nagoya. It was a two-hour journey, giving her time to relax and think about all the incidents that had transpired.

Angela planned to stay at Mie-ken with Barb for a couple of weeks, at least until everything blew over. But it was unclear what to do after that. Coming back to Tokyo would be returning to danger. For as long as Ariyoshi thought Angela was in Tokyo, he would be sending people around to deal with the problematic starlet.

Then, Angela had a brain wave. Angela thought she could call Ariyoshi from Australia, but he wouldn't believe she was actually phoning from Australia. There was only one way to trick Ariyoshi. If she sent a telegram to Ariyoshi from Australia, that would probably convince him that she was no longer in Tokyo. It seemed like a great idea, and the Voice confirmed it.

"It's good, Angela. Do it but wait one week. Give him time to doubt where you are."

Angela arrived at Mie-ken and stayed with Barb, who was frantic about Angela. After all, Angela had come to Japan to be a star, not to get herself killed. After everything that had happened, Angela now believed it wasn't really worth it, not when one risks her life with Yakuzas and AIDS. The issue of STDS and AIDS was something Angela hadn't even had time to think about because the Mafia was so prevalent. If she could escape the Yakuza, could she escape AIDS? That was the question running around Barb's mind.

It was good to be in Mie-ken with Barb, to be away from Tokyo. It gave Angela a chance to reassess her life direction and realised that she didn't need Ariyoshi. The sooner she could get him out of the picture, the better it would be. Angela may go back to the street, which wouldn't be a problem, but, at least, she had her career set, had a direction which had been missing for so long. Angela had been relying on other people, instead of relying on herself and the Voice within her. She now knew that the Voice was the only power she needed. It would be the power to help her find the dream, but not the people who made worthless promises. The pretenders she'd met on the street and in business dealings could not help, but only the Voice could.

The week passed by quickly. Angela rang Lyn in Australia and asked her to send a telegram to Ariyoshi in Tokyo. She told her sister precisely what to say.

The telegram read:

"Dear Ariyoshi, I have left Japan. You broke my heart. Cancel our contract. I give up. Angela."

It was sent from Australia and arrived in Tokyo the following day. Angela knew as the Voice has said, everything would now be back to normal.

"Ariyoshi is a stupid man, obsessed with his own desires. He will believe just what he wants to believe," the Voice told her.

Another week passed. In need of money, Angela had to return to Tokyo, whether she liked it or not. That meant going back to the street, but just where would she go now? It was unclear, but the Voice would know.

A few days afterwards, Angela caught the Shinkansen, bidding a sad, teary farewell to Barb and her babies. On arrival back at Tokyo, she boarded a bus to Hirai and soon reached her apartment. Angela looked at her door and noticed some scratch marks on the door, where someone was trying to pick the lock but had evidently stopped. Angela also saw a note under the door, a letter from Ariyoshi about how he refused to pay her any more money. Then, she saw the pile of newspapers stuffed into the post box. Nobody had been inside; it was clear as the dust had piled up against the front door. Junk mail was jammed in the corner of the doorway. Angela entered her apartment and slammed the door behind, securely. It was such a relief to be safe and inside.

The Voice said, "Don't worry, Angela. You'll be safe now. The bad man has gone out of your life, but you have found something more important, belief in yourself. It's as I told you. You will find something, and it's the direction and confidence in your life. Move on with it, and don't trust any more men, only trust Me."

The Voice repeated the same thing, so many times as if trying to programme Angela into a particular mindset. She believed and trusted that Voice. Angela would go on and would go to places she didn't even know. Angela needed money. The only way she could get a large amount of cash quickly was to go to the most dangerous place in all of Tokyo, in fact, all of Japan, Shinjuku. That sub-city would be hazardous, as there were many different Yakuza groups there, more than anywhere else. Thus far, if she had so much trouble, she was bound to find difficulty with Yakuza in Shinjuku. At least, that's what she thought.

The Voice said, "No, in fact, you won't have any trouble with Yakuza. There may be other problems, but it won't be Yakuza."

CHAPTER FOURTEEN
'From the Red, Into the Blue.'

~

ANGELA HAD ALWAYS been reluctant to go to an area like Shinjuku, for it was sleazy. She considered herself a high-class girl. Shinjuku was perhaps the most sensible location for work, even though it was low-class. Many Japanese men went to Shinjuku, looking for sex play. Shinjuku's Kabuki Cho was nestled among dozens of little strip clubs, erotic, pornographic clubs, video shops, sex aid shops and, of course, the massage parlours or 'Soapland'. All such establishments were controlled by Yakuza. In the street were many Asian prostitutes, most of whom appeared cheap and desperate. Usually, beautiful girls could only be found in areas such as Akasaka. A prostitute in this area would charge as little as go-sen-en (¥5,000, $50).

Shinjuku was not unlike Soho, Kings Cross or even the Hollywood strip. It was Japan's version of 'let's play sex.' That's what the Japanese used to say, 'Shinjuku is play town.'

Angela spent her first day in Shinjuku, just looking around, taking in her new surroundings. Soon, Angela found a reasonably good area, the high-class area of Shinjuku, where most of the expensive night clubs and exclusive member clubs were located. It was 'yon-chome' (area-four) on the hill. She had been there once before but hadn't worked there, until now. Angela stood in the street night after night, for at least one week. Many men approached her, but no one could afford go-man-en in Shinjuku. That was ten times the price of a street girl and was three times what they would pay in Soapland. No one could afford Angela, especially seeing as they had to pay for the hotel room, too.

Angela began to realise that she was a victim of circumstance and the prey of oppression. It would mean altering her price structure, just to survive. The Voice said, "High class is not determined by price, Angela. It's determined by attitude."

That meant that Angela would change her price system and her method of operation. If she were to do short times only, then, she'd have to charge a short time price.

After a considerable amount of thought, Angela finally decided to charge ni-man-en (¥20,000, A$200), for twenty minutes and san-man-en (¥30,000, A$300) for thirty minutes. Nothing less and, of course, more would be great. However, in Shinjuku, Angela would not find any more than this. Most men would want the lowest price and the best quality they could find. Angela realised that the best place to go to was near the Koma Theatre, where all the girls worked.

One businessman said, "Near Koma Theatre is no good, there are many Yakuza."

That sent a shiver down Angela's spine. The last thing she needed was more trouble with them.

Near Koma Theatre, in the quadrangle's centre, was a little park, surrounded by small trees and shrubs. There were seats there also. Angela had been there before. Most of the street girls stayed on the outskirts of that area. It was the place where men would look for a 'play' girl. Some were cheap, and some were very cheap, but most were of an average appearance. In the evenings, especially, the better girls would come out. However, in the daytime, only the desperate girls would be about.

It was about 7:00 p.m., and there were a couple of reasonably attractive, Japanese girls working in the area. Angela moved in and circled the quadrangle, slowly. She gazed carefully at everybody, checking out the situation. It seemed as though the Yakuza weren't around. There was no one in the quadrangle, except customers and playgirls. Angela watched as the girls leaned against the wall.

The men walked by, placed their hands around their mouths and asked, quietly, "Ikura desu ka? (How much?)" Then, if the price were right, they'd walk off together.

"It's so easy," Angela thought. "I could do two or three short times and go home while getting the same amount of money as if I'd spent all night in a hotel room with someone. For an all-nighter, I'd probably end up doing it two or three times, anyway, so what's the difference? The only thing is, I have to do it with two or three different men."

The Voice said, "Stick to the rules. Remember, all these situations were not chosen by you. They chose you. I will protect you, for, you are a victim of other peoples' sins."

Angela was beginning to have doubts about whether Shinjuku would be profitable. Still, the Voice was reasonably positive, except for one thing.

The Voice said, "Be careful."

Angela was very careful and stood near a Western-style picture theatre, where a Gaijin film played. In no time at all, the men noticed Angela. Like a flock of pigeons after food, they gathered around. Soon, Angela met a nice looking, reasonably high-class businessman. They went to a hotel, just around the corner. The hotels were only about two minutes away. There were more men there, wanting Angela more than she could ever imagine. It was a perfect spot. She went to do one, then came back, did another, then yet another, then another and so on. In a matter of four hours, Angela had made fifteen hundred dollars. It was staggering how quickly Angela could make money here.

"Perhaps I should've come here a long time ago," Angela thought.

The Voice said, "It is dangerous. Take care."

Angela listened to the Voice, but at the same time wanted to make more money. She thought everything would be alright now.

The next day, Angela came back to the same place and began

operating in the same way. There were two routes which Angela and her clients could take to go to the love hotel. One would be past the police station and the other, which was a little longer, was around the back. She made a mistake and wasn't careful enough. Angela carelessly walked past the police station with different men several times. The police began to take notice of her.

A little while later, Angela was eating in a restaurant when the police came in. They saw Angela and insisted she accompanies them to the police station.

"Just routine. I've been to the police station before, and I've paid the respect they need before. This is the same thing as Ginza," Angela thought to herself.

The Voice said, "It's not the same, but don't worry. I'll protect you. It is not the same here, it's different, it's dangerous."

Angela walked with the two policemen as if it was a joke. For, it was quite apparent that there were street prostitutes everywhere, and massage parlours in every building, some, virtually right next door to the police station. So, what difference did one extra Gaijin prostitute make? At the station, an officer pushed her into a chair and began to ask questions in Japanese, which she didn't understand. There were about eight policemen, laughing and kidding around. Then, the head policeman became very serious. He asked Angela to put her hands in the air, and took her bag, then, realising his mistake, gave her handbag back and began to speak in English.

"Open, open," the policeman commanded.

Angela opened it quickly. She was frightened because the man was incredibly aggressive. Just as she delved her into the handbag, the policeman lifted his sidearm. He pointed it directly at Angela's head as she began to panic.

"Why is this happening? Why are you doing this to me?" Angela asked as she froze. "I've done nothing wrong!"

The other police didn't like what he was doing but didn't stop him. The policeman was determined to make a point. He was the police, and she was nothing; he had the power, and she was helpless. Angela rummaged through her handbag, searching for identification as the policeman's finger lightly caressed the trigger.

He expressed a determined hostility while peering at the Gaijin prostitute. It was malice she'd never seen a Japanese person, let alone in law enforcement.

"You are Yakuza," he yelled.

Angela shook her head and quickly removed her hand from the bag.

Just then, another policeman touched his shoulder, and he placed his gun back into the holster.

Angela shook her head again. "I am not Yakuza. I am a Gaijin and alone."

The policeman shook his head and said, "No, you are Yakuza."

Angela didn't understand that she was accused of being a Yakuza, even though; she wasn't. However, to the police, anybody who committed a crime was Yakuza. Anybody who deliberately set their way to go out and break the law for profit or gain was Yakuza. Angela, in the eyes of the police, had become the thing she detested most. She could understand their hatred, for she had the same feeling for the Yakuza, which only seconded the police. However, Angela wasn't Yakuza and didn't operate unacceptably and didn't oppress, manipulate or persecute others. Angela was simply a businesswoman.

Angela shook her head, insistently, stood up and waved her finger at the policeman with the gun. "I am not Yakuza. I may be many things, but I am certainly not Yakuza. I hate them. They are bad people. You are mistaken."

The policeman didn't understand the English, but the sentiment was crystal clear. Then, he ripped Angela's handbag from her hands, tipped it upside down on the desk and began to search through the contents. The other policemen, standing around, were thrown different items from the bag. One inspected her cosmetics, another, her wallet. Then, the others stood, murmuring to themselves, as they gazed at Angela.

"Passport, passport. Where is your passport?" the head policeman asked.

He could speak enough English to be understood. Angela had forgotten her passport, as she looked through all the things on the table and couldn't find it anywhere. It was in the glass cabinet in her apartment. Angela attempted to explain to the head policeman, who was in an agitated mood. The policeman seemed to be very upset about this matter and wanted to lock Angela up. She pleaded that she stay in the front of the police station, after all, she'd committed no crime.

Then, one of the policemen opened Angela's beauty case, to reveal the condoms. The policeman pulled them out and spoke Japanese to the others. They all looked, then at Angela.

"Yes, so what? I like sex. There's no crime in liking sex. I don't want to get AIDS, after all, sex is dangerous, these days," Angela said.

The other policemen had understood what Angela was saying, started laughing and joking to each other. Angela was only a foolish Gaijin, for, the things she said and how she spoke gave that impression.

Angela slammed her fist on the table, for she'd had enough.

"Who do you think you are? Why don't you go arrest some Yakuza out there and leave me alone? I've done nothing wrong, and I've hurt nobody. I'm minding my own business!" Angela cried.

The mad policeman started pushing her in the breast. "You are Yakuza. You are who we want to catch. Go home, go to your country. Leave Japan!"

The policeman had a hatred in his eyes that Angela didn't quite understand. They knew that she wasn't Yakuza, yet they were trying to make a point. They were insisting what Angela was doing was highly illegal, even though, many others were doing it.

Angela furiously said, "There is nothing in here, no guns, no knives, nothing."

The other policemen, who had the wallet, opened it to show the head policeman the money inside. There was Ju-go-man-en ($1500).

"Many money," the policeman said in Japanese.

The other policemen looked and spoke in Japanese to each other, then looked at the blonde Gaijin from her toes to her head. They'd realised she had the potential to make a tremendous amount of cash, and they hated her for it. A Japanese policeman's salary was about three thousand dollars per month while Angela had earned half of that in only a couple of hours. The real reason, Angela could now see, was their jealousy. It wasn't the crime she was committing, but the money that could be made. They could never, ever make that kind of money, even if they were to be corrupted by some Yakuza. All the policemen gazed silently at Angela with a jealous, envying eye. They hated her Western-style, the fact that she wasn't Japanese, but blonde and beautiful. Until now, she appeared pure in many Japanese people's eyes, which made them detest her all the more. They were also appalled by her honesty. There was no exception to that law in Japan, not even for a Gaijin.

"Have you finished? Is that enough?" Angela asked as she started to gather the things back into her bag.

The Voice said, "Don't worry, it's just to prove their point. The point is, they consider what you are doing a serious crime in this country."

Angela listened to the Voice and then understood. She politely packed her bag, placed it on her arm and said, "If there's nothing else, I must go now."

The head policeman started waving his finger and added, "Did you know, that in this country, I can arrest you for not having a passport? Write your name and details down on this piece of paper. I won't arrest you this time, but I could have you put in jail for six months, for not carrying a passport. You are a foreigner, and this is Japan!"

Angela realised the mistake she'd made by not bringing her passport. She then began to write her particulars down. The Voice said, "Don't worry, now. Later, we will worry together."

Afterwards, the policeman made a telephone call to another police department and spoke Japanese. Angela was asked to sit down and wait, a little longer. She'd been there for over an hour, and now, they were going to keep her a little longer. The longer Angela was there, the more depressing it became. Street girls walked past the police station, but they were all Japanese. They were usually escorted by some man going to a hotel or Soapland. Yet, the police didn't pay any attention to them.

It was Angela they were interested in, perhaps, simply because she was Gaijin and even more so, probably, because she was open about what she did. They had never seen this kind of honesty before.

After about twenty minutes on the telephone, the policeman said, "You can go now. Go home, first, go to your home, then, return to your country."

"But I'm in Japan on business, and I don't have the means to go to my country, just now. I must stay in Japan a little longer."

The policeman insisted, "Go home!"

As she walked out of the police station, the policemen laughed, looked at her legs and obviously talked about sex, using rude Japanese words. The policemen were no different from any of the other men. Now, they were talking about how they would like to do something to her. They were merely men in police uniforms. Underneath it all, Angela could see that they were no different, perhaps, even more, perverse than the men she'd slept with every day.

To Angela, men didn't seem to be in control of their bodies or minds, but merely slaves to their body chemistry. She disliked that kind of body control. Men could be sensitive, only when they didn't need sex and could be emotional and loving, only when they didn't need sex. Angela's sexuality was changing, but she was quite unaware of it. She believed the experience made her bitter, but something else would be realised one day.

Angela walked past the quadrangle and noticed many street girls still working. None of the other girls had been taken to the police station. Angela walked across the square and saw many people gazing at her. She was a little shaken and needed to sit down and think.

Near the square, between two theatres, was a game parlour, with many hi-tech electronic game machines. Angela had been inside there, once before. A little frightened of the street, she entered the building, to watch people playing the machines, which was very entertaining. The devices were hi-tech computers, rather than childish play toys.

Angela turned to hear the machines, like synthesisers and space machines. It was another world, compared to the one she'd just left outside. It seemed to lighten her spirits. She could almost forget about the depressing police station, which she'd visited and hoped never to see again.

Angela walked around the room and noticed one of the street girls sitting near a space invader machine. She began to walk past the girl, who put her hand out and asked the Gaijin to sit down and talk. Angela sat down without saying a word. The girl sifted through Angela's hair and caressed it with her fingers as if it were fine silk.

"Bootiful," the girl said, over and over, as she looked deep into Angela's eyes.

The girl was obviously, very taken by Angela. The lonely Gaijin felt some kind of affinity with a girl who was working in the same profession. Perhaps, in some way, they were very much alike. Angela tried to communicate, but the girl was only interested in examining the foreigner. She inspected every detail of Angela, from eyes to hair to the bust shape and legs. The girl was without inhibition. Angela felt as if she'd been gazed at by a lustful man.

As Angela chatted away in broken English and Japanese, the girl became silent. After all, Angela didn't mind they had a lot in common and, even if the girl couldn't speak very much, it didn't matter.

Perhaps, the point was that Angela had made a new friend, someone with similar problems, and shared experiences. It seemed that way, at first. In any case, as fate would have it, this girl wasn't a friend. If she were, she would've helped Angela.

From time to time, many people sitting in the game room gazed at Angela as if she was an object of beauty, something to be admired. They then returned to play the noisy machines. All the people in the game room were young and dressed in casual clothes, except for Angela, who was so obviously out of place.

Just then, the side door opened, and a businessman walked in, wearing a trench coat. Angela didn't pay him much attention at first, after all, she'd seen her fair share of businessmen since arriving in Tokyo.

Sex Business Tokyo

The Voice said, "Now, go home."

Angela sat there for a while, looked around the room and saw the businessman. He was walking around, looking directly at Angela. Then, he began to smile. It was a charming smile, not unlike many smiles she'd seen before.

The Voice said, "Go home."

Angela resisted home, only because of Ariyoshi, her finances were in a terrible mess. She needed a lot more money, to put herself back in the same position before meeting Ariyoshi.

"One more," Angela said to herself, "Just one more. Everything will be alright."

The Voice didn't say anymore. Perhaps, it wasn't greed, after all, but just a burning desire to secure. Angela really didn't really need the money.

Then, the businessman walked past again and smiled very nicely. Angela turned to the girl next to her. She looked at the businessman, then her eyes fell to the ground. After that, she wouldn't look Angela in the eyes, as if the girl knew something. Then Angela stood up and walked towards the man. He made it abundantly clear that he was interested.

"Come with me," Angela uttered, as she left the building.

The man followed directly. Angela walked down the street a little way and stood on the corner, pretending to catch a taxi. Then, she began to speak to the businessman. "How are you? Genki?" Angela asked.

The man nodded and said nothing, only continued smiling, such a noticeable, attractive smile.

Just then, Angela had a cold feeling, as if a cold wind were blowing up the back of her leg. She had experienced this feeling, once before, with Yakuza and was sensing it now.

Then, the Voice said, "Use your instinct, Angela."

Angela could feel that something was not right but didn't know what. She looked at the man, who obviously didn't look like Yakuza. The only other group Angela need fear was the police.

Angela laughed and asked, "You're not Yakuza. Are you a policeman?"

The man stopped smiling, looked at the ground and shook his head. "No, salaryman." Angela's instinct was more correct than she cared to imagine, but nonetheless, curiosity got the better of her. She wanted to see just how far this could go.

Angela said, "I think it's okay. Alright then. Sex, ni-man-en, twenty minutes."

The man nodded but didn't speak. They walked together, to the hotel.

Along the way, Angela tried to engage the man in a little Japanese chatter. The man refused to talk with her.

Angela asked, in Japanese, "Would you like to go to America or Australia?"

"No, Japan only," as if he detested the rest of the world. Angela could feel that cold feeling creeping over again.

The Voice said, "Don't worry, it's inevitable. I am with you, and I'll be there when you need Me most."

Then, together, they entered the hotel. Angela had been to that hotel many times. The man would have to pay first and then they would go to the room. It was the same system every time.

They entered the foyer, then the man leaned over to speak to the hotel receptionist.

"Five thousand yen, please," the lady said.

The man reached for his wallet, but, instead, pulled out a badge.

"Police. You are under arrest." Then, he suddenly grabbed Angela by the hand and cuffed her.

Then, just behind him, another policeman entered, barging the door. He was of immense stature and grabbed Angela roughly by the back of her neck. Then he pushed her forward and held her other hand, cuffing both hands together.

"I knew you were a policeman. I told you so. The only reason I came here is that you lied to me. You are the police, and you're not supposed to lie," Angela uttered, nervously.

The man looked down at the ground. He didn't understand the English but understood what Angela had meant, as he'd obviously lied to her.

The policeman had committed a worse crime than Angela,

ironically enough. Yet, Angela was now the criminal, and he was the hero. The bigger policeman dragged her, cuffed and very shaken, out of the hotel and down the road. She tried to talk to him, but he pushed her along, quickly, with no respect at all. The other policeman had stayed back in the hotel to question the hotel staff. They wanted to know how many times Angela had been there and whether she was receiving a percentage of the hotel room money, as well. The hotel, it seems, was also under investigation now that Angela had been caught. Of all places, Angela had been arrested in Shinjuku. She began to feel a wave of anxiety that she'd never felt before. Her stomach turned to butterflies, followed by fear. Then, the detective pushed Angela into the police station, where she had been, only half an hour earlier.

"You're easy to catch. I told you to go home," The head policeman said, then the smile left his face and he looked at Angela with a deceitful, obscene expression.

For some reason, this policeman disliked what Angela represented. The other policemen continued talking about her legs and large bust, as if it were alright, now they'd caught her. It was permitted for them to degrade her among themselves. They talked about how they'd like to have sex with her, now that she was guilty. Angela was furious. Then, the arresting policeman pushed Angela into a back cell. It was a small cell, and as soon as Angela saw it, she rebuked.

"I get claustrophobia! Don't put me in there! I'll be sick!" Angela uttered.

The policeman didn't understand and tried to push Angela through the door. She jammed herself in the doorway.

"I can't go in there. It's too small! I'll be sick! I get claustrophobia!"

He didn't understand. Then, another policeman said, "But, you've committed a crime."

"What crime have I committed?" Angela asked.

"The crime of prostitution. You must go into the cell. You must go in there."

Angela insisted and pleaded. "Please don't put me in there. I'm not going to run away. Keep me in the front. I can't go in there. I'll be sick!"

The man carelessly hit Angela, then pushed her through the doorway, into the cell and entered himself, shutting the door behind him.

"I will stay in here for a little while you until they come."

"Until they come?" Angela asked. "Who are they?" The policeman refused to answer and just looked through the little window. The cell was tiny, dirty, and quite disgusting. There wasn't even enough room to lay down. It was like a lavatory without a toilet, merely a little, square room with one small window and bars. That same shiver Angela felt earlier was her instinct, and she had denied it. The Voice had told her to go, and she had refused to listen. Now, the Voice was needed more than ever. She made a mistake, for she knew the man was a policeman. Why did she go? Angela never knew.

Perhaps, she didn't fear the police but only Yakuza. Now Angela realised the Japanese police were just as fearful. She never, ever thought this day would come, yet here she was, arrested at Shinjuku. What would happen to Angela now? Her mind ran wild with all the possibilities of imprisonment and or deportation. She didn't even know the law. Fined, perhaps, all the money she had earnt, she may have to return. Probably, all the things that Angela had bought would be confiscated. Then, her stomach noticed the size of the room, and she started to heave. Angela could feel the lump in her throat, then, her hands began to shake, and her brow began to sweat.

Then, the Voice came. "Don't worry. It will be alright, really. Trust Me, don't worry."

Angela wanted to listen to the Voice but was weak and frightened. She'd never been in a situation like this, in her life. She didn't know what to do. Her body trembled with a nervous shiver, all over. Angela was shivering, as she spoke to the policeman, "I'm getting sick, being in this room. You must put me in a bigger room. Don't you understand? I have claustrophobia! You can't put me in a tiny room!" The man understood, but pretended not to, then laughed with delight.

"Why are you doing this?" Angela pleaded.

The policeman looked at Angela straight in the eye, squinted with hatred and said, "You are Yakuza."

Angela burst out crying. The man walked out of the room and bolted the door behind him. Then, a few minutes later, he re-entered. Angela was still standing there, shivering and thinking of all the things that may happen.

All the while, the Voice said, "Don't worry. It will be alright, don't worry." But Angela didn't think that it would be alright.

Then, the policeman said, "They've come for you, now. Let's go."

Angela didn't know where or with whom she was going. "Where am I going? Where are you taking me?"

Then, he brought Angela to the front of the police station. A squad car was parked directly out the front door. Four uniformed police had arrived to escort the criminal Gaijin.

"We are taking you to Shinjuku Police Headquarters for interrogation and imprisonment," the policeman said.

Angela really began to shake now and started to feel like vomiting but didn't. They pushed her into the back seat of the car, two policemen sat on either side of her. They were the two men who had arrested her. The one on the left was the man who claimed to be a salaryman. The one on the right was the man who had pretended not to understand anything she'd said.

Then, two uniformed police entered the front of the car. Angela felt claustrophobic in the police car as well. It was a frightening feeling.

Angela hated being in small rooms, let alone crowded cars. It appeared they wanted to torture her, as well as prosecute.

Then, one of the policemen in the front, wearing a hat with gold braiding on it, began to take charge. He was obviously the ranking officer.

He turned to Angela and casually looked at her as if it wasn't such a big deal.

"Where's your territory? Akasaka?" he asked.

Angela's teeth were chattering with anxiety. "No, no, Ginza."

Then, they all began to talk about Ginza among themselves and how there was plenty of money there. They tried to estimate how much Angela could earn per month. Then, Angela started to dry heave. The arresting policeman said, "That's because you have committed an offence."

"No. This is all because you lied," Angela replied.

All the while, the Voice said, "Don't worry. It will be alright." Yet, the reality of the situation was totally contradictory to what the Voice had said. Angela couldn't believe that the Voice may have made an error, especially in a case like this. It had saved her from Yakuza so many times and had helped her in so many ways every day. She didn't know if the Voice was going to be accurate this time. She hoped and prayed in her heart that it would not lie or make a mistake, but that somehow, it would help her.

The police car sped along, with its red emergency lights flashing. All the while, the policeman talked about Angela. The conversation was mainly about the fact that they had a witness and that Angela had held up two fingers while talking about sex. The other detective was to be the witness. This meant they had a perfect case and could, perhaps, put her in prison for a long time. One of the policemen mentioned that it may be for three to five years. As Angela wasn't carrying her passport, the sentence would be longer.

Upon arriving at the Police Headquarters, Angela was pushed out of the car, roughly, as if she were a hardened criminal. The arresting officer dragged Angela into the Police Headquarters and up the stairs.

There were three flights of stairs, and all the police walked behind, as they pushed her ahead. They wanted Angela to try to run away and commit yet another crime to add more charges. The arresting officer painfully grabbed her on the shoulder and started to pull her around.

Angela pulled away from him and said, "Leave me alone. Don't be stupid! You think I'm stupid enough to try to run away, do you? Just let me walk up the stairs by myself."

The man then let her go. Angela walked up the stairs, with a grace and sophistication that even surprised the police. Even in her darkest hour, this girl had class. They were amazed at just how strong she really was. Angela had cried before in the police station, for being locked in a small room, but now, she was determined. Angela knew the Voice would never let her down. Somehow, someway, the Voice would save her.

Then, they entered the detective's room. Many detectives were sitting around, whose eyes popped out when they saw Angela. Then, the other police began to explain that they had arrested Angela for selling her body in Shinjuku's Kabuki Cho. They put her into the interrogation room and took off the cuffs. Angela had red marks around her wrists from where the cuffs had pinched her skin. At least now, she was free from those devices, although, still locked in another room.

Two policemen came in. One was short and, at first, didn't seem offensive. The other was larger, who actually looked like a policeman and didn't speak any English, but just sat in the back. The smaller man sat opposite Angela. He was to be the interrogator. Then, yet another man entered, just for good measure. It had now become very crowded in that room, and Angela's fear of small spaces began to re-emerge. The extra man was to stand behind Angela and restrain her. It was ironical that three policemen were needed to interrogate one harmless call girl.

"You have been arrested for prostitution, and you are not carrying a passport. These are two grave crimes in Japan. You will be imprisoned for three to five years, and you may be fined three million yen. After which, you will be deported back to your country. Then, under recommendation from the Japanese government, you will also be prosecuted in your own country. This is a serious matter," the interrogator stated.

Angela felt that shiver come back to her body. The dry heaving in the back of the throat had started once again. This was a very frightening situation. The interrogator shouted, "Do you realise the seriousness of your crime?"

Angela said, "I am not going to admit to anything. I would just like to make an observation. In Shinjuku, there are many prostitutes, and there are very many places where prostitutes work. Why me? Why did you spend so much time and use so many men, merely to catch me?"

"Because you are a foreigner and because you have committed a crime against the government." The man smirked with disdain.

"What about all the other people out there, committing crimes? Just because they're Japanese, it's alright. Is that it?" Angela asked.

The man was obviously annoyed with the statement, for, there was some truth in it. He looked at Angela, rose from his chair and got very upset and shook his fingers at her. "That makes no difference now. It doesn't matter what you say. What we say matters. You are under arrest, and you will be prosecuted for prostitution under Japanese law. This is a very grave crime."

Angela realised she'd made her point and was happy not to add any more, "I would like legal advice, and I'd like to make a telephone call," Angela said.

The policeman laughed and walked around the room. He played with a ballpoint pen in his hands. "Ha! You would like legal advice, and you would like to make a telephone call, would you? Well, this is not Australia. This is Japan! You are not entitled to legal advice, nor are you entitled to communicate with anybody for the next ten days. That is Japanese law. We can put you in prison for ten days before you get any of those things, so you may as well just go along with us. Just be a good girl and then, when we're ready, we will let you make a telephone call and let you get legal advice. In the meantime, you belong to us, and we will do with you, as we please."

The interrogator was extraordinarily nasty and sarcastic and wouldn't listen to reason. Then, the policeman who had arrested Angela entered the room and began to write things down. He asked Angela her name, address, why she was in Japan and all kinds of personal questions. The only thing they couldn't establish was where she worked.

"I don't work. I'm a tourist. I have a tourist visa. I am here sightseeing," Angela said.

They laughed and asked, "Where do you get the money to do your sightseeing?"

"I have enough," Angela replied and said no more.

The interrogator opened Angela's wallet and threw the money in front of her face. "There is ju-ni-man-en (A$1,500)! Where did you get it?" the interrogator insisted.

"It's a gift from a friend."

They laughed and couldn't believe her answer. She had replied very politely. They began to talk amongst themselves about how smart Angela was. She wasn't prepared to admit to anything that might land her in more trouble. They continued the interrogation.

About an hour had passed. Then, the Voice came to Angela and said, "Don't worry. Just be strong and admit to nothing."

It was a very tiring hour and not real, but rather something from a film, where a spy had been caught by the KGB in Russia. They asked her name, address, and purpose in Japan, repeatedly. The police wanted to know where she lived and how many people she knew. Also, if she was involved in any organised crime in Japan or if she worked for Yakuza. Angela became furious. That was the tenth time they'd asked that question. Angela stood up, only to be pushed down into the chair, by the policeman standing behind her. Then, tears began to form in her eyes. "I detest Yakuza, probably more than you do. They've threatened to kill me, maim me, capture me and do anything they wish to me. Yet, when I go to the police to tell them, you can't do anything about it. So here I am, one person, while thousands of Yakuzas are running around, out there, hurting and killing innocent people. They extract money, illegally by ruthless means from others. You're wasting all this manpower and time, on one, little Gaijin, who you think is a prostitute."

They all went silent. It was evident that Angela had hit a nerve. She wasn't involved in any Yakuza but was simply one individual they had spent so much police power to capture and now interrogate. They all walked out of the room, leaving Angela alone for about an hour, clearly in discussion with each other.

Then, four police came back in, all the same officer, as well as the one who had arrested Angela. Then, he began to explain that

Angela had said, "sex, ni-man-en," and had held up two fingers. They wrote it in the report and typed it on her arrest record. Then, Angela was taken to another room and photographed, side and front. Soon afterwards, they put her back in the interrogation room.

It was now the third hour, and the Voice came once again. "Don't worry. Be strong. It's alright. They can't hurt you. Admit nothing."

The third hour was complete, and everyone, including Angela, was very frustrated. Then, they brought the fingerprinting equipment into the room, and the policeman started to fingerprint Angela's fingertips.

The police chief entered the room, saw Angela, looked at the report, and asked, "You're Australian, aren't you?" Angela replied, "Yes."

"Isn't prostitution legal in Sydney?"

"It's legal now, yes," Angela replied.

The chief ordered the policemen to stop fingerprinting Angela, to go out and come back a little later. He wanted to talk to Angela and seemed more reasonable than the other men.

The four policemen came into the room and began to go through the story, one more time. They talked of how the policeman had heard Angela say, "sex, ni-man-en" and had seen her hold up two fingers. The police chief looked straight at Angela and asked, "Now, is this correct, Miss Krokowski? Please tell me the truth."

"I will tell you the truth, but first, I will tell you a story."

The Voice said, "I'll help you choose the words. Remember, admit nothing and just say the words that come to your heart."

"I was minding my own business in a game room, talking to a girlfriend. Then, this man came into the room and smiled at me. He seemed very charming, and so I asked him to come with me. I went out in the street, and he followed. Then, we stood there for a while, and I told him that I knew he was a policeman. He said he wasn't, he lied. You are supposed to be the good guys, and I'm supposed to be the bad one, but it was you who lied. All is fair in love and war, and this is a war, so, therefore, I'm entitled to one lie. I didn't say, sex, ni-man-en. The two fingers meant 'peace,' peace of mind for me," Angela replied.

The chief policeman turned around and asked, "Is that correct? Did you lie?" The other policeman refused to comment and said that it made no difference because Angela had been caught red-handed, anyway.

Then, the chief policeman asked Angela, one more time, "Did you try to prostitute yourself?"

"I'm entitled to one lie. No, I didn't. At least, I'm honest about my lies, not like the policeman. I didn't know the man was telling me a lie. You know I'm telling a lie, so, therefore, you know the truth."

The police were perplexed. Here was a smart girl, who admitted the truth by telling a lie that Angela indirectly confessed to. It really confused them.

It was now the fourth hour, and the police were still more frustrated than ever, mainly, because Angela wouldn't admit to the crime. That was the hard part, but Angela didn't know that. All Angela knew was that the Voice inside her told her not to admit to anything.

The policemen chatted amongst themselves, then left the room, leaving Angela alone. They all went into another room and spent quite some time talking amongst themselves. They were upset and angry. Angela sat alone imprisoned in the tiny room, as the detectives who had just commenced duty entered, one by one, to look at her. After all, Angela was something special, a blonde Gaijin prostitute, something they'd not seen before, in Shinjuku. So, they all looked at her, but really it was Angela who was looking at them. They were supposed to be undercover detectives, but every one of them who entered that room, out of their own curiosity, revealed their true identity. Angela would remember all those faces. They'd burn in her memory, never to be forgotten. In fact, that whole night would never be forgotten.

The next hour passed, the fifth hour. Angela was locked in a cell, alone, which was cold and depressing. Then, a short time afterwards, a couple of detectives brought Angela back into the room, where a policewoman was waiting for her. The policewoman started to remove Angela's jewellery and adornment.

"You cannot go to prison with these things. You must remove them and place them in this tray. All your belongings must go. They will be held until the judge decides what to do with you," the policewoman said.

The situation looked dreadful for Angela. The prison downstairs housed some of the hardened, Asian prostitutes, who had the misfortune of being captured. Perhaps, they didn't work for Yakuza either, for, the girls who didn't work for Yakuza were always caught.

Then, the policewoman showed some kindness to Angela and said, "Please let our hair down." As Angela did, she added, "Now, brush it out, slowly. You understand?"

Angela began to brush her hair when the detectives saw her long, golden hair. It seemed to soften and move them a little closer towards compassion.

Then, one of the detectives asked, "Why are you crying?"

"Why do you think? Because everybody I've met in this God-forsaken country has tried to trick me. If it isn't the Yakuza trying to catch me and extract money from me, it's the police, trying to trap me with lies. This country must be the worst place in the world."

"Yakuza only want money. We want you."

Then, Angela added, "It's not so. Some Yakuza want to catch me."

"Who wants to catch you?"

"They not only want to catch me, but they also want to kill me." Then, Angela added, "Ginza Yakuza. The Toa-kai wants to kill me. They have wanted to kill me for a long time now. They have many different reasons for wanting it."

As soon as Angela said, 'Toa-kai,' everybody reacted in fear. That name even frightened the police. It was strange that they all cringed at the sound of that name. They weren't so brave, after all.

Then, the policewoman asked Angela to remove her make-up and place all her belongings into the tray.

The head policeman said, "You haven't got a passport. How

do we know that you are who you say you are? You could be lying about your identity."

"Then, take me to my home," said Angela, adding, "And I'll show you my passport. It's in Hirai, a little far from here. I promise that I'm telling you the truth about who I am."

The interrogator uttered dispassionately, "These days, one can never tell. Are you a man or a woman?"

Angela laughed and said, "Isn't that plainly obvious?"

The policeman said, "Just to be sure, you're must undergo a physical examination." Then, he ordered the policewoman to check Angela's sex after they left the room. It was yet another humiliation, designed to degrade and break Angela's spirit. The men left the room while the policewoman waited for Angela to remove every portion of her clothing. Then, she touched Angela's breasts and looked at Angela's vagina. She checked and double-checked, then asked Angela to dress. The men re-entered the room.

The interrogator asked, "Well, what is it?" He then looked at Angela, as if she weren't a person, but merely, an object designed for sex.

The policewoman replied, "Yes, definitely a woman."

Then, they brought the report and the file that they had. The policeman wrote details about how long she'd been in Japan and her real intention for staying there.

One policeman asked, "Are you a spy? Is that it? If you don't work with Yakuza and you're standing in the street, maybe it is because you're a spy?"

"The only thing I'm spying on is my neighbour's washing, next door. I'm not interested in espionage. I'm only interested in my career. I am in this country because, believe it or not, I felt it was the best thing to do. Even though the feeling may not be mutual, I do love Japanese people."

The policewoman laughed, shook her head and said, "I don't believe that for a moment. How could you, after all the things they've done to you?"

Angela said, "I don't know why. Maybe it's because Australia hasn't been very good to me in the past, and individually Japanese people have been really nice to me. I don't care whether you believe me or not. The main thing is that I believe myself."

The Voice said, "Be strong. It's alright, don't worry."

Then, the policewoman stood up, to take all of Angela's belongings away. The interrogator walked back into the room. He told the policewoman to leave Angela's things. Then, he said to Angela, "Prostitution is legal in Australia, isn't it?

"Yes, it is."

"Were you aware of the law in Japan?"

"Not really. I had a feeling that it wasn't exactly legal. But I didn't think it was such a serious crime. Especially when you consider that Japan has more prostitution than any other country around." Angela softly uttered.

It was now the sixth hour. The two detectives and supervisor came back into the room and began to interrogate Angela once more. The supervisor appeared to be a little softer than the other two but was still trying to trap Angela, just the same.

He began. "You understand the Japanese language pretty well, yes?"

"Not really. I know many Japanese words, but I really don't know what they mean, and I don't know the legal implication of them."

"So, when you said, to this detective, 'sex, ni-man-en,' did you know what it meant?"

Angela said, "Put it this way. I didn't know it would mean what you think it means."

That statement disturbed the other two detectives. They began to get really angry, and one of them started to breathe sluggishly, his nostrils flaring.

Angela said, "Lots of people have taught me Japanese, but I can't read or write Japanese, and I can only speak a little bit, so, sometimes, I'm prone to make mistakes."

The supervisor was convinced that Angela's Japanese wasn't great; then, said something to her in Japanese.

Angela responded, "Wakarimasen (I do not understand)." He

believed that Angela's Japanese ability was minimal but thought she'd understood what 'ni-man-en' meant.

Tears rolled down Angela's face as she felt the heat and pressure of almost the seventh hour. Tears flowed off her face and trickled onto her blouse, dampening it near her breasts. The supervisor, once more, asked the other detectives to leave the room. The room was designed to temporarily keep prisoners, but the central prison was in the building's basement. It was very dark and even cold down there, but at least there were other girls there with whom Angela could be with for company. Angela thought the idea of being locked in the basement prison wasn't such a bad idea after all. At least she would be away from those policemen.

A few minutes later, the two detectives re-entered, along with the supervisor.

The interrogator said, "Well, we've decided to let you go. Aren't we good policemen? Aren't we friendly policemen? Only because you're leaving on the twentieth of next month and only because you won't admit to the crime, but there is one stipulation before we let you go. You must sign an apology, that is Japanese law. We cannot release you unless you sign this form."

"Yes, I will do that," Angela replied.

They finished fingerprinting the Gaijin, while the other angry policeman was in the separate room, typing up the apology statement.

Angela was very relieved and said, to the interrogator, "Thank you, thank you. Don't worry, it won't happen again."

Angela began to feel relaxed and relieved, when the Voice came to her again, saying, "Don't worry. It's okay. Keep being strong. Don't give in."

It was only a trick. The policeman came in with the statement. "You must sign here."

They wanted Angela to sign without reading. Angela began to read it. "It's in Japanese. I can't understand what it says. You must type it in English," Angela insisted.

Then, the other policeman wrote down the same thing in English, and Angela read it.

"I apologise to the Japanese Police Department for asking a policeman to have sex with me, for twenty thousand yen and going to a hotel, so I could prostitute myself. I swear that I have a flight booked on the twentieth of next month. Signed..."

Angela refused to sign. "I will write my own statement of apology. I won't sign this."

The interrogator threw the papers on the floor and slammed his fist on the table. "You are a selfish person! All foreign people are selfish! You always want it your way!"

Angela cried intensely and said, "It's just another trick! I meet so many men in this country, and every one of them tries to trick me! This is just another trick. You want me to sign something that I don't know the legal implication of. If you want me to write a statement of apology, I will write it in my own words. If that's not good enough, then you better lock me away and let the judge decide. Still, you better be sure about what you're doing, because I'm not some little, Japanese prostitute, who can be pushed around. I am a Gaijin, and I think that maybe, you don't realise just how strong I am."

Angela was, indeed, becoming steadfast, because of the Voice.

The policeman began to kick the side of the wall, fiercely. "You are so selfish!"

The other policemen returned and asked him to leave. They went out and talked together. A few minutes later, after Angela had cried, and the remaining makeup had washed down her face, they all returned.

One of them had a mirror and passed it to Angela, with a box of tissues. "Wipe all that stuff off your face," he said.

Angela looked in the mirror to see herself, looking horrid and totally disgusting. She took off all that makeup and left her face bare, with red eyes bulging out, for all to see.

The policeman said, "We should lock you away, but because we are nice policemen, we're going to let you go."

It was the eighth hour. Angela sat back in the chair and sighed with relief. The Voice came and said, "See, I told you it would be okay. All you must do is always trust Me. Don't worry." The Voice had been right, all along, and Angela felt very relaxed, knowing that soon, she would be out of there. She wasn't so anxious anymore. She had won a fierce battle against a foreign country. Yet, Angela, with the help of only the Voice, had beaten them.

The policeman looked broken, but not Angela. She seemed slightly relaxed and at ease now. The policemen were the ones who felt drained. Then, the police asked, "Would you like some coffee?" They brought some coffee and began to chat with Angela differently. She was now a person and not a criminal.

One of them asked, "Tell me. Do you take drugs?"

Angela said, "No, I don't. Drugs are bad for you and can kill you."

"Hmm," he said, "Just as well, because I'm head of the Narcotics Department, and if I knew you were involved in drugs, I wouldn't let you go."

Angela laughed, "If I was involved with drugs, do you think I'd tell you?"

Japanese police were a little naïve in the ways they tried to trick Angela. It was impossible, and they'd given up. That was just a last attempt, and it had failed.

Then the interrogator became friendly and said, to Angela, "Please don't ask a policeman for sex again, alright? And it would be a good idea if you did go home to your country, because Japan is a dangerous place, if not because of us, but some Yakuza."

Angela scoffed. "You don't have to tell me the dangers of Yakuza. I'm already aware of that. It's just you guys I didn't know about." Angela was fairly open about her profession but didn't admit it in so many words.

The policeman said, "If you want to meet men, the best way to do it is not to talk to them in the street, but to go to a cafe with one for coffee and exchange telephone numbers."

It was as if he was trying to give Angela a clue, or was he just trying to be nice? One would never know, and Angela certainly would never understand.

Then, the other policeman said, "Come with me. I'll take you downstairs and ask the policewoman to bring your things back up to the room."

The policewoman smiled with delight. She liked Angela and didn't want to see her locked in a prison with the hardened prostitutes, for a worse crime may be committed in that case. Moments later, Angela's things arrived. She placed her jewellery back on, then opened her bag, to check her money. It was all there. Angela turned to the policeman in charge and said, "Well, at least Japanese police are honest with money."

He smiled as if it were a personal compliment. He was being kind to Angela, now. The business of the evening was over. He accompanied Angela down the stairs and out of the police station, along with the policewoman.

The other policeman walked past and asked, "I just have one question. How is it, you're so strong? How is it, you can withstand such a long interrogation?"

Angela smiled. "I have a strength within."

The policeman scratched his head. "I don't understand. It doesn't matter, anyway. The main thing is, just don't ask a policeman for sex anymore, okay?"

Angela smiled and agreed. "You bet I won't ever do that again, no way."

Then, Angela was left alone with the policewoman, who said, "Take care, especially take care of Yakuza." She smiled and walked away. Just as she was about to enter the building, she called out, across the road, to Angela, "Remember, if you have trouble with Yakuza, dial 001, any time of the day. Don't forget!"

Angela crossed the road to catch a taxi. As she did, she noticed a man in dark clothing, hiding near the side of the police building. He was trying to lure Angela around the corner. He was calling out to her. "Yukō! Yukō! (Come, come)."

Angela refused.

Then, he yelled out, "Sex, okay! Come, come!"

Angela looked at the man and thought, "Ah, perhaps it's the police's last attempt to catch me, all over again." However, he really did look like a Yakuza. It was hard to tell, after eight hours of interrogation. Angela was confused and wouldn't be involved in it, in any case. She was just curious as to which one it was. Was it the Red or the Blue? It was hard to tell.

Then a taxi arrived. Angela hailed it and quickly scrambled in the back seat, ordering, "Hirai, kudasai (please)."

The taxi whisked her away into the darkness. As the man's image and his waving hand faded, so did Angela's anxiety fade into the night.

CHAPTER FIFTEEN
'Two Dangerous Beasts'

ANGELA HAD BEEN through a great deal in the last thirteen months. Although it felt more like thirteen years and her work wasn't finished. Angela had been working on her dancing, singing and music, but still had a long way to go. There were many things to do. That meant, if she wanted to stay in Japan, she would have to return to the street.

Angela spent two days inside, thinking about the horror of the street, the fear of Yakuza and now the police. The police were a frightening new threat that, before now, Angela hadn't envisioned. The policemen were probably as dangerous, if not in some ways, more dangerous than the Yakuza. It was hard to say who was the most significant danger.

Then, she remembered what the policeman had said. "Yakuza usually want money, police want Angela." It was obviously much easier to part with money than spend one's life in a prison cell. So now, it was the police who took the number one position.

The Voice said, "Don't fear anybody. Trust Me. Only Me."

The next few days passed by quickly. Angela had worked hard, especially in dance and music. However, she was beginning to become anxious about stepping back on the street and perhaps into those handcuffs.

The Voice said, "From now on, don't utter any words, only gesture, for it's by the mouth that you can be condemned."

This made sense, for the police had arrested her because of what was said. If a call girl were to say nothing, but let the client do the talking and merely gesture, 'yes' or 'no,' perhaps, it would be safer. Of course, she must always follow her instinct and listen to the Voice. Angela had known that the man was from the police. Why did she go against her better judgement?

If there were to be the next time, Angela reconciled herself to only listen to the Voice, without fail. Her faith in the Voice was now total, no matter what anyone else said.

It was tricky to decide where to work next. Angela wasn't allowed to go to Ginza, nor Akasaka. Roppongi was out of the question and so too was Shinjuku. There were very few places left. Angela purchased a map of Tokyo and sat down. One by one, she ticked off all the places she'd already visited. Next, she located all the major 'play' areas, where there was plenty of nightlife. There were only two 'playtowns' left. They were Ueno and Ikebukuro. Ikebukuro was very far from Hirai, being on Tokyo's outskirts, so it would take over an hour by train. Ueno was closer but smaller.

The next night, Angela went to Ueno and looked around. There were many Yakuzas there, which frightened her no end. Anyone could tell they were Yakuza. They were open about their profession. Most of them were dressed in casual suits with their permed hair. Strangely, they all liked Angela and followed everywhere she went. That frightened her enormously. Angela sensed a cold feeling every time she saw one and every time one of their cars drove past. The cold feeling would go up and down her spine, just as before. When she felt it, it was time to find a side street to scramble down and make her way to another area.

Ueno was a quaint place and a little exciting, like Ginza and Shinjuku combined. However, one thing was sure. Business here was going to be very difficult, for the Yakuzas were everywhere.

The Voice said, "Don't worry, just continue as usual, but always take care and remember the rules."

The first rule was that all the clients must be Japanese. The second rule was to always practice safe sex. The third rule was to make no price cuts and only serve men who had good character and behaved well.

There was no mention of the police or Yakuza, that frustrated Angela. The rules weren't designed to protect her from the police or mafia, but only from the disease. Most people believed there wasn't an abundance of viruses in Japan. She thought Japan was probably the safest place in the world, particularly for AIDS.

Walking around Ueno on her second night, Angela didn't meet anybody. It was a tough place to work at, perhaps, because there were many Soaplands. The Yakuza had the business wrapped up, and they were very cheap. 'Playgirls' ranged from as little as ¥2,500 ($25) to ¥8,000 ($80).

That was exceedingly cheap, considering Angela was charging more than five to ten times that amount for a lot less. It was going to be exhausting getting clients in Ueno. Also, there wasn't the same amount of clientele as there had been Ginza. Nor did it have as many clients, willing and able, as in Shinjuku. For the first three nights, she was unsuccessful. After the third night, she returned home a little depressed.

The following evening, Angela spent a lot of time near the love hotels. Very soon, a man carrying a briefcase, who seemed quite wealthy, came to her. Angela didn't even have to say anything, just nodded and raised her fingers. The man took Angela to Ginza of all places, as he stayed in a business hotel there. He had coincidentally run into Angela, just when he needed someone most.

Together, they went up to his room. It was a deluxe suite, very appropriate for the evening. Angela sighed with relief, on entering the room, for she was off the street for the evening.

"Ah," Angela uttered while lying on the bed. She was exhausted after working for three nights in Ueno, without meeting anyone. The man was very well dressed and seemed to be a very ordinary businessman.

"Shall I pay you now? Is that right?" the man asked.

Angela nodded and didn't utter any words, at all. Then, Angela realised that this was the best way to do business because the men seemed to be doing most of the talking. The man presented Angela with fifty thousand yen. She placed it in the trusty handbag and began to undress.

First, they drank beer together; then, entered the shower. The man scrubbed Angela's body with a meticulous appreciation of her delicate, white skin. Then they slipped into the bed. Angela quickly reached for the condom and started to position it. He reacted very distastefully.

"I don't want this thing on me," the man said.

"Ah, but it's my rule. If you don't wear that, then no sex," Angela replied.

"Alright, then, we will use it."

Then, the man leaned over and switched off the light. They just lay in bed, cuddling, for about twenty or thirty minutes. Then, the man began to have sex with Angela and seemed to do something a little odd. She quickly switched on the light, looked down and noticed that the man had pulled the condom off. He was going to try penetration without it. Angela jumped out of bed and quickly shook her finger at him.

"Don't do that! I'll give you one last chance. If you do that again, I'm out of here, with the money! Do you understand?" Angela demanded.

The man laughed and pretended that it was an accident, "I didn't mean to do it."

Then he got back into bed and placed a second condom on himself. He attempted to have sex with Angela once again. This time, he found maintaining an erection quite tricky.

The man stepped out of bed, put a robe around himself and reached for another glass of beer, then asked Angela to come and join him. She had been there for about an hour. She was getting annoyed with the man's determination to remove the latex. To remove the condom was to break the most fundamental rule the Voice had given. It was also to personalise her business and Angela didn't wish to do that. To exchange body fluids with a stranger was abhorrent. The man sat down and poured Angela a beer, which she drunk. Then, the man poured her another.

"No, I don't want anymore, I might get drunk," Angela said, pushing the glass aside.

It seemed as though it was the man's intention. In any ease, Angela refused to drink anymore and placed her hand over the mouth of the glass. The man poured the rest of the beer into his own glass. Then they lay on the bed together, once again. The man attempted to remove the condom once more.

Angela said, "That's it. I'm leaving." Angela jumped up to get dressed. Then the man got out of bed, grabbed her by the arm and apologised, as he kissed her hand.

"I'm very, very sorry. We don't even have to have sex, it's alright, I'm sorry! I just don't like those terribly nasty things. Forgive me. Just stay with me. We won't even have sex," the man uttered softly.

Angela felt sorry for him. He obviously found the latex uncomfortable, and so, she sympathised with his situation. "Alright, I'll stay then, but if you do want to have sex, you must wear it, and if you take it off, then I'll slap your face as hard as I can, and I'll walk out of this room, never to come back," Angela said firmly.

There was something pitiful about the man, but she didn't know why. Her innate instinct made her pity him, for some reason. Then they lay on the bed together, and the light was half-lit this time. The man talked a great deal and asked Angela many questions, most of which she answered. He had a strange look about him, which Angela couldn't quite put her finger on. They lay there for a long time. Then, he kissed Angela along her arm, neck and tried to kiss her mouth. Angela placed her hand between his and her lips.

"I don't kiss clients," Angela said.

Then, he turned away, quickly turned back, grabbed Angela's mouth, and placed his mouth over it. Just as his tongue was about to enter, she pushed him away. "Don't do that! I told you!"

The man had only kissed her lips and nearly penetrated her mouth. Angela wiped her mouth clean of saliva. "Don't do that again!"

The man's watch had a large diamond on the twelfth digit. Everything about him was labelled by an expensive designer. There was a real air of money about him. She commented on how beautiful the watch was. It was a man's watch but looked more like a woman's, decorated with diamonds and solid gold. The man took the wristwatch off and placed it in Angela's hand.

"So, you really like this watch, do you?"

"Yes, of course."

Then the man became more welcoming and said with a smile, "This watch cost me one million yen. That's about ten thousand dollars, I believe, in your country."

Angela was amazed at the high price. Japanese people were so silly, to pay so much for merely a timepiece.

"Admittedly, the diamond is beautiful, but what an incredible waste of money!" Angela said.

"Would you like to have this watch?" He asked.

"What would I do with a watch like this?" She replied.

"Sell it, of course. Why would you want it for anything else, but its value?" He stated.

"But you wouldn't give me this watch, even if I did want it," Angela replied.

"It's yours, on one condition!"

"What's the condition?"

"Remove the plastic, and the watch is yours," the man said confidently.

For a moment, Angela thought about ten thousand dollars, for one incident with a without safe sex. Then, Angela remembered her little diary and the second rule, which always used safe sex. Then, for a moment, she thought about the ten thousand dollars. That would just about cure her financial problem.

It was very tempting. Angela thought about the watch, as she gazed at the diamond.

The man insisted, "Gee, it's not such a big thing. I know many Japanese girls, who would do it for a lot less," he stated. "I'm a rich man. I have money in the bank too, you know. Perhaps, instead of giving you the watch, I can give you the cash. Would you like that?

I just want to experience you, totally. I don't care how much it costs. It's a pleasure I'd like to know, at least once. So then is ten thousand American dollars enough?"

Angela burst out laughing. She couldn't believe what the man was saying. It was totally incomprehensible that a man would pay such money for sex without that barrier.

Then, the Voice said, "Under no circumstances, definitely not." Angela's faith in the Voice had become unshakable from the incidents she'd been through. Angela reacted automatically. "No, under no circumstances, ever. Absolutely not."

The man was totally amazed that Angela refused this generous offer so quickly.

The Voice said, "Even if it's a million, the answer is no. Angela, trust Me."

Angela reiterated the words. "Even if it's a million, the answer's still no. I'm sorry."

They had been talking for a lot longer than Angela had realised. It was now 4:30 a.m. The man had spent all night trying to persuade the blonde Gaijin street girl to have sex without protection. Angela, realising the time, gave back the watch.

The band had a calendar date attachment, made of leather. The man took it off and gave it to Angela. "This is a gift to remember the date. This date is important, well, at least, it's important to me," the man sadly said, as he placed it in Angela's hand.

Angela didn't know what he'd meant but placed it on the band of her watch. "Alright, if it's a present, I'll keep," Angela replied.

The calendar wasn't expensive and looked out of place on such a costly watch. Still, ironically the date reminder seemed to mean more than the wristwatch. After that, they just lay on the bed in their hotel robes. Silently they gazed out of the window, as the sun began to rise. The man looked at Angela, and she noticed his cheeks were quite sunken. As the sunlight penetrated the room, it shone on everything, except the man's eyes. They didn't glisten but were darkened.

It sent a cold shiver down Angela's back, the very same shiver she'd felt with the Yakuza and police.

The Voice said, "See, why now?"

Then, the man said, "I have a confession to make to you. I have AIDS." He looked down at the ground, then looked at his watch and said, "All these things, now, are meaningless. I am alone. It is so lonely, having AIDS."

Angela's hand began to tremble, as she realised that she'd been intimate with this man and had actually had sex with him briefly, although safely.

It was frightening to realise how close she had come to remove the latex, merely for money. Angela looked at the man, as tears formed in the corners of his eyes. "It wouldn't be so bad if I weren't so alone. If I were with someone who had it also, I would be happy. I'm sorry."

Angela slowly moved away from him, fearing any further risk of contamination. She became ill, thinking about all the times he'd touched and kissed her. It frightened her to a great deal.

The Voice said, "Don't worry. You are safe because you've followed the rule. Everything is safe, don't worry."

The man was agitated and said, "I think you should leave now. I think you should leave."

Then, Angela went to have a shower. She scrubbed her breasts, neck, arms, and every part of her body, remembering, precisely, every area the man had touched.

The man said, "I think you are a man, not a woman. You are too strong to be a woman. I think you must be a man."

"I am, indeed, a woman, but you aren't much of a man, for, you told the most horrendous lie that anyone could ever tell. You tried the most dishonest, wickedly deceitful trick that anyone could ever do to another person. I forgive you, but I don't know if God will." Angela quickly dressed, gathered her things, and started to leave the room. As she was going out the door, Angela looked at the calendar on her watchband and said, "I think I will remember this day longer than you."

The man looked down at the ground as Angela shut the door behind her. She walked out of the hotel, away from the third and most dangerous fear of all, AIDS. Walking down the street, towards the subway, she paused for a moment to gaze into the bright sunlight, then said to the Voice, "So, the serpent has diamond eyes."

Angela had the English paper delivered every morning. Browsing through, Angela noticed an article about AIDS. It stated that three thousand Japanese people in Tokyo had the disease. It also revealed that seventy-three per cent had contracted the virus through blood products. Nine per cent through homosexual activity and the remaining populace, through either, drug usage or heterosexual contact. It was clear that there were many more men in Tokyo, like the man with the diamonds in his watch. That night was like passing an examination.

It was a test of strength, where only information from a different type of person, could save her. It was like being in the 'Twilight Zone,' but at least, Angela had survived. Maybe she didn't receive high marks, but she did pass and was still alive to tell the tale. Angela knew there was no contamination, for, the Voice had told her so. She was free from AIDS and would remain so if she kept to the rules. However, her personal sex life wasn't subject to business rules. That was a different matter. Perhaps, in that instance, love could be the cause of infection. In any case, Angela knew that her love life had nothing to do with these Heaven-sent rules. The rules were designed to keep Angela safe and protect her in business only.

Angela didn't even think about her personal sex life, for that had ended for the time being. She had turned off her own need for love, ever since that incident with Ariyoshi. In fact, Angela had switched off her personal feelings, so much so, that she'd never love a man again. Angela used to be a normal girl. But her time in Japan had changed her in so many ways that were yet to be realised. In a way, she hadn't become bitter but more resilient. Her taste in things was changing too.

It was time to return to Ueno, either that or go to the other city far away. Ikebukuro was too far. It was a formidable task, going to and from work, let alone, working there. However, Angela believed that it might be worth a try, after all, Ikebukuro was new ground. It was one place she'd never been to before. So, that evening, instead of going to Ueno, she journeyed to Ikebukuro. It was a bit like

Shinjuku. When Angela arrived at the railway station, she noticed something. Ikebukuro was in the Aokama area, the same place where the policeman thought she had worked. Unintendedly, they'd given her excellent information on a new city to sex business.

Angela walked around this new place, which looked just like Shinjuku. There were many people wanting sex, and there was the police, too. There were also many Yakuzas. Her instinct now knew that there was probably an abundance of AIDS, as well. In any case, at least Angela could now recognise things for what they indeed were. She could see, by the way, people acted, which group they belonged to. She could establish who was part of the blue group, the police, the red, blood group of the Yakuza, and the ones who were dying were of the black group. Angela's world was strange, a world that other people couldn't see. These people walked past, in the street, in some fantasy world and couldn't see reality as Angela saw it. From all Angela's experiences, she had become streetwise, so much so, that no one would ever understand her again.

On the first night in Ikebukuro, Angela met four clients. She had made ¥100,000 in three hours, without any trouble from police or Yakuza. She never uttered any words, but merely gestured with her fingers. It was so easy. This was learning from experience. Night after night, she worked but refused to go with too many men, for it was too risky.

Every day, Angela practised her dancing, singing and music. It was working out just right, and there was progress. During the evenings, she met clients. Most of the clients were merely working-class men, salarymen, who wanted to experience a beautiful Gaijin for once in their lives. Even if the cost was totally unreasonable, they were still prepared to pay it. Ikebukuro was now the place where they could go to find that experience. Angela had been working in the Aoyama area for about a month. Her life was really in order, financially speaking. Angela was strong-willed, having a routine that was followed every night. On leaving the railway station, she'd slip around the corner and zigzag through the entertainment strip areas, near the Soaplands.

One evening Angela was going through the motions. A man was

standing near one of the night clubs, who seemed to be waiting for her. He was dressed quite expensively, wearing a gold watch and chain. It was easy to tell that this wasn't a salaryman. He dressed in an expensive, linen, brown suit and smoked through a cigarette holder. The man had a character about him that was different from all the other people around.

Angela walked by, then he began to speak, "May I have a date with you?"

His English was poor and mixed with Japanese. Angela found it interesting that he had been waiting for her. Her instinct suggested the man was not the police. As they walked a little further, Angela's intuition told her that she was talking to a Yakuza. She wasn't frightened of Yakuza now, because she knew who they were and how they operated. The police had convinced this Blonde Gaijin that Yakuza only wanted money, so there was no harm if they wanted sex. The meeting seemed safe. Anyway, there was no harm in having coffee with the man in a crowded coffee shop.

Angela said to herself, "After all, I don't have to fear them. If there is only one of them and he doesn't want money, only sex, it'll be safe."

The Voice said, "I'll tell you when to leave. It's alright. I'll tell you when."

Angela was in tune with the Voice entirely now. If the Voice said something, no matter how absurd it seemed, Angela would do it. If the Voice said, everything was okay, she would stake her life on those words blindly, believing, that everything was **OK**.

They went to a coffee shop and talked for about twenty minutes. The man asked her the same old questions, like, where she was from, what she was doing, and why Japan. He also asked whether she was married and what kind of visa she possessed. He was curious about all her personal details.

Quite unconsciously, Angela answered all the questions and then uttered, "You are a Yakuza, a different kind of Yakuza but Yakuza in any case."

As the man drank his coffee, his hand trembled. "Ah, if I'm Yakuza, it's no good," the man added. "For, I will either shoot someone or stab someone, then, I will be arrested and put in prison. I don't wish to be put in jail, so therefore, I am not Yakuza."

It was an odd thing to say, but he hadn't actually denied it. Angela's instinct didn't tell her anything on the contrary. In fact, it only reinforced the belief that he was, in fact, Yakuza.

The man asked, "Short time, sex, how much?"

Angela played with her hand on the table, as if wiping it, with three fingers.

The man looked at them and said, "I understand." Then he added, "Okay, let's go."

Angela said, "I know a very nice little love hotel, just around the corner."

They walked out of the coffee shop, when the Voice said, "I will tell you when."

Angela didn't understand the meaning, as everything seemed to be going well, except, the man was Yakuza. He didn't want money, so Angela thought it would be okay. On this particular evening, it was hard to go to her usual hotel. There were police driving around, booking parked cars. That was enough to deter her. Instead, they went to another location, across the railway line.

As they passed over the line, the man appeared to be looking for something or someone. "Excuse me for a moment," the man said, as he went to a public toilet.

While he near the toilet door, Angela noticed him chatting with another man, briefly. She was standing some distance away and saw him leave the bathroom with the other man. Then, they went separate ways.

The man returned to Angela and said, "Let's go." As they walked a little further, the man added, "I would like all night, not a short time and I will pay you ju-man-en (¥100,000, A$1,000). How do you feel about that? That's a thousand dollars!"

Angela thought that it was pretty good.

The man added, "Except, I don't like this area. I wish to go to Shinjuku."

Angela thought it would be alright and she would be okay until the Voice said otherwise. They walked together, then stood at a taxi stand for some time. Then, it was their turn to catch the next taxi in line. The man gestured for the people behind them to take it. For some reason, he wanted to delay. Then, another taxi quickly drove up, and he grabbed that one.

The Voice said, "Soon, you must go."

Angela got in the taxi and realised that the driver was obviously a Yakuza, she could tell. She didn't react, but instead, acted normal. The cab sped off and, as it did, Angela noticed that the driver hadn't even started the meter. In Tokyo, that was a very odd thing. She pretended not to notice. Then, she saw something else: there was a van following, taking every turn. When it came very close, almost touching the back of the bumper bar, at the lights, it was evident that the driver of the van was also, Yakuza. The three men were all looking at Angela, very intensely. She acted normally.

Then, the Voice said, "Don't worry. Soon, you must run away, but now realise that Yakuza don't only want money. They also want you. They want to capture you."

As the taxi drove along, the client asked, "Do you speak any Japanese?"

Angela denied understanding Japanese, for, it was a very advantageous position to be in. She pretended to not understand anything but knew what they were talking about more than they cared to imagine. Then, the man started talking to the taxi driver amicably. They talked about how they had many Thai girls and that they were ten thousand yen each. They were concerned because it was hard to make money, as most of the Soaplands had Thai girls. However, nobody had a beautiful Gaijin, like this. The client revealed that they would become rich and commented on how lucky he was to have caught her. Angela understood everything the man said to the driver. She knew the situation, but instead of reacting fearfully, Angela embraced the man, cuddled him, and began to kiss him on the cheek. The man was delighted and couldn't believe how sexy and willing the blonde Gaijin was. In fact, she was embracing the man, only to observe the van in the rear. She was a professional. And knew just how to get at a man, through his pants. Angela kissed the man's neck and stroked his leg, near his crotch, all while checking the rear window, only to see the Yakuza van. Angela noticed that the door on her side of the taxi had the two locks sealed with plastic. Angela then placed her leg in between the man's legs and started to gently rub his crutch. The man became excited and embedded his face in Angela's breasts. As he did, Angela reached over and removed the plastic cover on the first lock.

The man was too busy with Angela's breasts to even notice. Then, Angela began to work on the second lock, which was the door opener. It had a plastic cover moulded and taped over it. Angela slowly began to caress the man's hair as she removed the tape and plastic cover. She placed her body between the man and the door. What the Voice had told her, now clearly made sense. She had to wait until the right moment. The Voice would say when. At that moment, she would flee from the car and be away from the trap. At the other end of the line, Angela knew that was a needle, waiting with her name on it. Angela's instinct told her not to react positively. She was an actress, covering every step and detail, so the man would not notice the plastic lying on the floor.

The man did notice the tape on the floor. As he began to pick it up to see what it was, Angela grabbed his penis. That excited him, enormously. He yelled with delight and dropped the tape without another thought. It was clear that if she were injected with a relatively potent dose of heroin, the rest would just be a bad dream. Angela visualised it in her mind. It was confirmed that the slave trade of the Japanese sex industry was still alive at that time. The taxi was almost at Shinjuku, 'ichi-chome' and only had a little while to go. Then, suddenly, a police car drove past. All the members of the Yakuza reacted strangely. She continued to pretend not to notice and acted as if she were a little tipsy. Then, the taxi pulled up at the lights.

The Voice said, "Now! Go now!"

Angela didn't even look at the traffic, nor did she even care. She knew the Voice would take care of everything. Angela pulled the door lock, then kicked it open, grabbed her bag, then leapt out of the taxi, to the shock of the driver and the man in the back seat. She sprinted across the road, without even looking: a truck drove past inches from her path. Arriving at the other side, Angela turned to notice the man in the van had got out, but couldn't cross the road, as there were too many cars.

The Voice said, "Run! Run for your life!"

Angela ran down the road, like a gazelle leaping through a forest. The people walking up the street couldn't believe how tall and fast the Gaijin was. She entered a shop, ran right up the back and hid behind a fridge. Her heart was beating furiously.

The manager of the shop asked, "Dajobu desu ka (everything alright)?" Angela said, "Byoki desu. Sumimasen (I feel sick, excuse me)."

The man said, "I'll get you some water."

Then Angela looked up and noticed the taxi and Yakuza van slowly drive past. However, they hadn't seen her. Angela waited there for thirty minutes.

The Voice said, "You are safe, now. Very good. You trusted Me perfectly, for we are now one, and we will always be one."

This was a religious experience. Angela was in contact with a force, a power beyond one's self which could guide her in moments of danger or crisis when common sense and reality weren't enough. In moments such as these, when things are not as they seem, the unknown can be seen by someone from the unknown. The Voice was one such individual, a presence, an entity, a being, who could always guide Angela. This was another moment of danger that Angela had safely been shown through.

She hoped there wouldn't be too many more incidents like this. However, the main thing now was that she knew that Yakuza didn't only want money, but also her body. They tried to control, own, and manipulate her body, for the explicit purpose of making money out of her physical flesh.

After about thirty minutes more, the man came out from behind the fridge. The people in the shop obviously thought her to be a strange, crazy Gaijin. She crawled out from behind the refrigerator. "I'm sorry to have bothered you. Thank you," Angela said, as she walked out, onto the street. Then, Angela caught an average taxi home, all the while, looking out the back, making sure there was no one following. When Angela arrived home, she picked up her Bible. It read, "Fear not, for I am always with you."

CHAPTER SIXTEEN
'A Sequence of Inevitable Destinies'

AFTER THE LAST encounter, Angela didn't wish to return to Ueno. Ueno was just one of those random places, and it was better to avoid unpredictability. Life for Angela in Tokyo was complicated, always living in constant danger and fear.

Ikebukuro was the last place in Tokyo where Angela could now work. All the other 'play cities,' as they're called, had been used up. She was becoming quite infamous and a little too well known both by the police and Mafia. Ikebukuro was the new place; no one knew her there. It was far away enough from Shinjuku, Ginza and Akasaka to be completely new territory. It was either Ikebukuro or change cities completely. That meant going to Osaka, Hiroshima, or oven Kyoto. Angela had spent so much money on her apartment, that it was a pointless consideration to change cities at this time. Angela's initial encounter with Ikebukuro was rather profitable. There wasn't any reason she couldn't continue working in that area, as long as she was careful.

Angela went early to Ikebukuro on a Monday evening. In all of Tokyo, there were more Soaplands in Ikebukuro. This small, inner sub-city, had everything, including strip clubs, bars, and many 'sex toy' shops. The 'sex toy' shops had all kinds of sex aid products, vibrators, bondage equipment, artificial stimulators, videos, and magazines. Angela found her new territory rather curious and felt a strange kind of attraction to it. Ikebukuro was like Shinjuku, only prostitution was more rampant here. Many Taiwanese girls were everywhere, working as street prostitutes in large numbers, on several corners of the streets.

On the other hand, Shinjuku was very secretive. Ikebukuro appeared to be very 'upfront' and blatant. The main area was very well lit, so most street girls left that area to haunt the dark, dim-lit backstreets. Angela now knew why. It was the fear of the police. Angela would have to stick to those backstreets, too. The possibility of encountering something just as dangerous and perhaps, more deadly lurking in that dark area, in a backstreet in a place so very far from home, was the only problem that existed. Fear was Angela's primary instinct as she walked through Ikebukuro. Would Ikebukuro be the beginning of something new or the end? It was a very frightening situation for Angela. Ikebukuro represented the final challenge, the last chapter of Angela's sex business in Tokyo.

Angela had initially come to Tokyo to dance for the Japanese. Instead, she was dancing with them. Even though the dance style was not the kind she would wish for, it was still, in a way, dancing. 'Dancing in the bedroom,' Angela would say.

The first few nights in Ikebukuro were the hardest. A Yakuza man came to Angela and asked her for money. "Hey! Gaijin! You are a working girl here. Three nights now, business in this street. We want one month's payment, ju-man-en (A$1,000). If you pay it, everything will be okay. If you don't pay it, we won't care about you," the Yakuza man uttered, in broken English.

Angela pretended not to understand. This was a little different to her other encounters with Yakuza. "What do you mean, we won't care about you?" Angela asked.

The man looked at her and replied, "We won't care about you."

"Will you hurt me?"

The man laughed, then said, "No, we will not care about you, at all." Then, he laughed again.

Angela didn't really understand. It was different from the

other places, where they may threaten her at knifepoint. This was a different kind of Yakuza. A Yakuza that Angela felt she needed, more than they needed her.

"What makes you think I'm a prostitute, anyway?" Angela asked.

"I'm sorry. Are you an English teacher?"

Angela didn't reply and simply said, "Just be sure about who I am and what I am, before you ask for money."

Angela hadn't denied her profession but tried to confuse him with her words. If he saw her many times, he wouldn't be absolutely sure that she was engaged in the sex business. Angela was charging the same amount as in Shinjuku. It was a seedy area, and there were no rich men around. These were working-class men who came to get stimulation. Many overworked and frustrated salarymen came to find sexual release. Whether they were married or single, they all needed release. Angela would get one, two, or perhaps three clients a night, all for twenty to thirty thousand yen each. It was a little tricky going to the hotel. She had to be very careful about that and made sure no police were watching. Secondly, she made sure that the client wasn't a policeman or Yakuza. After being confident that the man genuinely was a client, the next step was to find a hotel that was clear of any Yakuza. Angela would also be always looking for police cars and plainclothes officers. It was as dangerous as Shinjuku, but Angela had more experience than in Shinjuku. Being in constant fear and apprehension, she believed prudence would be the best course. Fear would be the key to safety. Angela kept to the dark, backstreet areas and always kept her eyes open. When she'd go to the hotel with a client, she'd still follow the same routine: money first, and not much conversation.

By now, Angela's Japanese was routine. "O Genki desu ka? (Are you well?). AIDS, Anata motte imasen? (You don't have AIDS, do you?). Yakuza dame (No Yakuza)."

Every client was handled in the same way. Angela had a mental checklist. She would ask many questions before she'd even agree to go with the man. Angela consciously made the price cheap. So, there was less negotiation. This meant the least amount of contact with men as possible. If her price was high, that meant talking to many men about money. All working people had at least twenty-five thousand yen in their pocket, twenty for Angela and five for the hotel. Angela had now stepped into the realm of hardcore prostitution. That meant there were short time sessions only, usually twenty minutes. Sometimes, it would last up to an hour, in which case, Angela would charge thirty thousand. Businessmen who could afford such a price would spend an hour with Angela. Still, most working-class men found ni-man-en (¥20,000, A$200) quite expensive, considering some Taiwanese girls, who were quite attractive, would provide full service for as little for go-sen-en (¥5,000, A$50). Everything was different, and Angela would soon realise just how much. Each night, Angela went to Ikebukuro's dark area and walked down the streets, embraced by fear.

The Voice always said, "Don't worry, my child. I'm with you, I'm guiding you. Nothing will hurt you; I promise. I didn't let you go this far to get you into trouble now. We're almost there, a little while longer. Be patient."

Sometimes, the building's shadows cast on the road seemed to frighten Angela. She could see figures lurking in those shadows, yet the Voice would always calm her nerves. Usually, they were the shadows of other prostitutes, also walking the dark area. Like most of them, Angela wouldn't stick to a corner, but she'd walk around instead. In that way, it would be more difficult for the police to trap her, at least, that's what was believed.

All the prostitutes were owned by Yakuza. In books and videos of the girls at the sex toy shops, Angela noticed that they all had tattoos. When a Yakuza possessed a prostitute, they almost had their sign engraved, as if to say, "This is our property." Even if it is a small tattoo, it still represents a symbol of ownership. There was no way out once you got in. Once a Yakuza prostitute, always a Yakuza prostitute. The only way out was if they wanted you out and, if they did, then they had their methods of doing it quickly.

When Angela returned home, late in the evening, she'd write songs on her keyboard, play melodies and compose music. It was a special kind of music, expressing the fear, loneliness of the street and faith in the Voice, all the things that were Angela's life. She didn't want to write these songs but had to, as a responsibility. She had to get all these feelings and ideas about her life into some artistic form, to be free from their torment. Putting all these emotions into music and painting was the only way Angela knew. In fact, Angela could do many things, multi-talented. However, it was music and dancing that were Angela's preferred means of expression. Music was paramount over everything else. Each night after work, no matter how late, Angela would make herself rehearse. She'd cry as she sang songs of the lonely streets and of how all the men seemed to be just flickering images of spirits, which were really only physical animals. There was, indeed, a sadness in Angela's music, unique in character. Most of the men in Angela's life appeared to be bodies without souls.

One evening, after a rather depressing session, Angela had a dream and, in it, the Voice came to her. The Voice said, "Look, Angela. This is your life."

It was a strange dream. Angela was herself, a prostitute. In the dreamscape, she was with a client. The man was bad, old, and dirty looking. He represented the soul-less clients with whom she was beginning to encounter more often as of late. The Voice manifested itself in the dream as an Angel of Fire, who hovered above Angela's head and spoke to her in the usual way. It whispered just as in her waking moments. No one except Angela could see the Angel nor hear the Voice. It was as if the Voice really was an Angel of Fire, who stood over her, every night, guiding Angela from danger and misfortune.

In the dream, the Voice said, "Show a bad man his destiny, and he will change his ways."

Then, the Voice led Angela, who, in turn, led the client to a waterhole. The Voice told her to show the man his reflection in the water. It really was a waterhole of the future. It revealed to the man his destiny. The lot of the man could be seen only in that waterhole and only with Angela. As the man looked, he suddenly became horrified. All his hair fell out, and his skin became old and wrinkly.

Then, he died with horror, as his body turned to stone. Angela looked at the man, who just died before her eyes, then looked at the Angel of Fire.

"What does it mean?" Angela asked.

"You must teach the wisdom you have learnt so that death of the spirit is not inevitable," the Voice replied.

Angela awoke very fervently, drenched in a cold sweat. It was about 4:00 a.m. and dark. It was a little frightening just how real the Angel image had been. She wasn't dreaming of dancing now. This dream was filled with mixed emotion and confusion and was a dream link with the Voice. That was the first time that had happened. Not only was the Voice speaking to her in waking moments, but now in her dreams.

This was the single, most important, significant thing in Angela's life. However strange it was in the ordinary sense, for Angela, it was good, for, without the Voice, she was lost. Angela had not been a tough person. She appeared to be and did things only determined people could do, but the Voice provided that strength. Without its guidance, Angela was as helpless as a child, or so she believed and perhaps it was true. In any case, it didn't matter now. The Voice would be with her, always. Angela went back to sleep, and this time dreamt of dance.

Angela wasn't frightened of the Voice. However, when the Voice was in her dreamscape, it seemed to be very significant. All the other dreams were, merely dreams, or weren't they?

The next dream Angela had was off dancing with a woman, breast to breast, nipple to nipple, lips to lips. It was an exotically, beautiful dream. She woke to an orgasm. Angela hadn't experienced an orgasm for so long and almost forgot how it felt. The aim was a sexual dance encounter with a Japanese woman, who also had an orgasm. Afterwards, Angela lay in her bed, late in the night, touching her own body. All this time, with all the worry, fear and anxiety, Angela had forgotten about her own, physical needs.

"How ironic," Angela laughed. "Here I am, a prostitute, who sleeps with men every day, but I am so frustrated, so emotionally and sexually frustrated, I'm beginning to dream about women. I don't understand myself anymore."

The Voice said, "Don't worry, you'll understand, soon. It's only natural for you. Don't be frightened, you're just finding yourself."

Angela didn't understand, but always listened to the Voice and so, went back to sleep; only to dream about things she would never remember.

There was an inevitability about the Yakuza. The longer Angela stayed in Ikebukuro, the sooner they would own her. It wouldn't be too long before she had their tattooed mark of ownership on her beautiful, Gaijin ivory skin. That frightened Angela. Many people also believed that it was inevitable. Just how long that certainty would take, could only be determined with hindsight.

The next night, Angela met the same Ikebukuro Yakuza man. He came after her, grabbed her coat and started to pull her around. "Okane (Money)!"

Angela pulled away, denied understanding what he was talking about and pretended to not understand the Japanese language. If he bothered her anymore, Angela said she would go to the police.

The man laughed and replied in English, "Ikebukuro police are Yakuza."

Angela refused to believe him.

He added, "Dozo (Please). The police won't help you. The only ones who can help you are us, Kyokuto-kai."

Angela ran off, fearing that once she paid them, they'd expect her to always do so. They would probably bring her clients and know everything she did. If they knew where she went and who she was with, eventually they would run her. That inevitability scared Angela.

It was a constant danger. On the other hand, there was still the other danger, namely, the Police. Angela didn't know when she would meet them next. The fear was overwhelming. This was a foreign country with a foreign language and culture. Like a salmon swimming upstream, Angela stood out in the crowd, one blonde head amongst millions of blackheads.

Days turned slowly into weeks. Ikebukuro was like a vacuum. Although Angela's emotions were intact, the days always seemed the same, endless and uneventful. Angela didn't mind the lack of variety.

She didn't want one day to be paramount over another, which would increase the possibility of something terrible happening. One evening, as Angela walked down the street after leaving the hotel, she found herself looking at the other prostitutes. Some looked back at her. They sometimes looked at each other with a kind of passionate yearning. What it meant is obvious. Some were attracted to each other. They seemed to be attracted to the same sex, possessing some homosexual tendency. Many had been desensitized to men, after enumerable sexual encounters. Whether they chose to be lesbians or not, was entirely a matter of personal choice. Now Angela began to notice women. She never really saw them before but started to realise just how beautiful women really were. Men seemed to be dull and uninteresting to her, only appearing to want one thing from her.

On the other hand, women seemed passionate. They were motivated by an emotional need rather than lust. Even the prostitutes appeared to be friendlier people, than any of the clients. Occasionally, Angela would meet a nice guy. Still, after he had experienced release, there wasn't much more left to say, except, "See you again, perhaps." For Angela, men were merely a sexual encounter. The only man she ever really loved was Theo, and he was lost in the past. Theo was now a series of memories. Angela looked back at those memories with a tender fondness. Sometimes, life with Theo was a mixture of passion and pain. Mostly pain, yet there were beautiful memories that Angela would cherish on her darkest nights, in the street, alone. Yes, Angela was very frustrated and confused.

The Voice said, "Don't worry, it's only natural. After all, it's not important who you love. What's important is that you follow love. It doesn't matter the gender of the person. What's important is that its love, not lust."

Angela thought about that each night as she went to sleep. She began to dream of making love with women. It was certainly confusing. Through it all, Angela was starting to realise that she may be gay. It was a very twisted realisation for a prostitute to make.

Japan was certainly not the place to be for a gay woman. It had a very traditional society, full of the stoic role-played customs.

Men were, seemingly, men, even though sexist at the same time and women were, invariably, women. There was very little female homosexuality, that was visible. Homosexuality that did exist existed to fulfil the needs of men. Unlike a Western country, Japan's society was male-dominated, where sexual inequality is a central issue. To be a gay woman would mean being lonely, especially in Tokyo and even more notably, as a prostitute. Angela realised that she may, in fact, be bisexual. She was, sexually and emotionally, a victim of the game and profession of sex business. Rather than becoming hardened and bitter, as many do, Angela looked elsewhere for love. However, most of the men Angela met were considered to be the best clientele available. They indeed were, compared to who the other prostitutes received. Angela, still, only wanted money from men. Sex always seemed cumbersome, fragile and uncomfortable.

Angela went to Ikebukuro five nights a week. Her business was continuing very well. However, most people considered Ikebukuro as dangerous as Shinjuku.

One man said, "There are plainclothes policemen everywhere and, if you're not careful, you may get caught and be sent to prison."

As time passed, Angela began to realise that she was the only solo businesswoman on the street. Everyone who worked in Ikebukuro belonged to the Kyokuto-kai (Tokyo based Yakuza). Angela was a little different. Would she be able to survive in this environment? It was difficult to tell.

While talking on the phone with Barb, the same Ikebukuro Yakuza man, arrived again. This time, he started banging on the door of the telephone booth. Angela, very annoyed, finished her conversation, to open the door and hear the man's mutterings.

First, he began to say the same thing as before: he wanted a thousand dollars. Angela refused to give him any money and said she really would go to the police.

The man laughed and said, in half Japanese and English, "Look Gaijin. We own the police. If you don't pay us, we will not tell them to protect you. Then, they will arrest you, and you will go to prison. You must be a part of the group, or you will be caught. That is the way it's done here. It's always been like that."

Angela refused to give any money and pretended not to understand, then walked away from him. Angela had understood what he had said. It was such a difficult situation to be in. It was so stressful. Angela was always looking over her shoulder, wondering whether one of the two were following her and thinking, "Is this one safe? Is this safe?"

The Voice would say, "Yes, he's safe," or "No, he's not safe," depending on who approached.

Angela never went with anyone, unless the Voice said it was safe to do so. She refused to go with anyone if there was a shadow of a doubt. It limited the amount of money Angela could make, but at least it kept her out of prison and out of the hands of Yakuza.

There were many big Soaplands in Ikebukuro. One of the most famous ones was very glamorous. Angela had noticed it many times, in Kayo Street, yet her territory was Kayo Street. One night, while working, Angela saw something very odd. There were video cameras in Kayo Street, hidden everywhere. It didn't matter whether you came from the main street or the play centre and walked down Kayo Street, the cameras could see everything. The only reason she never noticed them before was that they were placed high and inconspicuously.

Angela said, under her breath, "It must be the police. They're watching. High-level security." Then, as she walked back onto the main street, it was apparent that the cameras were everywhere. As Angela turned around, she saw the big Soapland sign flashing. She said to herself, "Maybe Soapland owns those cameras, so they can see if the police are coming. Then again, that wouldn't be allowed. The police must have cameras all over the play area. That's why the crime rate is down because the cops see everything."

All she knew was that they could see everything she did. Whether it was the Blue or the Red, didn't really matter anymore. The only thing that mattered was the inevitability of it all.

When Angela was young, she developed Meningitis. She had been very ill and eventually drifted into a coma. Angela's mother took her to the hospital. The doctors didn't know what was wrong with her, and so rushed her by ambulance to a bigger city hospital far away. Close to death, the doctors diagnosed her condition as being a severe case of Spinal Meningitis. Angela had a dangerous fever, and her body began to go numb. It was very dire, indeed. In fact, the doctors thought she was already, brain dead. Angela would have died if it weren't for one Chinese doctor, who pushed through with a new type of treatment, using coma arousal associated with the medication.

Angela could remember the feeling of her spirit, leaving her body to go to a beach. At that beach, she met God. It was indeed God for, who else lives in Paradise? He lived in the clouds that hovered over a beach with water, like crystal. Ever since Angela's recovery; she'd been close to this Voice. It had spoken to her, ever since that time: Angela believed that the words that were heard were the Voice of *God*. Nothing in her mind could ever change that. No matter where Angela ended up, what happened to her or what she did, she always believed that God was with her. Indeed, He was, manifestly, in the form of a Voice.

After her illness, Angela was in high school and went to the priest, to confide in him. She told the priest about the Voice.

The priest clutching his cross and rubbing it firmly for strength looked at Angela with a frown on his face. He said, "Sometimes, one never knows who we really are talking to, you know." Then, he looked up at the altar, clasped and held the cross tightly around his waist and looked to the ceiling, then at Angela. The priest added, "Look, Angela. Most people don't have voices inside them. It could be God, or it could be the Devil. You'll never really know until it's absolutely certain. In either case, it's best not to do anything radical, and if I were you, I'd stop listening to voices."

That memory of the priest never cast doubt in Angela's mind. Angela continued to believe the Voice, ever since her little visit to Heaven. Nothing, not even a priest in a Church, could change that.

"When you know something inside your heart," Angela used to say, "You don't need anyone else to tell you what it is."

Working in Ikebukuro was a little bit like walking on a knife's edge. One could fall off either side, but just standing on the thin blade was the only way to survive. Every moment was razor-sharp.

Each night, she caught the last train from Ikebukuro. There was no point in paying five thousand yen for a taxi home. That was frivolous and unnecessary.

Angela always slept alone these days. She never trusted men enough, to do 'all-nighters' anymore, all clients were only 'short-timers.' Her savings were increasing. Still, her trust in men, particularly Japanese men, was dwindling by the day. When Angela first came to Japan, she was amazed by the average Japanese's distrustfulness towards everything around them. She had found that very humorous. After being in Tokyo's streets in the sex business, she now possessed the same prudent nature. Angela now understood, very well, why Japanese people were so distrusting. Tokyo was huge, yet was said to be the safest city in the world. Perhaps it was for an ordinary person, but it was the most dangerous place on earth for Angela. Working in the street was like being at the frontline of the war. Angela was one of the soldiers, fighting a personal war against failure. To be a casualty meant to be captured, owned or to become sick. Angela was still in one piece. She didn't have enough money to leave the street so nothing would change.

In any case, Angela continued to write songs, dance, and compose music. By now, she had a unique repertoire. No one knew about it. During her time in Japan, she had worked very hard on her talent. Angela knew that to really succeed, one's skill must be of an exceptionally high level. However, she never believed, for one moment, that her talent was star quality.

Her desire for stardom was the only aspect of Angela's life that seemed uncertain. In fact, Angela doubted that inevitability. As days passed, Angela looked at the soft hair, expressive eyes, and luscious lips of beautiful women. In fact, she now saw everything about women as beautiful, not in a purely sexual manner, but appreciatively, as for a flower and women were flowers. Of course, Angela's tendency was growing to the point of irreversibility. She had many desires that needed realisation.

Perhaps the street had altered her sexuality or was it in fact, that Angela had always had a lesbian tendency. And now she was only beginning to realise it? In any case, it didn't matter. All that mattered was that Angela didn't see men as being anything, but friends.

Very early, one morning, Angela had an awful dream. In the centre of a frying pan, she stood on a pin, with flames surrounding it. Outside was a bottomless pit. There was no way out. If Angela jumped out, she'd fall down the abyss, and if she jumped into it, she'd surely burn. It was difficult standing on the pin for any length of time, for it was harrowing, like standing on broken glass. However, Angela stood there and looked up to see the sky. Through the clouds, a rope fell from Heaven and touched her hand.

The Voice said, "Follow Me."

Angela clasped the rope with one hand, then another. She couldn't see through the clouds but knew that the pain had gone. The threaded cable was firm. It was impossible to see through the clouds but guided by the Voice, she climbed higher and away from danger. Upon waking, Angela realised that the dream symbolised her life.

Angela ran into the Yakuza man again the next evening in Ikebukuro. He was being friendly now, instead of nasty. In fact, strangely, the man seemed to respect the Gaijin's strength. He added, "Listen, Gaijin. If you don't join us, you'll go to jail. The police don't like Gaijins here, and they are Yakuza. So, you must come with us and do as we say, or they will put you in the monkey house."

Angela realised that she was standing on the pin of her life but had no idea where the rope may be. She believed there was a rope but couldn't see it. That night, Angela saw a police car slowly drive by as the men inside stared at her. It was just a matter of time. She went home upset.

It was that time of the month, and so Angela felt exceptionally uptight. She felt so alone, especially after having a close encounter with a police car. Even though there were Barb and Lyn, she still felt alone. No one experienced these things, no one else knew her desires nor understood her fear, which was the loneliest part.

Angela looked across the room to see all her keyboard and recorded tapes. She picked up a recent cassette, and suddenly realised that her music must be the rope. A tear formed in Angela's eye, believing the music must be the rope. It felt as if a light was shining down on her. Angela clutched the cassette tape so tightly thinking, that it was, indeed, the rope.

The next day, Angela copied the tape and sent them to three different recording companies. She was beginning to climb. Now she waited for the next handgrip. Angela continued to work in the street, but inside, stayed. A little time passed, and nothing arrived.

When Angela returned home from Ikebukuro, she noticed a gorgeous Japanese girl standing alone in the railway station. The girl was leaning against one of the concrete pillars. Angela looked across at the girl, as a surprised expression came over the girl's face. Angela's immediate response was to smile. The girl stood away from against the pillar and smiled back. Then, Angela happily waved at the girl, who waved back. It was as if they had known each other from a previous encounter. Then, Angela remembered she'd seen the girl before. They'd even said hello, as a matter of fact.

This was the second time they'd seen each other and were both so delighted. Neither spoke but just gazed into each other's eyes. Angela knew what was in her heart, but walked away, for fear of rejection. She would probably never see the girl again. So, despite her business success, Angela had the potential to fail herself.

Despite the difficulty of working on the street, Angela continued. Ironically, there were many clients. One particular night, Angela met a businessman on vacation, dressed very casually. They went to the hotel, showered, and got into bed.

"I'm sure I've seen your face before," Angela said.

The man laughed, nodded, and replied, "Yes. I'm sure you've seen my face a lot."

Angela couldn't remember where. Then, during sex, she looked at the man's face once again.

"What's the matter?" he asked.

"Now, I remember where I've seen your face."

"Then, where was that?"

"In a police car," Angela said.

"That's right."

Angela was now terrified. She didn't know if he could be trusted. She had sex with a cop. Now sex business was frightening. A terrified Angela wondered where it would all end.

Fortunately, the policeman really liked having sex with her and told her there would be no problem from him, as long as she made him feel good from time to time.

Soon after the business, Angela looked for the girl in the railway station and would do so every night. She had a strange new feeling inside when she had seen her before. It was some innate feeling, an enchanting emotion that Angela very much wanted to maintain. Angela kept going to work every night and soon forgot all about the rope. Instead, searching for the girl at the station. She was never seen again.

Some evenings, Angela would come home tearful. Then, one evening, she arrived home to find a small parcel, with one of her cassette tapes in it, returned from the most prominent recording studio. She opened it. There was just a simple letter.

"Thank you for your submission." Nothing more was written. The letter seemed to fall out of Angela's hand and float down to the floor. With it, Angela's ego went, too.

The Voice said, "Keep looking for the rope."

Angela's dream seemed an impossible one. The only reality was the street. The longer she walked it, the more unrealistic the idea of being anything else seemed. Yet, the Voice still said that the dream would be realised. Angela now believed that her work wasn't any good.

The following evening, Angela returned to work. By now, she was totally desensitised to men. They didn't even seem to make an impression upon her. She had feared that insensitivity, the fact that she could have sex with a man without feeling anything. However, when nights turned late on the street, beautiful women would excite Angela.

Angela pondered, "If I like looking at women so much, imagine how wonderful it would be to make love to one!"

The police were now onto her. They knew she wasn't part of the Yakuza. A Gaijin like her stuck out, which made sex business more obvious. The Japanese were extremely good at covering up the truth. Even though there were street prostitutes everywhere, it was done in such an unobvious manner. As such, the police didn't mind, because the general public wasn't totally aware that prostitution existed on such a broad scale. However, one blonde, honest Gaijin like Angela was just enough to rock the Ikebukuro police boat. The police were determined to get her off the street. The only way they could do that was to put her in prison. Angela knew the police car that cruised past each night would soon stop. They looked at her as they talked on the two-way radio. Someone at the top was pulling strings. He would be the one who decided when and how. All Angela could do was wait.

Every time that car cruised past, it felt like a shark swimming by. Angela could feel it touch her personal space and scrape along her psychic body, as ripples of fear tingled along her flesh. It was an experience full of terror.

The Voice always said, "Don't worry, it's alright. You're safe." It still said that, even in the most precarious situations. The Voice seemed to exclaim the opposite. Yet, Angela had believed the Voice. However, this time it appeared that the Voice may be wrong. It talked about the rope, but it had been cut. It had been severed because the hope Angela trusted in was gone. What would she do now?

Angela's life was a mixture of different realities. There was a kind of urgency about her activities. She knew that something was going to happen soon. One of those inevitable destinies would be realised. The only question that remained was which one would it be?

CHAPTER SEVENTEEN
'A Rope Made in Heaven'

THE FOLLOWING WEEK, the other two cassettes were returned from the other studios. Angela opened them very slowly. The first letter read:

"Thank you for your application. However, we have no place for someone with this kind of talent. Please contact us again when you are more commercial."

Angela laughed as she ripped up the letter into hundreds of little pieces. "How commercial can you get?" she said. "Standing on the street, putting everything I have into my music! Selling my body to play music! It must be ultimate in commercialism in itself."

Angela threw the cassette into the corner with her dirty washing and quickly opened the second parcel. The next one was packaged more roughly and was written by hand, while the first was typed. It seemed that this studio was a little unprofessional or maybe they didn't have a typewriter. The second letter read:

"Dear Miss Angela. We liked listening to your cassette. To be honest, we were amazed at the originality of your work. It was quite unusual to learn that you alone wrote and played all the music. You are quite a talented young lady. Unfortunately, we do not have the funds, nor the ability to promote and market you as a new artist. We are sorry."

That letter was the last straw. Tears ran down Angela's face and fell onto the letter. She crumpled it up and threw it along with the cassette.

Angela uttered, out aloud, "That's all my work is – dirty washing. All of my songs and dance routines are only dirty washing, from my dirty job."

It was morning, and the light shone through the window, hitting the crystal lampshade next to Angela's bed. A piece of light scattered and fell onto the Bible, resting near the bedhead.

The wind blew softly through the window, making the crystal lampshade shiver and so, the piece of light flickered. Angela noticed it, out of the corner of her eye. It illuminated the word 'Bible.'

The Voice said, "Read my letter."

Angela was feeling very sorry for herself and continued to cry for no particular reason. Perhaps it was just to release the pressure.

Angela turned, reached over the side of the bed, opened the 'Book' with one finger and began to read, "Fear not, for it is I. I am always with you till the end." Angela's eyes fell to the bottom of the page and read the last line. "Be patient, My child. Be patient."

Angela had always known, instinctively, that the Voice was God, and now she was sure. She felt humbled that God had taken such a personal interest in her life, even in the state of sin. She now cried for the crime of compromise and prayed for forgiveness.

Angela opened the Voice's letter, once again. She read the story of how Jesus was led into the wilderness and tempted by the Devil for forty days and nights. The Devil showed Him amazing things and commanded Jesus to deny the Voice. Jesus refuted the Devil, and he went away. Ironically, Angela felt the same way. She could understand being tempted in the wilderness. Instead of forty days in the desert, it had been years in sex business Tokyo.

Angela now believed that to be patient would mean to continue street work. She never considered returning home. Tokyo had almost beaten her with the fear it instilled from its streets, the problems it created from the police. Her dreams seemed to be at her fingertips, yet to go home would mean giving up on everything she believed in. It would be considered a failure. It was the thing that frightened Angela the most, more than AIDS, police or Yakuza. Angela's dream seemed broken now. However, she wouldn't admit that to the Voice.

A few weeks past and Angela continued to go to Ikebukuro. Her reputation had grown; she was getting four, and sometimes five clients a day. Any more than five were considered, too many. Every night, she dreamt erotic, sexual dreams of women all night and masturbated in her sleep. It seemed that she had become emotionally fragile and frustrated. The only thing that would work would be to leave the street altogether.

In the morning, the Voice said, "Now, it's time. It's time." It said nothing more. That seemed to confuse Angela. She was a little apprehensive and little emotionally uptight. Angela thought, "Perhaps it meant it's time to relocate to Osaka." Then she began to pack her things. There was so much to do. Where would she start? Angela felt sure it was time to leave. Slowly, she packed away the things that had been with her, during her stay in Tokyo, one by one, into little boxes. As she did, she cried.

Again, Angela went back to her workplace. The territory was extremely crowded. Nowadays, there were too many street girls in Ikebukuro. Perhaps Osaka would be better. There were a couple of street girls that hated Angela. She thought, "If the police or Yakuza don't get me, one of these street girls are likely to."

A few of the older girls were extremely jealous. They believed that the best way to eliminate the competition was to get rid of Angela. After all, the blond Gaijin took all the best clients, while some of the older girls never got anybody. It was these girls who Angela should have feared most. Those girls hated her and were prepared to do anything. Those hardened ladies had been in jail several times and had nothing to lose. A couple had hardened faces with eyes that penetrated Angela's soul. It was becoming apparent that the street, apart from being a place to make money, was also a place where she could die. She never thought of the other girls as enemies before. Would Angela finish prostitution, or would it finish her? Only the Voice knew, and no one else did, not even Angela Krokowski.

The Voice continued to say the same things, daily. It was as if the Voice was in a different reality. However, it had helped Angela so much, which was bizarre. It now seemed out of touch. Strangely, Angela never doubted the Voice, only herself.

Then, the Voice said, "Keep holding on a little longer, Angela, just a tiny bit longer."

Angela was walking down the street the next evening when a police car pulled up. The police seemed hesitant. One of the police officers started to open his door. They were obviously going to approach Angela, perhaps, with the intention of an arrest. The other policeman stopped him, possibly because he was reluctant to speak English. Then, they both exited the car.

The Voice said, "Go, quickly go."

Angela ducked down a side street and ran, as she heard the car door slam. They re-entered the car and continued on their way. She hid in the darkened doorway of an office building, as her heart pounded loudly.

"Boom, boom." It had the same beat of a song she had written, called, 'Standing on Broken Glass.' She could hear the song playing in her mind as her heartbeat. "Thump thump, standing on broken glass."

Angela stood in that doorway for at least an hour. The police had long gone, but she clung to the darkness. It was complicated, and it challenging to know what to do next. She had become so well-known very quickly in Ikebukuro. There wasn't anywhere else to go, in Tokyo.

"There are far more Yakuza in Osaka, but it's better than jail," Angela thought. After all, it was well known that all the big Yakuza crime syndicates originated in Osaka. Tokyo certainly had many Yakuza, but it was far less than those operating in the second-largest city in Japan, Osaka.

The Voice said, "Trust Me. Just a little patience, and you will realise your dream."

The waiting eventually took its toll on Angela, and it showed in her eyes.

Even the clients were beginning to say, "You are so beautiful! Why are you so sad?"

Angela would smile, push it aside and reply, "I'm okay." However, she was despondent.

Angela didn't bother working anymore that night. Another close encounter was the last thing she wanted. Like any other night, it was a matter of catching a taxi to the railway station to return home by train. While travelling, she listened to the Walkman, in fact, she always listened to music, as it was the only excitement in her life. With those headphones on and the volume up high, it was as if Angela was in another place. Usually, the Walkman played other peoples' music, but tonight it played her own. It was the first time she had played her own music for leisure. In a relaxed mood, she listened as the songs played, one by one; 'Standing on Broken Glass,' 'It's Cold on the Street,' 'Whales Cry,' 'It's Only Paper Money' and many others. Angela loved the songs and, for a moment, forgot whose music it really was. It made the sadness go away, if only for a short while.

When Angela arrived at Hirai, she planned to book her flight to Osaka in the next couple of days. That night, Angela didn't sleep, but instead, finished packing.

The Voice said, "A surprise is coming."

Angela wondered what the surprise may be. She packed all her things away and only left out what she needed for the following couple of days. Looking around her little flat, the place that such a high price had been paid, Angela began to cry. The apartment seemed so bare and unimportant to her now. It was as though she'd only just arrived, experienced all this emotion in a day and it was now time to leave. The last thing to be packed was her music. Tears flowed as she bundled the music away; she was tired and weak. She lay on the bed and gazed out of the window to see the bright stars shining in the twilight sky.

Then, the Voice came to Angela. "Now is the time."

Angela fell asleep as she listened and looked at the stars. The stars were always so beautiful, and that's what Angela was - a star. Even if the world never knew it, at least Angela knew that if she had been given a chance, she could have made it.

The next morning, Angela walked down to the public telephone to call the airline company. She noticed a letter for her. Taking the envelope out, she saw it was from Australia, written by hand. Perhaps it was from one of her relatives or friends. She wasn't in the mood for a cheery letter, so she pushed it into her handbag and proceeded to the telephone. The flight was three days later, Osaka Itami Airport. Then she went back to the apartment and forgot all about the letter.

It was amazing to see how many things she had accumulated. Then, a person came to the door to collect the monthly payment for the newspaper daily delivery. Angela told the man she wouldn't be needing the paper anymore, then went to her handbag to pay the money. As she did, she noticed the letter scrunched up in the corner. She pulled it out and placed it on the benchtop near the kitchen, to read it after work that evening.

Angela went to work that night but was more concerned with finding the girl at the railway station than finding clients. However, she never found her and would probably never see her again. Tokyo has twenty million people. The chances of finding one person at random at a particular time and place were astronomical. Soon, Angela met a couple of friendly clients. One of them gave her a substantial tip. After which she, very wearily, returned to the apartment. Upon entering the room, she noticed the letter which had been neglected all day. She shut the door behind her and switched on the kitchen light.

The Voice said, "Have you forgotten about the rope? Now is the time, be happy."

Angela walked in and picked up the letter without a second thought.

She was more concerned with analysing what the Voice had just said. Angela automatically opened the envelope and, at the same time, thought to herself, "What does it mean, now is the time?" She then ripped the envelope open as a single piece of paper fell to the floor. She went to pick up the letter but noticed that the stars were out. She looked up to see a bright star and felt a soft warmth inside. She gazed endlessly at the starlight.

The Voice said, "It's here! How wonderful it is!"

Then she picked up the letter, and it read:

"My Darling Daughter, it's time to come home! Love Mum xxx"

Angela began to cry with joy but didn't know why, as she clutched the letter tight to her heart. A wave of happiness rippled through her that almost paralysed body. Angela knew that something significant was happening and gazed at that single star.

The Voice said, "The rope, Angela, in your hands."

In the twilight of that starlight, Angela knew her mother was right. All this time, she had dismissed the idea of returning home because of the failures she'd experienced. That short piece of writing was so precious and beautiful. She cried with joy and relief, for the first time in two years.

Within days Angela was on board a night flight from Tokyo to Sydney. The night sky outside the plane window was filled with stars, and in Angela's mind, turned into thousands of stage lights. She imagined a grand stage, and in the twinkle of an eye, Angela was on it. The music played as she danced. Angela was not the same person anymore. Upon returning to Australia, the new Angela knew she had the strength, talent, and business sense to succeed in a world she had never entered, the music business.

The Voice had guided her home, safely, oh, so carefully. In her heart, Angela knew she would be successful. Still, it would be in Australia and not Japan and on her own terms without any room for compromise. She thought of all the things she'd been through and how the Voice had never, ever lied to her. She was safe now and would never need the street again. How happy, indeed, Angela was, finally embarking on her dream.

Well, that's the end of a true story, but for Angela, it was only the beginning.

www.ingramcontent.com/pod-product-compliance
Lightning Source LLC
Chambersburg PA
CBHW070419010526
44118CB00014B/1827